BENOIT BUCKS

BRYCE M. TOWSLEY

Skyhorse Publishing

Skyhorse Publishing books may be purchased in bulk at special discounts for sales promotion, corporate gifts, fund-raising, or educational purposes. Special editions can also be created to specifications. For details, contact the Special Sales Department, Skyhorse Publishing, 307 West 36th Street, 11th Floor, New York, NY 10018 or info@skyhorsepublishing.com.

Skyhorse® and Skyhorse Publishing® are registered trademarks of Skyhorse Publishing, Inc.®, a Delaware corporation.

Visit our website at www.skyhorsepublishing.com.

10 9 8 7 6 5 4 3 2

Library of Congress Cataloging-in-Publication Data is available on file.

Cover design by Tom Lau
Cover photo credit: Donald M. Jones

Print ISBN: 978-1-5107-1460-1
Ebook ISBN: 978-1-5107-1461-8

Printed in China

Dedication

This one is for my mother, Patricia Ann Towsley.
She never doubted it could happen—
I just wish she could have stuck around to see it.

Table of Contents

Acknowledgments

First, I want to thank my wife, Robin. She is my copy editor, sounding board, critic, spell checker, and the person who keeps everything else working so I can stay focused on writing. Without her there wouldn't be any book.

Tom Blais was a great help in all things Benoit. Thanks also to Dave Coker and Craig Jaques for their help with photos, and for their advice in hunting camp.

A special thanks to all the magazine editors who have put up with me for all these years while I learned how to do this writing and photography thing. Particular thanks to Bob Beaupre with the *Vermont Sportsman* for letting me run with it all those years and to Russell Thornberry at Buckmasters for taking a chance on an unknown writer from Vermont. Isn't it ironic that the first article I ever did for him was on tracking whitetails?

Thanks to Dave Henderson for taking time out of a very busy schedule to write the foreword.

Finally, thanks to the Benoit family. It's difficult when all those "alpha dogs" gather for a project as stressful as this one has been. They handled it, and me, with admirable professionalism.

If I missed anybody and I am sure that I have, you who you are and I hope you know that I appreciate everything.

Foreword

It may seem odd that I would be the one to write the Foreword to this book. After all, I don't know the Benoits.

Oh, I shared seminar billing with the family patriarch, Larry, at shows in the late 1970s and have been in the audience at a few Benoit presentations over the years, but we don't really know each other personally. I do, however, know who they are and what they are through the book *Big Bucks the Benoit Way*. Published in 1998, it sold better than any deer book that Krause Publications has ever printed.

It requires only minor literary license to call the Benoits deer hunting legends. They are a singular breed of New Englanders with a fascinating story to tell. The popularity of that book, however, came largely from how the story was told by its author, Bryce Towsley.

Bryce was a logical choice to write that book and this one. He is a fellow Vermonter and a veteran deer hunter, so he is familiar with the "where" and "how" of the Benoit Way. He is also a truly professional writer with a conversational style that is easy to read while at the same time being informative and entertaining. He is a master not only of the "how-to" but also of the "how-it-was."

He's also my best friend.

We first met when Bryce was still a part-time writer making his actual living in retail. When he subsequently closed the business and became a full-time freelance writer, he would come to me for advice and guidance, since I'd been living that life for a while already.

I was glad to help and, from those beginnings, have had a ringside seat as Bryce shot past my station and steadily ascended the ladder into this industry's major leagues. Today, he is a field editor and/or columnist for the top six shooting and/or hunting magazines in the country. Needless to say, I now go to him for advice.

The circumstances of this business have afforded us the opportunity to experience and savor the outdoors on a broader plane than most folks. But while Bryce and I have shared countless hunting camps, hotel rooms, rental cars, close calls, and bottles of Jack Daniels, our personal escapades are, undoubtedly, interesting only to us.

A rarity among modern outdoor writers, Bryce is dedicated, conscientious, truly experienced, and genuinely knowledgeable. His books on rifles and muzzleloaders are veritable textbooks on the subjects, written in such a way that you didn't even know you were being educated.

This is a guy who is passionate about what he does and how he does it. You never have to wonder what Bryce is thinking; he wears it on his sleeve and is quite willing to tell you about it. He wants things done the right way and is willing to step forward and face the heat. At the same time, this otherwise intense man regularly passes up prime assignments to take his kids, Erin and Nathan, on hunting or fishing trips.

Above all, he takes pride in what he does and wants to leave a legacy. And this book is yet another step toward that eventuality.

Dave Henderson
March 2003

About the Author

Bryce M. Towsley is an award-winning writer and photographer living in Vermont. His work covers a wide diversity of subjects, but none more than the field of hunting and the firearms.

He published his first article in 1980 and in the time since has published thousands of articles and photos in most of the major outdoor and gun magazines.

He is a field editor for *NRA American Rifleman*, *American Hunter*, and *Shooting Illustrated* magazines.

He has published six other hunting or gun related books and contributed to several others. He also published an action adventure novel, *The 14th Reinstated*.

Towsley has hunted extensively throughout the United States and Canada, Mexico, Africa, South America, Russia, and Europe for a wide variety of game. Towsley has competed in several shooting disciplines and currently is active in 3-gun shooting and USPSA.

www.brycetowsley.com

Bryce M. Towsley shot this 8-point Texas whitetail with a prototype Thompson Center Contender G2 in 2001. Bryce M. Towsley photo.

Cabela's

Introduction

There is something in the human psyche that causes us to focus on the memories of any "first" in our lives. We all remember our first kiss, our first car, or our first whitetail buck. As a writer, it is inevitable that prominent on my personal list of "firsts" would be my first book.

These "firsts" are milestones in our lives and they serve as a measure of how life is unfolding. Right or wrong, they are symbols of our successes and our failures. They mark the progress of our lives and are either proud trophies or shameful reminders of what could have been. I think that while we all want any "first" to be a wonderful memory, the reality is that those memories are often haunted with the echoes of disaster. After all, it's our first time at these things. How can we expect to get it right, let alone perfect?

Maybe sometimes we just get lucky.

My first book was by any measure a success and, in the final analysis, it was truly a good and successful event in my life.

That book was *Big Bucks the Benoit Way*. It was published in 1998 and has gone on to become the bestselling whitetail hunting book in history.

A typical buck pole after a season of tracking by the Benoits. Benoit Brothers photo.

You can find it on websites or in bookstores now, in trade paper, from Skyhorse Publishing.

Five years later I wrote this, my second book with the Benoits.

As it was with *Big Bucks the Benoit Way*, the challenge was primarily on me. The Benoits are incredible deer hunters, of that there is no dispute. They have an infinite storehouse of whitetail hunting knowledge locked in their heads, but extracting it is like mining for gold while drilling through solid granite. To say it is difficult would be an understatement of historic, perhaps even Biblical, proportions. It would be a challenge for me to "mine" their knowledge and turn it into words that made at least a little sense to the reader. But I knew that when I signed on and I was confident I could succeed.

However, the greater and more troubling challenge was, how would I follow the first book? When I started *Big Bucks the Benoit Way*, I wanted it to be the best and most comprehensive book on tracking whitetail deer in existence.

The question loomed: How do I tackle the same subject matter again without being too repetitive and without stealing from the soul of the first book? I didn't want just another "second book" that would cash in on the success of the first while cheating the reader of any genuinely new material. As an avid reader myself, I have collected far too many of those and I know the dirty feeling of having been swindled that follows the last chapter.

My challenge was to write a book that was as good as or better than the first. I wanted this to be a book that could stand on its own legs and still be a faithful companion to *Big Bucks the Benoit Way*. In that light, it had to not only provide information on the Benoit way of hunting, but it also must contain new and worthwhile information. This new book would have to dig deeper into the heart and soul of the Benoit way of deer hunting. If *Big Bucks the Benoit Way* was the textbook of the basics, this book should be the advanced study.

Larry Benoit was almost eighty years old when I wrote this book and had retired from the limelight. He just wanted to make knives and hunt deer. So the book deals with the next generation of Benoits, the *Benoit Brothers* as they call themselves: Lanny, Shane, and Lane.

They took the Benoit style of deer hunting and infused it with new thinking, new technology, and new enthusiasm. When working on the book, I came up with the catch tag *Hunt Smarter, Not Harder*. That went on to become the motto for the Benoit Brothers and it epitomizes the concept of this book.

This book is not just for trackers. The success of the Benoit family spawns from far more than just simple deer hunting skill and knowledge. Much of the secret to their success is founded in their approach and attitude about deer hunting and in their single-minded focus and drive to succeed. This is a book that explores those success-driving themes again and again. It explains why they are important if you want to bend the game pole with big-bodied whitetail bucks, while offering advice on how readers can adapt them to their own style of hunting to achieve that goal.

Part of the mandate I imposed on myself when accepting the contract for the book was that I wanted to include whitetail hunting information that would be useful to anybody who hunts deer. Without question, the book would need to focus on tracking big bucks in the snow; after all, that is the "Benoit Way." But I also wanted to include information that would help deer hunters shoot big bucks no matter what their hunting style and no matter where they hunt. There is a lot of information in the book that will prove useful to not only trackers, but to any whitetail hunters.

As with *Big Bucks the Benoit Way*, *Benoit Bucks* has endured. It was available in hardcover from 2003 to 2016, which is a very long time for a hunting book.

Now it's being reintroduced in softcover for a new generation of readers. That's a strong tribute for a hunting book and proof that the Benoit style of hunting big whitetails is timeless.

This is in all probability the last book about hunting deer with the Benoits. Larry Benoit passed away on October 16, 2013, at the age of eighty-nine. Lane Benoit left us February 12, 2015, at the age of sixty.

Shane and Lanny are still hunting, but are slowing down from the business of hunting and making fewer personal appearances. Besides, half of the Benoit franchise has left us and they took the magic with them. The Beatles would never be the same without John and George and so too will the Benoits never be quite the same without Larry and Lane.

The good news though is that with this book, *Benoit Bucks,* along with its predecessor, *Big Bucks the Benoit Way*, the Benoit legacy and their style of hunting big woods lunker whitetails lives on forever.

Bryce M. Towsley
March 8, 2016

THE BENOITS

An Introduction to the Benoit Brothers

When it comes to deer hunting, for many years the Benoit name has primarily been associated with Larry Benoit. This legendary buck tracker was well known throughout the whitetail-hunting world for his ability to track down and shoot huge northern whitetail deer.

Larry probably became the first true whitetail deer hunting celebrity in America when he rose to fame just before the whitetail deer hunting boom took off, and he rode that fame throughout the early years. The book he did with Peter Miller in 1975, *How to Bag the Biggest Buck of Your Life,* is a whitetail-hunting classic. It's been long out of print and used copies are selling for "big bucks" if you are lucky enough to find one for sale.

Larry was a big part of my first book, *Big Bucks the Benoit Way*, but astute readers will note that unlike *How to Bag the Biggest Buck of Your Life, Big Bucks The Benoit Way* dealt with the entire Benoit deer hunting family, rather than Larry alone. While Larry has earned the well-deserved reputation for deer hunting that he has long enjoyed, the acorn doesn't fall far from the tree as they say, and three of his four sons are also serious deer hunters.

As each generation picks up the banner, they learn from the last and apply their own thinking and experience to take it to the next level. Larry gave credit to his father, Leo, for being a great deer tracker and for teaching him how it's done. Larry learned all he could from his father and added a lifetime of his own hunting to that knowledge; then he continued that tradition by teaching his own sons how to track whitetail bucks. Now they have added their own life experiences to that knowledge and have taken deer tracking to the next level. While it may be a source of argument, I'll stick my neck out and state here that I think they may well have evolved into even better deer hunters and collectively they are probably the three best whitetail deer hunters alive today.

All things must end and it has come time for the torch to pass from Larry to the next generation of Benoit deer hunters. Larry was almost 80 years old and still whitetail hunting when he shot his best-racked buck ever in 2001.

The book you now hold in your hands is about the next generation of Benoits: Lanny, Lane, and Shane—the "Benoit Brothers." In the pages of this book, you will learn about how they hunt and how they have adapted to the changing world of whitetail deer hunting. You will also learn a little about who they are and what makes them tick, both as both deer hunters and as men.

The Benoit Brothers—Shane, Lanny, and Lane, from left to right—with their father, Larry, after a successful season.

Benoit Brothers photo.

CHAPTER ONE

Lanny

"Lanny is a phenom," Shane says with obvious sibling pride. "Anything he decides he is going to do, he will excel at it."

From what I can see, that's not just idolizing his big brother; it's true. Lanny really is a phenomenal guy and I believe he is the best whitetail deer hunter alive today. He hunts in the toughest places and with some of the most difficult methods, and still manages to take the best bucks in the area almost with ease.

Lanny will look a long time to find an exceptionally large track before seriously hunting. This makes a huge difference in the trophy quality of his bucks. Over the past several years, the average dressed weight of his bucks has consistently been more than 240 pounds.

One story that I think illustrates this point well almost didn't make the cut for this book. Lanny was worried that he would be thought of as a game hog if I told it here and felt strongly I should not. But what he did was completely legal and is just too good to leave out. However, I will say that Lanny is not happy about it appearing here. He really is a rather humble guy and worries about the image he projects in the deer hunting industry. So it's with his reservations and at my insistence that this story is being told. Please take it in the spirit I intend to convey–that is, to illustrate how phenomenally good he is at hunting whitetail deer–and not to brag about how many bucks he can kill.

They were hunting in an area that allows "party hunting," where hunters can fill each other's tags, so one hunter shooting multiple deer is legal. There was a cameraman filming for video, and as he usually does, Lanny had been keeping his finger off the trigger in order to drag out the season a little longer. But that's not how videos are produced and the cameraman started to complain. It's been my experience that cameramen in general like to complain and they tend to do it a lot, but in this case, he actually had a point. They had been at it for a couple of weeks and they didn't have a single kill shot. It may be subject to some ideological debate, but the undeniable truth known by any video producer is that the kill scenes sell the tape. Without them, you might as well be filming a grade school Christmas pageant and trying to pawn that off as a deer hunting video. It's easier and the sales results will be about the same. So this guy was starting to complain about Lanny not shooting and with good reason. They were paying him to produce a deer hunting video, and he needed the material to do it right.

The conditions for tracking were not good, with old snow that was crusty and very noisy, but Lanny finally had listened enough to realize the guy had a point.

"Fine," he said. "Starting tomorrow, we are hunting for the camera."

Over the course of the next four days, and while hunting on public land, Lanny shot three trophy whitetail bucks. All of them dressed more than 200 pounds and every single one had what any honest deer hunter would call trophy-quality antlers. Every kill was filmed and anybody who has ever worked with a video crew while hunting will tell you that the degree of difficulty is elevated exponentially by adding a camera to the mix. Most guys film their deer hunts from treestands; doing it the "Benoit Way" puts the filming difficulty factor someplace far off the charts. I have met most of the big-name, famous whitetail hunters in the industry and, while some are a joke, most are outstanding deer hunters who have my respect and admiration. However, I am confident in saying that I don't know another person who could have done what Lanny did on demand. But like anybody who is truly great at something, he made it look easy.

Lanny decided to take up skeet shooting years ago. "My goal was to win the state championship," he told me. Most shooters will work for decades at something like that, even in a small state like Vermont. It only took

Lanny Benoit. Bryce M. Towsley photo.

Lanny two years.

He decided to become a snowmobile racer, and starting with a few barnyard races, he ended up a dominant force at the world championships and setting a record for the most wins in a weekend. He was so good that he was embarrassing the big-time nationally sponsored teams, so Ski-Doo put him on the payroll. Lanny went on to win 12 world championships, 19 world series titles, and endless points titles in multiple circuits during his 19-year snowmobile racing career.

Today Lanny, along with his son Landon (a champion drag-racing competitor himself), builds high-performance engines for snowmobile drag racing. They have an international reputation and enjoy a huge demand for their products. These are engines that cost thousands of dollars, but may only have a few hours or less of working life and no guarantees. Yet high-level racing enthusiasts seek them out for the simple reason that they win.

Lanny has been married to his wife, Lynn, for 28 years. They have three boys, including Landon, who is also Lanny's favorite hunting buddy. Landon recently had a son named Tagen, making Lanny a grandfather.

Lanny has a dry and often subtle sense of humor that is a hit with the seminar crowds. He is good-natured and a lot of fun to hunt with. And like he says, every time you head out the camp door with him, it's likely to be an adventure!

I asked Lanny to share some of his most memorable deer hunting stories and here are but a few of the many hunting tales he told me.

ADVANCING THE LEGEND

"I was in this restaurant/bar in Stratton, Maine, when somebody recognized me," Lanny told me as we were bumping down a rutted logging road in northern New Hampshire in Casper, his friendly Suburban. "Pretty

Top: Landon Benoit. Bryce M. Towsley photo.

Bottom: Lanny & Landon Benoit on the track in New Hampshire 2002. Bryce M. Towsley photo.

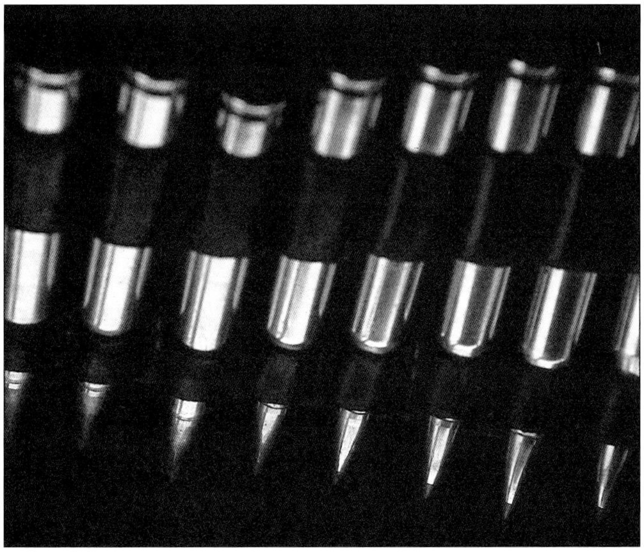

Top: Lanny and Landon make a very effective team when it comes to tracking and killing big bucks. Tom Blais photo. **Bottom: Cartridge belt with red-tipped Hornady ammo.** Bryce M. Towsley photo.

soon a crowd had gathered and we were all talking deer hunting. Everybody was telling me how their season was going and when we got to this one guy, he was crying the blues. He had experienced just about everything that could go wrong and he wasn't even seeing deer. So I asked him what caliber gun he was shooting.

"'Why, a 270 Winchester, of course,' he said. 'The same as you.'

"'Just a minute,' I told him. 'Wait here, I might have something in the truck that will help.'

"I went out to the parking lot and got my gun belt. I brought it in, laid it out on the table and started looking over all the cartridges in the belt with a puzzled look on my face.

"'One of these is a magic cartridge,' I said, 'but I can't remember which one it is.' I picked and poked at the cartridges in the belt, pulling out one then another, looking them over and shaking my head at each one before putting it back. Then I finally picked one near the center of the belt and took it out. I handed the guy the 270 Winchester cartridge, and amid the laughter of everybody there, I told him, 'This is a magic cartridge. Its destiny is to kill a 200-pound Maine buck. I was saving it for myself, but I already got my deer. I don't think they keep from year to year so you might as well have it.'

"The next night, I was in that place eating again when the guy came sliding sideways into the parking lot, throwing gravel and dust into the air, blowing his horn and yelling out the window. Wouldn't you know, he had a 200-and-something-pound, big-racked buck in the back of the truck that he had shot that afternoon with the cartridge I gave him. Stuff like that helps ensure you don't have to buy many drinks."

It's also the kind of things legends are made of!

THE "TERMINATOR" BUCK (I'LL BE BACK!)

"It was 1991 or 1992, I really can't remember for sure, but I do recall that it was the second week of the Maine deer season. I woke up during the night to answer the call of nature and as you know, in hunting camp, that usually means you have to step outside. It turned out to be a cold chore, but I was pleased to see that it was snowing.

"I was kind of excited and having trouble sleeping after that, so I finally got up and passed the time making a good, big breakfast. I couldn't wait for the sun to come up and left the camp before it was light enough to see a track. After only about half an hour of riding the roads and looking with the headlights I found about 12 buck tracks crossing the roads. It was clear that there had been a lot of deer on the move during the night and this was shaping up to be a great day.

"About 15 minutes after daylight, I found a really big track and I told the guy riding with me that I was going to check it out and follow it for a while. I was lucky because I only had to follow it for about 100 yards before I could tell it had a good rack. I went back and told my buddy that I was going after this buck. I didn't know where I would end up or even if I would get the deer or not, but I wanted him to make sure to find me at the end of the day.

"I tracked that buck from just after daylight until about 10:30 in the morning. I saw then that he was feeding, so I slowed down and started looking for him. It was only a few minutes before I saw him stand up from behind a spruce tree. I could see his neck and his backside and I told myself, *Now take your time and be really careful to place this shot well.* I wanted to shoot him in the chest, so I took my time and I pulled back just a tiny bit into the branches of that tree where his shoulder should have been before I carefully squeezed off a shot. It looked like the deer went down, but I guess he didn't. Actually, he went down all right; he went down the hill! I went to the spruce tree to find my buck and he wasn't there. I found a big stump that they had pushed up when they were logging in there. I had shot right into the stump. It was only about a 40-yard shot, but in the poor light and with the branches of the tree, I was fooled. I could see his back and his front, but I couldn't see that log. The bullet never went through the log, of course.

"I could see his rack before I shot so I knew he was a good 10-pointer, and I was so sure I had him that I was reaching for my tag as I walked over there, but all I got was a surprise."

"Why didn't you shoot him in the neck if you could see it?" I asked.

"That's a good question. Obviously, I should have," Lanny replied. "But I wanted to shoot him in the shoulder and it seemed like a good idea at the time. Also, I just don't like neck shots and you will see why in a minute.

"So I started tracking the buck and he took me into this big swamp, where he went through a bunch of blowdowns. He didn't know what that bullet was and all he heard was a loud noise. He didn't know where that came from and when it wasn't repeated, he kind of forgot his initial scare and calmed down pretty quick. He wasn't very spooked and he was just ahead of me most of the time. We got into that big swamp where there were spruces and blowdowns that you could hardly get through. The deer was just in front of me, but it was so thick I couldn't see him. So I crawled up on this big log to get higher with hopes I could get a look at him. I do that a lot in these situations, where I climb up on a vantage point when I am tracking. It can be a stump, a rock or a blowdown, but the higher perspective often lets you see the buck. This log got me up higher than all that brush and junk and I could see him about 125 yards in front of me. There I am, teetering on this log and all I could see was just his neck. I am not about to make the same mistake twice, and if the neck is all I can see, then that's where I'll shoot him. I go 'kerpow' and down he goes, for good. Or so I thought.

"I guess this is kind of a 'happy/sad' story. I am happy in the morning when I find this great big buck track. But by late morning, I am starting to get a little sad because I haven't seen him yet. Then, suddenly I do see him and I am happy again. I shoot him and thinking I got him, I am really happy. Then he's not there and I discover I killed a log, so I get really sad again. I am still sad as I track him through this thick swamp hole, but I see him and shoot and now I think I have him and it's happy time again.

"It takes me a long time to get over to him through all that thick stuff and when I get there I am very sad because once again there is no buck, only tracks running away. I can see where he fell down, but he got up again. I am tracking him for 10 minutes and I have a good blood trail coming out both sides of the deer, but somehow he is still going.

Lanny's getting close to this buck! Tom Blais photo.

"Finally after about a quarter of a mile I came to a big brook. The deer went right across it, but it's too deep for me. I thought about taking off all my clothes and my boots and wading across, holding them above my head. But first I start walking the bank. I wandered downstream about 300 to 400 yards and found a place where a tree had fallen across the brook, and I crossed on that. I am thankful for staying warm and soon I am back on the buck's track.

"I followed him for a long way across this flat area and across a cutting. Somewhere along the way, he stops bleeding. Then he starts up a mountain and he keeps going up, which goes to show that the old idea they won't go up hill when they are hurt isn't right. By now, it's early afternoon and I know that it's a long way back to the truck because I have been walking steadily away from the rig since daylight. I know there are very few other roads in this area where I could walk out and hope to catch a ride back to my truck, so I was starting to think about heading back. I figured I could cut him off at a road the next morning if he kept moving or at least find a shorter way in with the truck so I could take up his track again.

"But then I noticed from his tracks that he was starting to get a little wobbly, so I decided to give it some more time. I am walking along, looking ahead for the deer when he suddenly exploded out from under a spruce tree about 20 feet from me. He surprised me and I shot from the hip, but I got him through the lungs that time.

"That neck shot had hit him high in the neck and actually broke three vertebrae along the top, but without damaging the spinal cord enough to keep him down. I suppose if I could have run right over to him, I would have gotten him. I am sure that he lay there long enough that I could have shot him again, but it took so long to get through that brush that he must have recovered

Lanny is always looking for that next big buck track.

Benoit Brothers photo.

from the shock and got back on his feet. It was amazing how he managed to keep going, but those big bucks are tough. Once they get traveling, they often seem to get their second wind.

"It was about 12:30 when I shot him. I gutted him and piled some brush over him, then pointed my nose at the truck. I walked hard and steady until 4 p.m. before I hit the road. Even after I hit the road, I still had four or five miles to go to the rig. I had told the guy with me to drive around and fire a signal shot every now and then, starting at 4 o'clock. I heard him shoot just as I hit the road. I fired a shot back and he came to get me. I was pretty thankful for that, as I had put in a long day and I was pretty tired. I had tracked that buck about 12 miles, three of them after I shot him. Then I had to walk out for that same distance, so I was tired.

"He was a good buck, and I really didn't want to leave him all night, so we took the truck and started four-wheeling to find another way into the deer. After a while, we found an old logging road that got us close, but we still had a long drag and didn't get back to camp until about 10:30 that night.

PREVENTING BUCK ATTACKS!

"Hear that you are going to be doing product endorsements for deer scent," I said with a smile. "Is that true?"

"Not exactly," Lanny said, "but there is a good story about that.

"Several years ago (Shane interrupts to tell us it was 1989), Landon and I had the boys drop us off about 10 miles down the road, and I told them we would hunt to the top of the mountain because there was a logging road going to the top and they could leave the rig up there.

Lanny with "The Terminator" buck, which weighed in at 268 pounds. Benoit Brothers photo.

It was bare ground and we were mostly just scouting, but about a half a mile from where the rig was parked, we found where these two big bucks had had a hell of a fight. It was the end of the day, but I told Landon that I wanted to come back the next day.

"That night back at camp, some guy showed up who was marketing a new deer lure and he wanted one of us to try it. Of course, we are not the right guys to test deer lures because we don't use them and don't know much about them. I told him that the only lure I use is when I try to charm them into not running off on me, and I don't do that with my good looks."

"Well then," I asked Lanny, "what do you charm them with?"

"My 270," he replied with a grin. "It works pretty good at charming them into sticking around.

"Anyway it was pretty comical because I was reading the back of the package for this scent and it said not to put any on yourself because the buck might attack you. I thought that was pretty good because it would be a lot different going into the woods and having to worry about a big buck sneaking up on your backside while you were hunting. It would be a little different having them chase you instead of the other way around. So I decided not to put any on me because it could be dangerous. I didn't want to have to fight my way back to the Suburban that night, and I didn't want to become an illegal deer hunter by being forced to shoot more than one buck in self defense.

"So we got back down in there in the morning and we found where those big bucks were fighting. We had been there about 10 minutes when I remembered the deer scent. I told Landon that we would pour it on a tree. That way, if they wanted to attack the tree instead of us, we would be all set. So I sprayed some on the tree and I stepped back to wait. It wasn't a minute before we saw

Lanny and Landon with the "Preventing Buck Attacks!" buck. Benoit Brothers photo.

a big ol' 8-pointer coming up the trail. I whispered to Landon, 'Boy, that stuff works fast!' So we shot that buck and he weighed 228 pounds.

"I never did get my endorsement contract because when we were dragging the buck out, the scent fell out of my pocket and we never found it. That guy never came around the camp again and nobody could remember his name."

"That buck was down at the bottom of a real steep bank," Shane added. "Then, when we got that buck to the top, we still had a thousand yards of cuttings (clear-cut) to drag him through. So we drove the Suburban across that, bumping over stumps and banging off logs. Most normal guys wouldn't think of driving through that, but 'Big Red' (the name Lanny had given that Suburban) handled it without a hitch."

WATERFALL BUCK, PART ONE

"This is another of those two-day adventure things. Back in 1998, Dennis Grifthen and I got up early in the morning and drove way back in to this place in Maine. I parked and got out of my rig and hadn't walked very far before there was this huge buck track. So I start tracking him. While I am tracking him, I can hear this huge waterfall, which eventually the track went right by. You may wonder what a waterfall had to do with tracking a deer, but I'll get to that. I remember that on the map there is a big pond in this area, but somehow I always miss it and have never found the pond.

"Anyway, I tracked this deer until about noon and shot the buck. I had tracked him through some really nasty places, full of blowdowns and thick brush. It was hard work and I remember that I had gotten awful hungry, so I opened a can of beans. I can remember thinking that I shouldn't be opening those beans because the buck was close; it was the wrong time to be doing that, but like I said I was hungry. I am one of those guys who, when I am hungry, I am going to eat, no matter what. So I am tracking this buck with a white plastic fork in one hand and the can with the top sticking up in the other. My gun was under my arm and I am sneaking along and things were perfect. The day had warmed up a little and the snow was sliding off the trees, making a lot of noise. This helped to hide the noise I was making and pretty soon I could see just the chest of that buck as he was standing in front of me. Just as I went to move a little, a big bunch of snow slid off a tree just to the right of me. The buck turned his head to look at the snow and he was looking right at me. I dropped the beans and I remember it landed right-side up in the snow with the fork sticking out of the top, so you might say I didn't spill the beans! I shot the buck in the chest and he dropped.

"While I was gutting the buck, I was thinking that I couldn't be too far from the road because I could hear a truck. But I knew there wasn't any road over there. I did know that the brook near where I'd shot the deer went down to the river I had crossed and that the river was big enough to float a boat down.

"I had tracked this buck from daylight to noon almost in a straight line, so we had gone a long way. That's too far to drag him back and I went to look for the road, but I knew there couldn't be one because I knew the woods and there just weren't any roads. Finally, I left the buck and hiked back to the truck.

"When I got to the truck, I was pretty worn out because I was walking through the blowdowns and spruces that had grown together until they were almost a solid mass. My buddy wanted to go get the deer, but I pointed out to him that I had been walking without stopping since 12:30 just to get back to the truck, and it was now 4 o'clock. We would have been two days dragging that buck out.

"I explained that we were going to get a boat and come down that river to get the buck. I had never been down it before, of course, but there were some landmarks. The first was the brook that came into the river and marked where the buck was. Then, of course, there was the waterfall. We couldn't go past it and I knew if we got to it, we had gone way too far. The buck was upriver from the falls, so if we made it to there, we needed to turn around.

"Dave Coker had a 12-foot boat with a little motor with him. So the next day, we do some tough four-wheeling to get back in there as far as we can and then we launch the boat. We went down this river and saw a lot of ravens flying around a spot that I recognized, and I

Three views of the "Basset Hound Buck" killed in Maine in 1995, which weighed 247 pounds and was more than eleven years old. Benoit Brothers photos.

realized that it was where I had walked yesterday. There were three of us in the boat, which was dangerous, especially when we hit several rocks that were hidden under the black water. We kept going down the river looking for that brook, and we kept going and going, but we never found where it joined the river. Finally, we came to the falls and realized that somehow we had passed the brook. It was a struggle back upstream from the falls, and even when we went back, we couldn't find that damn brook. It turns out that it had gone underground before it reached the river, so it never joined it in any visible way.

"We finally found the buck and put him in the boat and started back up the river. The current going back up the river was so strong that the little motor couldn't push the boat. Shane had on some waders and had to get out of the boat into the November-cold river and push the boat upstream. At times the water was up to his chest and, with the swift current, it was a lot of work.

"We got to the place where I had walked to the river the day before, and we stopped for a breather. I told the guys, 'You know, yesterday I stood right here and I could swear I heard a vehicle.' They all laughed at me, but then I said, 'Hey, there goes one now!' A yellow truck was driving through the brush on the other side of the river, miles from any road. It turns out there was a railroad track over there, and it was a railroad maintenance truck driving down the tracks.

"That buck weighed 247 pounds, but he should have been a lot heavier. His track was huge. This buck must have been over 300 pounds in his prime, but he was a very old buck and was all worn out. It didn't have anything to do with the rut; he was just old and worn

Lanny Benoit looks across the river the "Waterfall Buck" was swept through. Tom Blais photo.

out. His skin hung so loose that he looked like a basset hound. The state guys couldn't age the deer for sure, but they said he was definitely more than 11 years old."

WATERFALL BUCK, THE SEQUEL

"We were hunting Ontario in 2000 and all it had done for weeks was rain. It wasn't even bare-ground hunting anymore; it was bare-mud hunting.

"Finally we got some snow. I got up early that next morning, all excited and raring to go. I walked out of my tent and headed for cameraman Tom Blais's tent, calling his name to make sure he was up. When I got in the tent, I found that not only was he up, he was making me a big breakfast of my favorite foods: eggs, bacon, and toast with peanut butter. Already this was looking like a great day.

"We got out of camp early and drove way up into

Lanny Benoit crosses the river the "Waterfall Buck" was swept through. Tom Blais photo.

Above: Lanny Benoit & Tom Blais with the Ontario "Waterfall Buck."

Tom Blais photo.

Left: A tired Lanny with his Ontario "Waterfall Buck."

Tom Blais photo.

some country that we had scouted earlier in the season and knew held some big bucks. We found a big track right off and got on it. We tracked it for about four or five hours and had a couple of chances to shoot him, but the camera was never quite right. Making videos has really changed things in our hunting. It's hard enough to track and shoot a big buck, but now we have to make sure the cameraman has the buck in the viewfinder and in focus before we shoot. That creates a huge gap in how often we get to shoot.

"Finally we pushed this buck too hard, and he panicked and crossed this river just above where it funnels down between some ledges. He didn't realize how deep it was and how fast the current was flowing. The river narrowed down through this funnel at these ledges and the current really picked up. He jumped into the river in about the worst place he could have picked. He got swept into the funnel, through the rapids and down over a waterfall. The river was raging from all the rain and he got dragged through boulders and all that for about 250 feet. He got swept into a basin at the bottom of the waterfall where finally the water was calm enough for him to swim out the other side.

"We went down the river looking for the buck, expecting to find his body because I didn't think he could have survived that swim. He really had to have taken a beating going down through all that mess. We kept sneaking down the river and finally I spotted a little movement on the other side of the river about 100 yards below the waterfall. It was clear that he wasn't feeling too good, as he hadn't gone very far. As soon as Tom had the buck in the camera's viewfinder, I shot him. But then we had a big problem. He was on the other side of this big, cold river. We didn't have any way to cross, and because it was late in the day and we were pretty worn out, we headed back to Casper.

"We hiked back in there the next day with a chainsaw and we cut a tree down to make a bridge. Then we crossed on that and got a rope tied on the buck to pull him back across the river.

"That hunt is in the first video we made, and you can see how fast the river is and what that deer went through."

THE CHARGING BUFFALO BUCK

"The buck weighed 205 and was built like a buffalo," Lanny started this story. "He had short little legs in the front that were bowed. He had a huge chest and massive, paddle feet. He was a strange buck, in more ways than one.

"We had about four feet of snow in Vermont that year and it was hard to walk in the woods. I followed the brook because it was easier to walk in the brook, which was still open, than it was to try to wallow through all that snow. It took me a couple of hours to work my way up the brook to the headwaters high in the mountains, but when I got there I found this big buck track.

"I started tracking him and he was headed up the mountain. We got up on top in the spruces and the snow was really deep. I couldn't believe this buck was headed up the mountain in this deep snow. Of course, we had gotten all that snow in a day and a half, so I don't think the deer quite understood what was happening yet and were still way up in the mountains rather than headed for their winter range like they should have been. Anyway, we got up on top and I jumped him and another buck up at the same time. I saw the first one and it distracted me while the big buck ran off before I could get a shot. I got confused and sidetracked before I realized it was a different buck. He was still a nice buck, but he had a smaller rack.

"I tried to run after the better buck and catch him as he went through the open hardwoods on the side of the mountain. I took after the buck, running as best as I could in that deep snow. Finally I caught up to where I could see him trying to run ahead of me through that snow. But he had those short little legs and was having a hard time. He would take a jump or two then would stop and catch his breath. He was leaping along like that about 150 yards in front of me, and I was trying to shoot him. But I was all out of breath and kept missing him. He would run and I would run, then I would shoot and I would miss and he would run some more.

"He was running back toward the parking lot, where my dad and Uncle Windy were standing by the truck listening. Every time I would shoot, one of them would say, 'Well, he is getting closer.'

"This went on for a while; I would reload my gun,

run until I caught up with the buck, and shoot at him some more. But the problem was that every time I could see him, he was a long way off in the hardwoods and moving. I was always out of breath and just couldn't hit him. This went on for about an hour before we finally got down in the spruces near the bottom of the mountain. The buck started circling around in this thicker cover and we went round and round for a while. Finally I caught him, and while I didn't have the greatest shot, I did manage to hit him. I didn't hit him very hard; I just kind of ticked him. It got him mad or something because he did something I have never seen a deer do before: He turned around and blew a little bit and ran right at me with his head down. I honestly think that deer was charging me. He was just sick of running and he let me get close. I think he had simply had enough. I remember shooting as he was coming for me and he fell over. I walked over and made sure he was dead, then I fell over myself and laid on my back staring at the sky for about 20 minutes. I was just trying to get some air and get my breathing back to normal. I remember the steam was just rolling right off me from being all heated up from running so long in that heavy, deep snow. I laid there for a long time thinking, *What a chase.* That chase had lasted a couple of hours and I must have shot at him six or seven times.

"Then I staggered my way back to the truck. I didn't even gut the deer out. I just went back to see if I could get some help. We found a farmer with a tractor to drag him out.

"That was in 1965. I was a lot younger then. I was 19 years old and a lot tougher in those days."

Lanny's heaviest buck, a 13-point brute taken in 1979, is shown here hanging on the left. Benoit Brothers photo.

MY BIGGEST BUCK

"The heaviest buck I ever shot weighed 271 pounds. I was looking for a track part of the morning, riding the roads and looking hard, but I couldn't find one. My dad had left a big buck the day before, so he took me over to where he had quit the track. I took that old track from the day before and caught up with the buck about noon.

"We started into a swamp and he got down in there and mixed up with a lot of does, and I had a hard time keeping track of him. Then he started crossing a lot of water that was deeper than my boots, so I had to keep making big swings to go around the water. Then I found where he got into a fight with another buck, but it didn't last too long and I don't suppose there were many bucks around big enough to stand up to him. I guess it was sometime around late-morning when he left the swamp and went up to the top of the mountain and across the Appalachian Trail. He got mixed up with another bunch of deer and that took a while to sort out. But he also stopped to do some scraping and rubbing, which slowed him down some. Then I could see where he was puttering around feeding here and there. He would lie down for a while, then move and feed and lie down some more. I planned to come along and lie him down again, this time permanently.

"He was back in some big shelves along the top of the mountain. It was in some of those black spruces they have in Maine and it's very dark in them. All of a sudden I could see some movement and spotted part of an antler. I snapped my safety off and thought, *I got you now,* but something didn't look right. It turned out to be a small moose with antlers that had long points like a deer. I was glad I didn't shoot because they frown on shooting moose out of season up there.

"I kept on his track, sneaking through some spruces where the snow was about a foot deep and it was quiet going. I came around a spruce tree and there he was, feeding. He hadn't heard me, but when I stepped around that tree he saw me and picked his head up. I shot him and he ran off, so I shot him again. I knew I had hit him good, but you never want to take a chance, so I shot him again.

"I remember it was early in the 1979 season, when I was young and full of piss and vinegar. But after I shot him, I starting dragging and before long I was thinking, *Boy, I am out of shape. I can hardly drag this buck.* But it wasn't because I was out of shape; it was because he was so big."

THE LOGGING TRUCK BUCK

"One year up in Maine, Landon and I were tracking this big buck during a blizzard. It was cold, windy and snowing hard. We found a buck track and had tracked him maybe an hour before we caught him in his bed. But it was a long shot and we really didn't see enough of him. We hit him, but not as well as we should have, and he ran off. We kept tracking him and he went to a logging road, where he was standing when a logging truck came along and scared him off.

"Then he went down into this big beaver bog that was all full of swale grass about 2½ feet high and with one spruce tree in the middle of it that was about 10 feet tall. There was this big canal running though the center of the swale grass that was frozen enough to walk on. I stood on that canal and saw his tracks going out into the swale grass, but then they disappeared. I said to Landon, 'That buck has to be here someplace.' I couldn't see where he had crossed the canal and I couldn't see where he had left that patch of grass. We followed his tracks into that swale grass to that spruce tree. The buck was under the tree and he came out from there like a big jackrabbit. We got the deer, and after gutting him, we hid him back under that spruce tree and hiked back to the logging road.

"As soon as we got to the road that same logging truck came back down and stopped to give us a ride. The driver was all excited and started telling us about the 300-pound, 15-point buck he had seen standing in the road. He was stretching his arms out like a moose rack when he was showing us how big he was. He thought we should go find his tracks and get him. I remember bouncing along in that truck as he told that story and Landon and I looked at each other and winked. We never told him that we already had a tag in his ear.

"That was 1989 and the buck was a 10-point that weighed 225 pounds."

GRANNY'S CAP BUCK

"Shane and I went into this mountain called Granny's Cap. This was back in 1990 before they cut all the timber off up there. There was an old camp up there, but nobody used it anymore, so we parked the rig in the dooryard. We walked for three-quarters of the day without finding a track. But if we had walked in the other direction, we would have found the deer just 400 yards from the rig. For some reason, they were all herded up there together. Probably a doe in heat or something like that.

"As we made a big swing and circled back to come in behind the truck, we finally started finding all these buck tracks and they were all headed for the same place. One 150-pound buck we followed had walked up to a log and stuck his horns into it. That buck had at least a 20-inch spread on his antlers, but we were looking for older bucks with more weight. We followed that little buck's track and he took us to where there were a lot more deer. One was a great big buck that was really tearing things up in there. He was scraping and rubbing and fighting with all the smaller bucks. It was pretty late in the afternoon, so we decided to leave him alone and come back the next day. He had all those deer in there and we didn't think he would be going anyplace.

Shane and Lanny double-teamed the "Granny's Cap Buck." Benoit Brothers photo.

"We came in the next morning and picked up his track right where we had left it the night before. That buck never laid down all night long. All he did was run and fight. We tracked him until about 11:30 and all he had done was just run up the ridge and back down and around, but he never left that little area. We stopped up on top of this little ridge about that time and all of a sudden here came two does on a dead run. They went flying by us and never knew we were there, so we just took our safeties off and waited. Pretty soon we could hear him crashing and he was coming. He came running up along the trail the does were on and Shane shot him. That buck was a 7-pointer that weighed 220 pounds.

"But the point of the story is, keep looking. We might just as well have packed up and left the area thinking there were no deer around. But we stuck with it and near the end of the day we finally found them all together in a bunch."

DOLE POND BUCK

"We got up in there and we found this big old buck track. We saw that another guy was tracking a buck up in there too, but it was a different buck. His buck headed up toward Canada. Pretty soon, we jumped this bunch of deer and one of them was the buck we were after, but all I could see was his rack, which left me nothing to shoot at. He sure did have a big ol' rack on him, though.

"We tracked the buck out of the spruces and through a cutting. Somehow we got ahead of him, although I don't know how. The next thing we knew, the buck was coming right at us; and when I tried to shoot him, my gun wouldn't go off. The trigger was clogged up with some pine needles. The buck took advantage of the situation and tried to get out of there. Shane wound up shooting him with a really long shot out across the clear-cut.

"We got back to the camp that night and a guy who was camped down the road came over to our camp and threw his hat on the floor and screamed, 'You shot my **$&&% ##!!@$#* buck on me!' We had seen his tracks and it wasn't his buck, but we couldn't convince him of that. He finally went away, but he went away mad.

"That was in 1981. The buck had a huge 11-point rack and weighed 218 pounds. His face and antlers were covered with ice from where he had gotten all sweated up running during the night, and he looked like some of those bucks you've seen in the calendars."

Lanny Benoit driving "Casper." Bryce M. Towsley photo.

Lanny with his 2002 New Hampshire buck. Benoit Brothers photo.

I spent a week hunting with Lanny in northern New Hampshire late in the 2002 season. The deer were sparse and big bucks hard to find, so we had a lot of "windshield time," which allowed me to pick his brain about deer hunting. We finally found the one big track that Lanny was looking for late on the day I had to leave for another trip. Lanny told me that night that he would shoot the buck in the morning. He went back the next morning and tracked that buck successfully. The buck weighed 225, even in December when he was as "rutted out" as he could be and still survive; he carried a big, 7-point rack.

Pay Attention to the Weather

One day in New Hampshire, it was relatively warm, cloudy and overcast with low-light conditions. We saw a lot more deer activity that day and Lanny pointed out to me that these are the kinds of days deer like. They don't really like bright sunlight, but rather prefer low-light, overcast days.

The very next day was bitter cold, and although it was snowing, the sun was shining brightly down through the falling snow and reflecting off the snow on the ground. It was a "sunglasses" kind of day and the deer activity took a drastic decline, reinforcing his point.

"You take a dark, rainy day," Lanny said, "and the deer are usually roaming everyplace. It makes no difference if it's a half-moon, quarter-moon or no moon. Slice the moon in sections if you want to, it makes no difference. It's the weather. And if it's a rainy, overcast day, the deer will be moving.

"Let's say you have had three days of sunshine and three nights of full moon. It's been warm and the deer haven't moved much. Then you get a rainy, overcast day that's a little cooler and they are going to move. On those kinds of days, the scent will hang in the air longer and a doe-in-heat's scent will really hang around. Those bucks go nuts."

Don't Overcomplicate Things

"A lot of these deer experts try to make this deer hunting thing too complicated," Lanny chuckled. "They all try to make a deer out to be more than it really is. They talk about how majestic it is, which it is. They are wonderful animals. Then they talk about how smart they are. But they are just animals. They aren't really smart; they just learn how to survive. You might say they get smart by accident. If they get shot at and maybe ticked a little, I don't suppose they get "smarter," but they sure do get wary. If you get a buck that's 8 or 9 years old that's never gotten dinged up by hunters and has not had a lot of experience with them, then he's not really a very smart buck. He is a lucky buck because he has lived that long, but that doesn't mean he is smart. My experience in tracking an old buck like that is that he is easier to get than a 3-year-old because he is less wary of you. He has gone through all the battles and, who knows, maybe he has even been shot at and missed. It's just part of his life and I think he doesn't worry so much anymore. Those old bucks, too, they don't want to run any more than you do. You jump them out of their beds and they only run a little way before they start walking. You jump some of those young bucks and they come out of their bed at full bore and they run for half an hour before they stop. But the old bucks tend not to run so much. I'd rather track an old, 8-year-old buck than a 3-year-old. They are just easier to get."

Use the Rut to Your Advantage

"When the rut is on, the best kind of buck to get on is one that's with a hot doe because he is not going to leave that doe. If you ran her over with your truck and left her body lying in the road, that buck would stay with her. He just won't leave her. The will to breed is stronger than the fear of humans.

"One of the bucks we shot in Ontario a while ago was a good example. We jumped them up, and the doe ran one way while the buck ran the other. We just waited and pretty soon that buck came right back past us, trying to get back with that doe. He knew we were there, but he wanted that doe. The only real skill we used was in being smart enough to stand there and wait because we knew he wanted that doe. If we hadn't done that, we might not have gotten that deer.

"If it were legal and you shot that doe, the buck would stand right there and try to make her get up. (Author's Note: I have actually seen this happen when culling does in Texas.) He will even horn her a little to make her stand up. If you jump up a buck and a doe, and the doe circles back like they often do, just wait, because he will be right behind her."

The snow in the Northwoods, while always beautiful, can be quite heavy at times. Benoit Brothers photo.

This buck track headed through thick brush, indicating that he probably does not have a large set of antlers. Bryce M. Towsley photo.

"I think that if you could make a doe scent that really did smell like a doe in heat, there would be hunters being attacked. I don't hear of any hunters being attacked, so I don't think they really have a scent that smells right yet."

"Now you take a big area like here in New Hampshire and you have, say, 10 or 15 does in this entire big basin and three of them come into estrus, it's still going to be hard to find them. There is just too much area and too few deer.

"But in places like Canada where we often hunt, a basin like this will hold 40 or 50 does and maybe 10 or 15 are in heat at the same time, so you have a lot better chance of finding a hot doe. It's always better to find as many deer as you can. It's simply a matter of numbers."

Hunt the Right Habitat

"In the North Country, the deer need to have good winter habitat. They need lowlands with evergreen trees. This keeps the snow cover from getting too deep, as the trees catch a lot of the snow and the branches hold it until the sun and wind evaporate it. Also, the closeness of the trees combine with the canopy to keep the areas protected from the wind and warmer because of less radiational cooling. The deer for miles around will depend on these areas to make it through the tough northern winters. They may live close by, or they may travel 20 miles to get to the yard.

Lanny explained how that plays into his hunting strategy.

"A lot of these mountains in New Hampshire don't have a lot of nice, swampy lowlands for the deer to winter in, so they don't hold a lot of deer. I look for the winter yards to locate good hunting places. They aren't using these yards during the hunting season, but they won't be too far from them, particularly during these late-season hunts.

Lanny Benoit shooting at a buck in northern New Hampshire. Bryce M. Towsley photo.

Lanny Benoit on the trail of a New Hampshire buck. Bryce M. Towsley photo.

"Some bucks will not yard with the rest of the deer–sometimes because they are loners and sometimes because they just don't know about the yard. If they have never yarded up with their mama when they were still young and with her, they may not know about the yard. If it was an easy winter and they didn't yard, the next year, when he is on his own at a year-and-a-half old, he may not find the yard. Most of them follow the other deer and do yard, but some simply find a place of their own to winter. But that doesn't matter; the does all know about the yards and the bucks usually live close by them, so you can be sure that the bucks will find them when it's breeding season. So I always look for good winter habitat when I am hunting new country in the North.

"Of course, that only matters where the winters are severe enough that the deer will yard up. In places just a little farther south, they don't need to yard up to survive the winter, so none of this applies. But anytime you are within 200 miles or so south of the Canadian border or any place north of it, chances are the deer use winter yarding areas to survive the winters."

Learn the Habits of Old Bucks

"There is one way to tell a young buck, even one with big feet and maybe even a big deer that's young. A young buck has never had much for antlers and he is used to dipping under branches without getting them tangled. When they are fawns, they are used to scooting under branches and stuff and it takes a while to get

Craig Jaques films Lanny & Landon Benoit while on the track in northern New Hampshire 2002. While filming this, the buck they were tracking was shot by another hunter just ahead of them. Bryce M. Towsley photo.

out of that habit. But an old buck, one that's had big antlers for a few years, won't go under any branches he doesn't have to. He is also more interested in walking in a straight line and not fooling around. He won't be zigzagging around and wasting time like a young buck that still has a little 'kid' in him.

"Also, a big old buck has been walking these woods for a long time and he is not going to work any harder than he needs to. He knows all the best and easiest routes around and that's what he is going to take.

"A lot of times those old bucks have nothing to do but sleep, eat, and wander around. He may walk around all day, but he also won't use any more energy than necessary and he will always take the easiest route."

Learn to Track at the Proper Speed

"One of the mistakes that people make when tracking is they go too slowly when they are close and give the deer time to get nervous. If he knows you are after him and maybe has seen you, it's better to keep moving at a fast pace. If you slow down, the deer has too much time to think about it; and if he knows you are there, he will probably decide to run. If you move fast enough, he may wait to see you and if you step into the right opening, you may get a shot.

"The death creep is only good if the deer doesn't know you are there. It's meant to surprise a buck that isn't aware of you. But if that deer has already heard you coming, you won't get him with the death creep. If he is 100 yards or 200 yards away and he has heard you going into the death creep and trying to sneak up on him, it won't work. You are better off to keep going along at a fast pace. Sure, he will run off most times, but sooner or later, you will see him.

"It's like when you are driving down the road. Those deer can hear you coming for a long time before they see the truck, but a lot of times they wait until they see you or even until you stop before they run away. It's the same when you are tracking bucks. They are going to hear you, but if you just keep going, they may wait long enough for a shot. Going into the death creep in this situation is a lot like stopping the truck. It's a change, and to them, that signifies danger.

"When there are noisy hunting conditions, you are better off to move right along at a good pace. The deer are usually going to hear you anyway. I have had lots of bucks I didn't want to shoot stand and watch me walk on by them. As long as you don't make eye contact and they don't realize you have seen them, a lot of times they will stand still and let you walk by.

"I know it sounds crazy, but probably 85 percent of the bucks I have shot, I just walked up and shot them. The key is in seeing the buck. You have to be watching for the deer. You can't keep your eyes down on the ground looking at the track.

"Those old bucks are kind of cranky anyway, particularly when they are in the rut. Just because they can hear you doesn't necessarily mean that they know you are a man. They might just think you are a rival buck and they will stick around to kick your butt or try to intimidate you."

Shoot Quickly

"One thing is that when you do see him, you have to make up your mind quick and shoot him. The minute you stop to shoot, the buck is going to go into high alert. You can't fool around, and if you are sure it's the buck you want, shoot him. You can't try to judge his antlers to see if he is big enough. You simply don't have time. You need to shoot him and hope his antlers are as good as you expected they might be from the sign along the track. Also, shoot at what you can see. Don't look around or wait around for a better shot, because chances are you won't get one."

We were on a New Hampshire buck and tracking him for a while when we stopped for Lanny to explain about some sign we had found and to shoot an on-camera interview about what it meant. We were just getting started when a shot rang out about 200 yards in front of us. We had chased that buck out of his "favorite spot" and run him right into another hunter. Lanny was philosophical about it, though, when he said, "Sometimes that's what happens and there is simply no way to avoid it. The buck's going to go where the buck's going to go!"

Don't Give Up on the Late Season

"Late-season hunts are a double-edged0 sword. The buck activity has dropped off quite a bit and it's harder to find a track. But on the other hand, the bucks are not wandering as much, so they are easier to catch up with.

"I get a kick when I read these experts who say that a buck will live his entire life in a square mile," Lanny said. "That expert sure doesn't know much about big-country bucks. They will often roam for miles and their home is everywhere. They are going to roam wherever it takes them to find a doe in heat. They wander all over the place, and they remember where they found deer and go back there during the rut.

"In this country, you can roam for a long way without seeing any deer, then you will find an area that seems to be full of deer. The bucks will roam for miles looking for these 'pockets' of does. So, when the rut is on, you can sometimes follow a buck track for a long way. On the other hand, though, you will also find lots of tracks crossing the roads and in travel areas, so locating a big buck is easier.

"But after the rut in the late-season, the bucks are resting and looking for food. They are trying to recover from the rut so they can survive the winter, and they are not traveling any more than they need to—just enough to find food and shelter. Finding a track is harder and big buck tracks crossing the road can become scarce. But if you can find a track, usually it's a lot shorter walk to find the buck that made it than it is when the rut is cranking up."

Read the Wind

It's a cold, windy day with the snow falling and blowing. Lanny points out that it's hard to tell how old a track is because the snow and wind are filling them in fast. He says that the best thing to do is to get out of the wind-swept hardwood ridges and find some sheltered land with spruces and thick brush. Not only is that probably where the deer are, so they can keep out of the cold wind, but the tracks will also be protected and easier to see and read.

Also on the subject of wind, he has this to say:

"If I am tracking a buck and the wind is behind me, it does concern me, because that's one more tool he has to know where I am," Lanny said. "But you have to stay with the track and just deal with it; you can't stop tracking him because the wind is at your back. Besides, he may even become curious about how you smell. I have had bucks that could smell me and wanted to see what I was. It depends a lot on where you are hunting and how much interaction with man that deer has had in his lifetime."

"Oh," I said. "Foolish me. All this time I thought they waited because you smell so sweet after a month in deer camp!"

Chapter Two

Lane

Lane is the "middle" Benoit brother. At the time of this book's first printing, he was a 49-year-old sheetrock hanger who was proud to wear the crown of the "bad boy" of the clan. He approached most things in life the same say way he did deer hunting—wide open and straight ahead. He was a big, burly guy with wild hair and a bushy, fierce-looking beard that displayed his belief that brawn coupled with a full-ahead charge will solve most problems in life.

Lane enjoyed tossing horseshoes competitively and liked to bass fish. He was a competitive skeet shooter for years and liked nothing better than teaching his son Zeb about the outdoors.

Of the three brothers, Lane was the most like their father, Larry, in many ways (including personality). Like Larry, he was a good storyteller, animated, colorful, and possessing a great memory for details. As a hunter, he was a loner, preferring most often to go his own way. He was excitable and passionate about most things, and that includes deer hunting. The first time I hunted with him, I could see a visible change occur as soon as we stepped into the woods. He stood straighter, his eyes became brighter, and his movements more defined. When we hit a buck track, he locked into an even more intense predatory attitude that made me very glad I wasn't a whitetail buck.

Lane moved very quickly through the woods, but is surprisingly quiet for a big man. He slipped through the brush with a catlike grace that you would never guess he possessed from looking at him. He had a way of pulling success out of a tough season near the end and is known as the "last day" leader of the family. Often he was down to the very last hours of the season when he pulled the trigger. A buck Lane shot in Maine some years back holds the all-time title for the heaviest Benoit buck to be officially weighed, at 284 pounds. In addition, the buck Lane shot in Canada in 2002 is one of the best-racked bucks taken by the family in many years.

Until his passing in 2015, he was still using the same 760 Remington pump rifle in 30-.06 Springfield that he has owned for nearly 30 years. It's equipped with a peep sight, adorned with primitive art, and looks like a road kill. It's clearly a rifle that has seen a lot of hard use, but it's also killed a lot of bucks.

Even Lane's lifestyle was shaped by his demand for independence. He lived with his "woman," Irene, and his

Lane Benoit. Bryce M. Towsley photo.

Artwork on the stock of Lane Benoit's rifle. Bryce M. Towsley photo.

son Zeb in a beautiful log cabin that he and Irene built themselves. It's situated deep in the woods of central Vermont and is "off the grid," as the back-to-nature movement here likes to call it. A generator provides electricity and Lane sees little use for a telephone.

Lane had the first Benoit buck to ever be officially scored, and I asked him to tell me about how he got the big fella.

THE TWISTED-KNEE BUCK

"It was back in 1986, and it was one of my most memorable hunts. It was a pretty unique season because I saw lots of bucks and the season went good, then it went bad and finally it turned good again.

"It started out when Dave Coker and I decided to hunt in this place we called 'the Shark's Tooth.' That's not the actual name, but because I still like to hunt that place, and because there are still some big bucks there, I am not going to tell you the real name.

"We camped out the night before the season opened. We knew that Lanny was coming by in a day or two, so we told him where we were going to be so he could find us. The first morning, we woke up to find snow—not a lot of snow, but we were pretty excited because we woke up and there was the white stuff. We went up this old logging trail that takes you right up into the saddle that forms one side of the Shark's Tooth. The first thing we did was jump some deer. One was a small buck, so we passed on him. Dave and I split up, and as I headed up into the sag in that big mountain range, I found a big buck track following a doe. I thought, *Great, fresh snow, high up on the mountain, and headed up. I shouldn't have any trouble tracking and getting him.* He didn't have an extremely big track, but I could tell he was a good buck. He had a long stride and a lot of width between the tracks, showing he had a big chest. A little farther on, he stuck his head down to eat some fiddlehead ferns and I could see his horn prints in the snow. There were a whole bunch of points on one side, but the other antler only made a swipe, so I didn't really know what he had on that side. But going by the imprint on the snow, I knew he had to be at least a 10-point and maybe bigger, so I was pretty excited.

"It wasn't long before I was close, and as I moved along on the track, sneaking up on the deer, I heard the crack of a branch breaking. It was the doe running away and she drew my attention for just a split second. Then I saw the buck out of the corner of my eye. I had one quick shot just as he went over the top of the mountain. I pulled the trigger just as he dropped down over the other side of that steep ridge top and I shot right over the top of him.

Lane Benoit on the track of a buck in Ontario 2002. Bryce M. Towsley photo

So now the chase was on.

"I had gotten a good look at his antlers as he headed up over the top and I knew he was a dandy with a lot of points. He looked like a 12-point and I decided I wanted this buck. When he got tired of running around the mountain, he headed down into the low country where there wasn't much snow. It was slow going, but I was able to track him in the wet leaves and the smattering of snow and I followed him all day. I got a couple of more cracks at him, but he just never gave me a good shot.

"It got towards the end of the day and the buck had headed high up to the Shark's Tooth, and I thought that would be a good place to leave him for the day. I knew there were some other hunters down low, but I didn't think any of them would come up this high.

"As I was walking out, headed towards the campsite, I stopped for a second to 'answer the call of nature,' and as soon as I was busy a big 8-pointer popped out. I had my gun over my shoulder, so I didn't get a shot. I almost did get a chance as he ran through the hardwoods, but I couldn't get a clean shot, so I didn't pull the trigger.

"But I was all excited. I got a crack at a big 12-point in the morning, almost got a shot at a big 8-pointer, and saw a small buck. I just figured, *What a day! This season is starting out grand.* I decided then and there that I was going shoot that big buck if it was the last thing I did.

"I got to the road and along came Lanny in his old brown van. I told him about my day and about how excited I was about it all. He said, 'Well, that's good. I just came from up north and they have lots of snow, so if this snow melts, you can always go up there to track. You are welcome to come up with me and the rest of the guys who are camped up there.' Which we had planned to do later anyway.

"Lanny left, and as soon as he was out of sight, I heard gunshots. I just figured he was shooting at a partridge or something. Pretty soon, Lanny's van came flying back up the road. It's getting dark by now and he says, 'I've got good news and I've got bad news, which do you want first?'

"I said, 'Give me the good news first.'

"'OK,' he says, 'the place I am hunting up north has a lot of snow and there are a bunch of big bucks.'

"'And the bad news is?'

"'Your 12-pointer's dead. He is down the road in the back of some-guy-from-Maryland's truck.'

"It turns out that he shot it 200 yards from the road. The buck followed a doe down off the Shark's Tooth and got himself blasted. The guy got it just before the end of shooting time.

"The guy almost lost the buck. He hit it in the antler, which stunned the buck and knocked him down. When he ran over to it to see if it was dead, the buck got up on his feet and started to run. But the guy was close, so he shot him again. It was a hell of a rack, a beautiful 12-pointer. I hear it scored really well with lots of mass and long tines.

"My knee started to bother me that night. I didn't realize it in the excitement of chasing the buck, but I guess I must have hurt it going up and down that mountain so many times. By morning, it had swelled up and I could hardly walk. My grand season suddenly wasn't going too good after that. I was feeling kind of depressed; my big 12-point buck was dead and my knee hurt so bad that I couldn't walk. So we pulled out and headed up to where Lanny was camped.

"First thing the next day, he and a good friend tracked a big buck and shot it. So now one of the good bucks was gone, which didn't do much for my mood. Then Coker got wheeling around by this big river where he found a lot of buck sign and he shot a good buck. After that, he decided to tell me about the place.

"'Lane,' he said, 'there is a lot of buck sign down in there. The land is pretty flat and you should be able to get around with that bum knee. You can just hobble around in there and you can probably get a big buck. There are plenty of them running around.'

"So the next morning we headed up the road past where he was talking about and sure enough, there were some big buck tracks headed down into that lowland area by the river where all the trails were. It turns out that I already knew about those trail systems because I had followed a big buck partway down in there the day before, so I knew what he was talking about. So we headed back down with the truck. I hoped to run into a buck coming up the trail as I was limping down it. I figured it might save me a lot of walking because as I said, I could barely walk. Mostly I was just hobbling along and I knew I couldn't go far or into any rough country. As we parked, Lanny and all his pals came along and asked, 'What are you guys doing?'

"I said, 'We are going river buck hunting.'

"Lanny laughed and said, 'All the buck tracks are up on top.'

"'Yeah I know,' I said, 'you guys go track them. I can't go, my knee is shot.'

"So they went up there and split up. They found a track that Lanny started to follow, but before long one of his buddies cut him off so he left the track to him. Meanwhile, we went down to the bottom. There was a camp full of hunters down there, but we knew they weren't hunting near their camp because nobody saw any man tracks the day before. We didn't want to interfere with them, so we asked if they minded if we hunted behind their place. The guy said, 'No, if that's deer hunting, you can have it. It's a hellhole in there and I don't want any part of it. You go ahead.'

"So Coker and I head in and we had gone about 1,500 yards when we heard a branch crack. Coker said, 'It's a buck and he's coming from your left.' I climbed up on a hummock to get some elevation so I could see and there was a trail that was open from all the deer using it. That buck came out about 15 paces from me, following a doe track. He came by with his nose stuffed

A good friend of the Benoits, Dave Coker often shares their hunting adventures as well as their hunting camps. Tom Blais photo.

right in a doe's footprints. It was cold and you could see the steam puffing as he blew the snow out of the track. He turned and came right at us, and all I could think of was that great big rack, which was about 24 inches wide. I thought, *Don't pick your head up*, as I shot between the rack and hit him right between the shoulder blades. He dropped and didn't even quiver. Dave and I danced there hooting and hollering for 10 minutes, even with my bad knee.

"Even to this day when I tell this story, it makes the hair stand up on the back of my neck because it was such a close encounter with a big buck. He was just a few feet from me and I had never been that close to a live big buck before.

"I had him measured and he scored $142^7/_8$ in the Maine Trophy Antler & Skull Club's perfect category. The net was $140^5/_8$, so he was almost perfect, with only 2 inches of deductions. That was the first Benoit buck that's ever been officially scored. That buck weighed 242 pounds.

"The next year, in the same riverbed swamp, I pulled out another buck that weighed 284 pounds, the heaviest buck any of us has weighed. That place was really good hunting, but then word got around we were hunting there and it was goodbye hunting area, because they all moved in and started hunting our spot. That's why I am so protective about my hunting locations these days.

"Not only was this a memorable hunt because of having all the elements of a great hunt, but it was even better because I was hunting with my best friend. It's a rare thing to share a moment like that with a good friend. Dave Coker and I have been hunting together since 1979. Dave shot his first buck with us in 1980. He has done well ever since. He works hard at it and shoots a big buck every year."

THE NUMB-BUTT BUCK

In the 2002 season, Lane shot the best-racked buck of his life. It was also the first buck he has ever taken while sitting on a stand. Once again, I asked him to tell the story.

"It actually started the year before, in 2001. Craig Jaques had a crack at this buck that year, but the cameraman couldn't get the deer into the viewfinder, and they let the buck walk off. We later nicknamed the buck 'Booner' because we thought it would make the record book. When I arrived in camp, Craig was switching roles from hunter to cameraman and he was going to film me. 'This is a buck we should be hunting,' he told me. And he was right. After he described the deer to me, I knew that we were going to track that deer and shoot that buck.

"The first morning out, we had a little bit of snow; it wasn't a lot of snow, but it was enough. We found his track right off. He didn't have a big track, but it was distinctive in the way he walked and the way it looked. We ended up tracking the buck for about four hours and we were getting really close. But the day had warmed up and the snow was melting fast, and finally the track was gone.

"But the buck made a mistake when he took me through this particular place where I finally ended up shooting him. Whenever I am tracking a buck, I am always cataloging these places as a good spot to come back to when the conditions are not great for tracking.

"This one was full of rubs and scrapes of different ages, so it was clear that he was using it often. Several of the rubs were 'shaggy,' which is something I like to see. The rubs that are polished up smooth are often smaller bucks with rather plain, less coarse antlers. But those big, shaggy-looking rubs are usually an older buck. That's because as bucks grow older they start to develop more 'character' in their antlers. They grow more and longer points and they often start to develop little 'sticker' points around the base of their antlers. All this extra bone results in making those shaggy rubs, and that's why I like to see them.

"The spot was a high knob that was surrounded by swampy lowlands with thick vegetation. This knob was the only high ground around and it formed a good travel corridor for bucks coming through there. It also was situated along a natural funnel that was absolutely covered with rubs and scrapes. It was clearly being used by a lot of bucks, but none more than our 'Booner.'

"These are the kinds of places I like to find and remember for when I am hunting on bare ground. It's tough to track much on bare ground, so I try to concentrate

Above: Lane Benoit looks at a buck's rub. Bryce M. Towsley photo.

Left: Lane's 2002 buck. Tom Blais photo.

Above: Lane loves to see big, "shaggy" rubs like this one. Benoit Brothers photo.

my efforts in locations with the most buck activity. Often I'll just still-hunt through them, moving slowly and keeping my eyes moving and searching. I try to follow the main deer trails so that I can move quietly, because a well-used trail will not have a lot of sticks to break.

"When you are tracking a buck, you will find that he will take you through these places time and time again. Often, too, you will find that different bucks will take you to the same place. They are simply places that bucks like. I always try to remember them so that I can use them to locate a buck track when the snow is good, or I can go and hunt there when the snow is not good for tracking. With the climate changes and the resulting unreliable snow cover, trying to film our hunting and I suppose because I am getting a little older, I also think of them as places to go and sit to wait for a buck. I don't do it very often, but I recognize that these are great places when I do.

"The snow melted, and we were back to bare-ground hunting, so we moved out of that place and went to another area with a little snow and a lot of bucks. I shot a good buck in there and was done for the year.

"In the 2002 season we found him again and as soon as we started tracking that same buck, he took us right back through that same place. It looked just like it did a year ago, full of shaggy rubs and littered with lots of big tracks and scrapes.

"As the season progressed, the snow conditions were getting progressively worse. Craig and I were trying to film shooting a buck and so we were 'walking the rocks' as we called it. The rocks are the open bedrock ridges in a burned-out area we hunt in Canada. They are the ridges that run through the woods and are exposed bedrock in

A "shaggy rub." Craig Jaques photo.

most places. It's easier walking, as the cover is not as thick as in the valleys. Also, because they are higher, you often have a better view of the valley floor; sort of like using a treestand to get above the vegetation. We hiked for 15 miles one day, but it just wasn't working. Craig headed back to camp late in the afternoon, and I hiked up into this place to check it out. I could see that there was still a lot of deer activity, and as I was poking along, a nice 10-pointer jumped out in front of me and ran up on the bank. I could have easily shot him, but I wanted to shoot my buck on camera so I let him go. This was very likely the same buck that Craig wound up shooting later.

"It was late in the season and things were cold and crunchy, with the snow old and poor. But that night we had a warm front move in and it got a lot warmer. When we woke up, it was foggy and misty. Bucks love those conditions and they will be on the move, freshening scrapes and looking for does. I had never shot a buck in my life when sitting and I always wanted to try it, so I told Craig, 'We are going to go sit in that place we found.'

"As soon as it was light enough to see, we started up the trail. We quickly found a good place and sat down. It wasn't long before a doe came through acting like she was in heat, and we knew that conditions were looking right to shoot a big buck that day.

"After about 45 minutes, we started raking a tree with an old dry stick to sound like a buck rubbing his antlers. We broke some brush and blew a few times on the grunt tube. Pretty soon, we could hear deer moving around. Then all of a sudden, a nice buck popped up in front of us in the farthest point of view that we could see. It was a good buck, probably the same one I had seen the day before, and I was going to shoot him. But Craig couldn't get him in the camera's viewfinder. I had a perfect broadside shot, but because of the slightly different angle that Craig was looking at him from, he couldn't see the buck at all. We had a tense whispering conversation about it and decided to wait him out and maybe try to coax the buck out to where we could film shooting him. We waited and worked the grunt tube a little bit and suddenly I could hear a deer coming from behind us, running toward the other buck. I saw that he had a huge rack, but I didn't shoot at first so that Craig would have time to get the camera on him. The camera takes about 8 seconds to turn on, and I wanted to make sure he had enough time. Then the buck stopped for a minute in the exact spot we were trying to bring the other buck into to film him. I was waiting for the signal from Craig, but I figured he must have him now, so I put the bead behind his shoulder and let him have it. He took off running and I shot three more times, but I really didn't need any of them.

"It turned out to be the largest racked buck I have ever shot. It has an official net B&C score of $163^7/_8$, which qualifies for the annual B&C awards. The gross was just short of 170 points. He weighed 212 pounds and had 11 scorable points. Maybe I didn't shoot him in the traditional 'Benoit' way of tracking, but it was one of the most exciting hunts in my life. That's because the nearly half hour we spent trying to coax that other buck close enough to shoot was pretty intense. There was a lot of anticipation building to a climax here and I remember getting so excited that my right leg was starting to quiver. Then the big guy came out and I really got excited! When you are tracking, things usually happen fast so you don't have a chance to think about it too much and you don't get wound up until after the shot. This was definitely different.

"Lanny, Shane, and Tom Blais were close enough that they heard my shooting and they showed up a little while later. Tom wanted to film how we got the buck, so we were going back to where I had shot from to do the cutaways and all that other stuff that you have to do for the camera when you are making a video. Tom wanted some footage of me shooting so I had reloaded my rifle, and it's a good thing that I did. As we were walking back and were about 10 yards from the spot, I was in the lead—with Tom behind me with the camera rolling and Craig behind him—when a 10-point buck popped up over the hill. I spotted the buck first and you can hear me on the video say, 'Will you look at that!' I stepped aside and handed the gun to Craig while Tom continued to film the buck. Craig wailed him through the heart and Tom got it all. That buck came right up that doe's trail with his nose in her tracks and he didn't even notice we were there until it was too late."

Craig's buck was a 10-point that weighed 218 pounds.

ANSWERING A CHALLENGE

The Benoits live in Vermont, and although they've shot a lot of big bucks in the Green Mountain State years ago, they rarely hunt there anymore. The reasons are simple enough: If you are going to shoot big bucks, you have to hunt where they live, and Vermont is no longer one of those places. Mismanagement of the deer herd, hunting pressure, and changing habitat due to social pressures have pretty much spoiled the trophy buck hunting in the Green Mountain State.

But two things related to this converged in 2002. First was a hunter who is like a lot of others in that they just don't get it. They refuse to believe that there are few, if any, big bucks left in most of the Vermont woods. They ignore the lack of big tracks and other sign in the woods and the even stronger evidence at the check stations where very few big bucks arrive with tags in their ears. These guys think the bucks are still out there, but

Lane Benoit and Craig Jaques with bucks shot at the same place just a few minutes apart. Tom Blais photo.

they are too hard for mere mortals to hunt. (Actually, I have been on some guided hunts where the outfitter had the same "head in the sand" outlook on the deer situation. Do you suppose it's something in the water?)

The other factor that converged is simply that you don't challenge Lane unless you really mean it.

"Usually I don't hunt in Vermont much anymore," Lane told me. "And I sure wasn't planning to hunt that day. But I stopped at the Duxbury Country Story near my home for coffee early that morning and there was a fella in there running his mouth. He was spouting off about how we hunt in Canada, Maine, and all those places because we can't do it anymore in Vermont. He implied that we were all washed up. I told him, no, that wasn't true, but that the class of deer just wasn't here in Vermont. There are a few good bucks, but the chances of finding one and then tracking him without running him into another hunter are just not that good. We hunt in other places because they have better bucks and areas that are better suited to our style of hunting, which of course is tracking.

"I took this guy out on the porch and I pointed up at the big mountain you can see from the store. 'I am going to climb up on that mountain today,' I said. 'And I am going to shoot a buck, just to show you I can do it. It probably won't be a great buck, but he will be a good buck.'

"'Yeah, sure,' he said. 'You are just going to go shoot a buck, just like that? It's that easy, is it?'

"'It's not that easy,' I said. 'But if I have a little luck on my side, I'll guarantee you I'll have at least a crack at one today. There's a big, flat plateau area up there with some little hummocks on it. When hunting season is on, the deer get pushed up on there and they stay. Every time I have climbed that mountain I have found a buck or two. I am sure I will find some today.'

"It was about 9:30 by then. It was one of those cold, noisy days when the snow is crunchy. There were guys talking about how they weren't even going hunting that day because it was too noisy to walk in the snow. I tried to explain to them that nobody likes crunchy snow, but you can still shoot deer. If you aren't in the woods, of course you aren't going to get a deer, that's guaranteed. But if you work at it and keep trying, you can still shoot bucks even in crunchy snow. I told them we get deer every year in crunchy snow, but I don't think they were listening.

"By 10 o'clock, I was parked, suited up in my hunting gear and headed up on the mountain. When I was

Craig Jaques with his Ontario 2002 buck.

Benoit Brothers photo.

Lane Benoit looks at a buck's trail. Bryce M. Towsley photo.

last up on that mountain, I was a lot younger and it took me at least an hour back then, so I knew I would be a while getting up there. It was crunchy and noisy and terrible conditions for tracking a buck and I'm starting to think I might have made a mistake. I knew that I had run my mouth, but to shoot a buck today I would really have to earn it.

"About halfway up, I found a buck working his way up the mountain ahead of me. I found where he had rubbed a tree and where his antlers had left a mark in the snow. I could see it wasn't a huge buck, but by Vermont standards he was pretty good.

"The farther up the mountain I climbed, the better the conditions became. There was some fresh powder snow on top of the crusty snow and the higher I climbed, the deeper that powder got. At the top, there was 6 inches of powder on top of the frozen snow. It was still noisy, but that soft powder snow was muffling the noise to where it was pretty good for hunting and pretty quiet.

"The track I was following was pretty old. It had been made during the night and it was snowed in and tough to follow. He had gone up the mountain, then back down part way, then up again. But I stayed with it, and when he finally got up on top, he got in with a bunch of other deer. I was working my way through some spruces and it was nice and quiet going. I am just poking along, taking a few steps at a time, then stopping and looking. I kept thinking to myself that these tracks have to freshen up pretty soon. Then suddenly they were smoking fresh and I knew I was right into the deer. All of a sudden I jumped a buck to my right and as he ran off, I snapped my gun up, but I didn't shoot. Instead, I just watched him run away. He had a nice rack; not a great rack, but a good one. I thought to myself, *Lane, why didn't you shoot that buck? You are in Vermont and he was a good buck for here; you aren't likely to find anything better.* In my mind, I was going to get on his track and try to remedy my mistake and eventually shoot him. But I didn't get two steps when I heard a deer blow and off to my left another buck was running. He was almost identical to the first one and I wasn't about to make the same mistake again. I shot one time and I had my first Vermont buck in years laid down there in the snow.

"He wasn't a huge deer, but I was pretty tickled with that buck. I was hunting by myself with no cameraman, back to my roots you might say. I sat down for a while and reminisced about hunting this place back in the '70s when I was a lot younger. Just as it had been back then, there simply wasn't anybody else hunting up in there. The bucks knew that and felt safe. That's why they were hanging out up there.

"This was one of those places that the average hunter will think of as inaccessible because it's too much work to get up there. It's just too far, too steep, and full of ledges. But no matter what kind of shape you are in, you can make it if you want to; just keep putting one foot in front of the other and sooner or later you will make it. It's worth the effort and I can guarantee if I go back next year, there will be bucks up there. Even in states with lots of hunting pressure, you can usually find a spot like this, the country nobody else is hunting and that's where the bucks will be.

"There was a big ravine on the way out and I was trying to avoid it when I was dragging the buck, but somehow I managed to find it anyway. I didn't have a clue how I was going to get that buck through there without getting killed, so I just dragged him to the edge, pushed him over and prayed he wouldn't smash his antlers on the way down. Somehow he found his way all the way to the bottom in one piece. I worked my way down behind him nice and slow. I had to be careful because I have a bad knee, and the ravine was full of pitfalls. It was all ledge and full of holes and snags. They were all covered with snow so you couldn't see them, so it took me quite a while to get to the bottom, but I finally did.

"I dragged the buck to a snowmobile trail and decided to leave him. I normally don't worry about doing that because if you pile some brush on the buck and urinate around it, the coyotes will leave it alone. But there are a lot of coyotes in Vermont now and they are acclimated to men and not spooked by the scent, so I really didn't want to leave the buck overnight. I got home and called around, but everybody had things to do and couldn't help me.

"So I went to Irene and said, 'Honey, would you like to go for a nice moonlight walk?' She knows I am not the most romantic guy around and she figured out pretty quickly that I had a buck up in the woods. I told her it wasn't that far and that when she heard the big brook running, we would almost be there. So Irene, our son Zeb, and I headed back up the snowmobile trail to get the buck. We grabbed a six-pack of beer and some Mountain Dew for Zeb and we made a picnic out of it.

"We didn't go very far before we came to a small brook and Irene said, 'Well, this wasn't too bad.' I laughed and said that this was just a little stream and there wouldn't be any doubt when she heard the big brook. Well, you can hear it a long time before you get to it, so even after she

Above Right: Lane Benoit with his son, Zeb, in Vermont in 2002.

Lane Benoit photo.

Right: Lane Benoit with Irene in Vermont in 2002.

Lane Benoit photo.

heard the brook, we had a long way to go. Then I took her over a steep bank that was snow covered and slippery and she didn't like that much.

"But we finally got to the deer. It was a nice moonlit night and we made an adventure of it. If I got tired dragging, we would stop and sit on the deer while we drank one of the beers. We even let Zeb drag the buck by himself. It was comical to watch as he got run over by the sliding buck on the downhill trails. He really liked dragging that deer; he thought it was fun, which is a good thing. It's always a good idea to have a well-trained young fella waiting to drag your deer for you when you get older. It was a great night and we all had a really good time!

"That weekend, I brought Zeb back up to where I shot the buck to show him what it takes to get a big buck. I wanted to show him that to get good deer, you need to work hard and get into places where the other hunters won't go. He is a great little hunter and we got his first turkey last spring. I know that he listens to me and this lesson will probably stick. It won't be long before he will be representing the next generation of Benoit buck hunters."

WHY THE CHAINS?

During our long drive back to camp one night in Canada, the subject of chaining the bucks to the porch of Larry's house came up. I knew it was because of some attempted theft, but I had never gotten "the rest of the story."

Lane chuckled and said, "I am not sure we want this story in print. But it was a long time ago and nobody got hurt, so I guess it's safe to tell now.

"It was after a successful season in Vermont and Maine and we had all the bucks strung up on the porch at Pop's house. It was a cold night and we were all in the house. With all those deer hanging on the porch, there was a lot of weight stressing the support beam. All of a sudden, we heard a big cracking noise. We realized later that it was the sound made by the weight coming off the porch beam and the beam cracking as the stress was released when this guy cut the rope that was holding one of the biggest bucks. My sister Zana was just a little shaver back then, about 6 or 7 years old, and she opened the door and counted the deer really quick. 'One, two, three, four, five, six . . . hey . . . there's a deer gone!' This kid named John was there visiting with us and he grabbed this old 10-gauge shotgun that was by the door. It was one of those old-fashioned guns with external hammers, and he leveled it at the guy who was just loading the buck into his van and cocked both hammers. The guy dropped the buck and dove into his van. He took off down the road with the door still open and swinging in the breeze. We got his plate number and reported him, but the cops didn't do a damn thing because he never got the deer into the rig, so they said we couldn't prove he was stealing anything. After that, we started chaining the bucks to the porch.

"But the untold part of the story is that the shotgun was loaded with double-ought buckshot and it had a hair trigger. If that kid had even breathed on the trigger, he would have cut that guy in half. That thief doesn't have a clue how close he came to death."

THE "TURNING POINT" BUCK

"Perhaps my most memorable buck was the one that finally got me pointed straight on the road to becoming

Deer chained to the Benoit family porch. Benoit Brothers photo.

a tracker. This buck was when tracking finally came around for me, when I finally got the confidence to do it on my own. Before that I was hanging around with Lanny and my dad to learn how to do it, but this was my first big test on my own.

"We had been hunting Maine for a while that season. Actually, it was the first time I ever hunted in Maine, and I was a little bit intimidated by those big woods. There wasn't any snow for the whole season and hunting the entire season on bare ground was starting to wear us down. Then finally we got a snowstorm. Maine didn't get much snow, just a dusting that went away pretty quick, but Vermont got hammered; they got a pile of snow. Shane and I had to get back pretty soon anyway because of work. I had an old 1958 Ford that was kind of a Flintstone rig where your feet almost hit the pavement through the rusted-out floorboards, and we pointed it toward Vermont.

"As soon as we got back, Shane and I forgot about work and headed up to South America Pond in the Northeast Kingdom of Vermont. It was a nasty day and the weather was terrible. We had an awful time on the roads and it wasn't until about 9 o'clock before we got up into where we wanted to be. But as soon as we got there, we cut a set of tracks from a buck and a doe.

"I followed the tracks and caught them in their beds. All I could see was the doe, but she kept looking over her shoulder, so I knew the buck was right there; I just couldn't see him. Well, they jumped up and ran off and I followed. They got in with a bunch of other deer and I lost the track for a while. I thought they were headed up on the mountain, so I swung out from all those other deer and headed on a swing up on the mountain to try to pick up their tracks again. Up on that mountain, I bumped into Shane and asked him if he had seen any tracks, because he had come from another direction and it would save me from going over there to check.

"'No, I haven't seen any fresh tracks at all,' he said.

"So I headed back down into that mess of thick brush and deer tracks and circled around all the tracks until I found where that buck and doe had come out. That's where I learned the method to find the track after it gets in with a mess of deer. You just keep circling around and around like a beagle dog looking for the scent, until you find the track.

"After the deer came out of that spot, I didn't track them 1000 yards when they both ran out in front of me and I got a shot at the buck. I could have easily have taken a couple more good shots, but I was using a semi-auto in those days and the damn thing jammed after the first shot. So I cleared the jam and got back on the track and sure enough, I had a blood trail. I followed it for a little way, and there he was leaning up against a tree looking pretty sickly, so I gave him another one and that finished it.

"He was a nice 200-pound 8-point buck, and I was pretty proud of him because I got him all on my own and by tracking. It was the turning point for me becoming a big-buck tracker. I was hooked for life.

"The next day, Shane and I decided we would go back and double team. We hiked up into the same valley and we found another buck track. We followed that one and snuck up on him in his bed. Shane shot that buck. We dragged him out and we had both bucks hung up on the porch. Dad and Lanny were both still in Maine, so this cured a lot of the problems we had been having. People were saying things like, 'Your dad is shooting your deer for you,' or 'Lanny is shooting your bucks for you,' but after that, it stopped. They knew we shot these bucks on our own.

"Before they got back to Vermont, Lanny and Dad had heard about the big bucks we had gotten. When they drove up, my dad had the proudest look in his eyes. I remember saying, 'Dad, I finally get it. I understand about tracking now!' From that day on, I have been a tracker. It was the turning point in becoming a trophy-buck hunter.

"I had actually shot a buck up in those same woods with my dad the year before. We had been tracking when I spotted the buck bedded down in some real thick stuff and said, 'Dad, there's the deer!' He dropped to his knees and I shot the buck. That is the reason why I went back up in there. I knew it was pretty good deer hunting, and I knew the woods and where to find the deer."

LAST-DAY BUCKS

Lane has a reputation in the family for pulling it out on the last day of the hunt. In talking with him we

Lane and Larry with one of Lane's recent bucks. Lane Benoit photo.

figured out that around 10 or 15 percent of the bucks he has shot over the years were on the last day. I asked him to tell me about the year he did it twice.

"In 1988, I shot a pair of last-day bucks. One was in Maine and the other in New Hampshire. One year before in Maine, in 1987, I had shot the 284-pound buck, and then in 1986 I shot a 242-pound buck with a giant rack. Those were pretty hard acts to follow and in 1988 I wandered around all season trying to find one as big or bigger. I did find one wide-racked buck when Pop and I were riding around scouting and looking at buck tracks. We came up to this notch at the top of the mountain, and I remember saying, 'Boy, this has to be a great place for them to cross.' Just as we got up there, this great big buck popped out in front of us and ran across the road. I knew it probably wasn't as good as those other two, but he was still real good, and in Maine you have to be realistic. It was too late in the day to hunt the buck, and we didn't have any snow then anyway, so we moved on. But as soon as we had snow, I went out and found the buck again. He was using that notch pretty regularly to travel across the mountain, and I tracked that buck off and on several times throughout the season. I guess I tracked him four or five times, but nothing ever worked out right. I got a couple of shots at him, but nothing very good and I just didn't connect.

"Then all of a sudden, it's the last day. The guys were giving me a hard time in camp about not having a buck yet, but I just took it and told them, 'You know me, I never give up. I have shot them on the last day before.'

"It was cold when we got up that last day and the snow was crunchy and noisy. It wasn't looking all that good, but as the day progressed, it warmed up. I started tracking the buck about 10 o'clock in the morning and by 11 or 12, it was just about perfect. You could really read a track in that snow to tell how far ahead of you the buck was. I came to his bed, then another bed and another. At that last one, I could see that he wasn't spooked when he left, but was just traveling along feeding. I remember it was the last day and I was trying to make no mistakes. I was being very careful and sneaky and wasn't leaving anything to chance. One step at a time, and I was very careful not to break any branches.

"I knew I was close to the buck and I looked over to see a rabbit sitting there looking at me. I remember thinking, *Now don't you go spooking and running off, scaring that buck*, because weird things like that had been happening to me all year. But the rabbit stayed in his spot, and as I stepped around some spruces, there was the buck 25 yards in front of me, feeding along without a clue I was there.

"I shot him behind the shoulder and as he ran, I threw a couple more after him anyway, like I always do. I remember thinking that if the guys are listening to me they will be calling me 'pow-pow' again for shooting so much. But the first shot did the trick and the buck only went 20 yards before he piled up.

"The best thing was that even though I had tracked that buck for almost 4 hours, I was only a quarter of a mile from the road. He just never went anywhere too far. So I dragged him out to the road and sat on the buck to wait for Coker to come give me a ride.

"I remember later the boys coming up the road and there was my buck in the back of the truck. I remember, too, Pop coming over with that famous grin of his and giving me a hug. He was pretty proud that I never gave up and it paid off. That buck weighed 215 pounds. He was an 8-point with a 21-inch spread.

"That's the moral of the story: never give up. Even if it is the last day, you can't get discouraged and give up. I have shot a lot of bucks on the last day. Part of that is because I am not as fussy then, but most of it is because I don't give up.

Lane with two last-day bucks from Maine and New Hampshire 1988. Lane Benoit Photo.

"The next day Coker and I headed to New Hampshire to hunt because their season ran for another week. Once again, it got down to the last day, which was also the last day I would be hunting anyplace that year.

"I picked up a buck track crossing a logging road. He wasn't a great buck, but it was the only track I could find because the deer just weren't moving that day. It was, of course, the last day, so I took it.

"To a lot of hunters it would have looked hopeless. The snow was frozen and crunchy and every time you stepped, it sounded like cornflakes crunching. But I knew that the buck would probably head up the mountain. He did and soon enough he started feeding heavily and climbing higher. Near the top of the mountain, the crusty snow gave way to powder that was a lot quieter to walk in. I suppose that the higher elevation maintained cooler temperatures, and when it warmed up enough to melt the snow down lower, up high, it stayed powder.

Lane's 2001 buck. Lane Benoit photo.

Lane and cameraman Craig Jaques with Lane's 2001 buck.

Lane Benoit photo.

So when it got cold again, it didn't freeze into crusty ice like the melting snow down lower did.

"The buck was bedded on top where walking was just as quiet as could be and I caught him in his bed. When he ran off, he kept a spruce tree between us as he ran straight away. I emptied the gun at him and cut that spruce tree right off in the process. But I got the buck. I didn't let that tree bother me; I just kept shooting. He wasn't a great buck. He weighed 178 pounds and had an 8-point rack, but he sure was a trophy for the last day."

CHARGING AT THREE BUCKS

"In the 2001 season we had to deal with the lack of snow. So as I always do on bare ground, I covered a lot of ground looking for bucks. I found this good spot, and if you remember, Bryce, you and I hunted there in 2002. We didn't find many deer then, but in 2001 I found a bunch of buck sign in there.

"Craig and I were trying to film, so we went in and found a high spot overlooking a lot of buck sign and we tried rattling, but nothing showed up. So we left and moved on toward a lower spot I knew about. As we moved on through the woods, a buck suddenly broke out to my left. It was a nice little 8-pointer and I remember telling Craig that he would be a good one next year. Then all of a sudden, another buck took off from my right. He was a good one too, but I knew there was a bigger one in there someplace. We had found lots of big tracks and plenty of big, shaggy rubs and I knew the buck making them was bigger than these two, so I let him go too.

"Then I could hear another buck, or at least another deer. He was pacing back and forth, nervous about what was happening, but not wanting to leave. Craig said, 'Let's run right at him, rather than trying to sneak up.' So we did; we ran like hell right at him. The two smaller bucks busted out to the right and left, but the big buck just stood there looking at us. He was standing there watching those younger bucks and he must have thought I was another buck running up to chase them off. This time, I shot three times and I shot down another tree, but I got the buck! He weighed 231 pounds and was a 9-pointer that scored 150.

"You just never know if you hit the deer good or not. Even if it appears that you did, if he is still running, I believe you should keep shooting. Sometimes you might

Lane and "The Hangover Buck," a 10-pointer that weighed 235 pounds. Benoit Brothers photo.

have hit a tree branch or something with your first shot, so keep putting the lead to them."

HANGOVER BUCK

For obvious reasons Lane debated about telling this one, but it's a good story and illustrates how the whimsy of fate can deliver a big buck when you are least expecting it and perhaps even when you are secretly hoping against it!

"This was a Maine buck," Lane started. "There was this fella named Bruce hunting with us and I had to go back to Vermont, so he volunteered to drive me. We had planned to return to Vermont, take care of the business, and then drive back all in the same night, even though it was about a 5-hour drive each way. He had a case of Millhouse beer in the truck and because he was driving, I was free to imbibe, which I did. That turned out to be pretty potent beer.

"We got in late, of course, and we were up early to hunt. I had been seeing a bunch of does in this pie-shaped piece of woods. It was surrounded on two sides by roads and by a big clearcut on the end. We found a set of big buck tracks going in, but they didn't come out. So Coker and I were going to work the piece of woods as a team. He was going in on one side and I was going in on the other. We were just getting ready when Bruce, Pop, and Shane showed up and decided they wanted in on the action. There was this big rock overlooking the clearcut that would be the perfect place for a shooter. We all flipped a coin and kept flipping until there was one man standing, which turned out to be me, so I was the 'designated shooter.' The other guys spread out to work that piece of woods and somebody was going to get a shot. We figured if he was going to escape, it would be out that big clearcut where I would be watching.

"I ran to get to that rock early so I could catch my breath before things started happening. Of course, my head was pounding when I got there, but I climbed up on the rock, and as soon as I did, there was that buck out in the clearcut and headed for the guys in the woods. He had been out in the clearcut all the time and was headed for those does in the woods without a clue those guys were there waiting.

"I was all out of breath from running and my head was pounding. He was out there about 250 yards and the big-bead front sight I use is designed for shooting fast up close, not for those long shots. But I started shooting and he looked like the duck in the carnival shoot. I would shoot and he would reverse direction; I would shoot again and he would run back the other way. Back and forth he went, with me shooting at him. Every time I pulled the trigger, it was excruciating because the recoil would jar my head and make the headache worse. I shot at him six times, emptying the gun and then hand-feeding the last shot. I knew I hit him several times, but I didn't know how many or how hard. Finally on the last shot, he went down. He was out there quite a ways by then. I jumped off the rock and reloaded my gun. Pop was there by then and he helped me find the blood trail. There was hair and blood all over the place and Pop remarked, 'He is hit hard. He's not going anyplace.' He didn't either; we found him right where he dropped on that last shot. I had to finish him off with another shot, which I really didn't want to do. He was a big-racked buck that was worth the effort and pain."

Lane Benoit looks at where a buck went under a log. Bryce M. Towsley photo.

Lane had a different approach to hunting than Lanny or Shane. While it's hard to pin down exactly, it might be best described as "more direct." While Shane uses finesse, Lane's style was closer to a full frontal attack. But, that's not exactly right either, or at least not complete. He may have hunted aggressively, but he didn't just blunder ahead blindly. Lane was always thinking and reacting to the changing situations. He hunted hard and he hunted aggressively, but he also hunted smart.

Lane was a student of the whitetail and is a great teacher with a gift for description and narration. On the long ride back to camp one night, I asked him to tell me about some of his best tips, tactics, and techniques.

Watch What You Drink

"Well, my first advice is do not drink Millhouse beer if you are hunting in the morning! Especially if you think you will need to shoot your gun!"

Catalog the Good Spots

"One of my biggest tips is to cover a lot of ground and catalog in your mind all the good spots you find with lots of buck sign. Go back to them to find the buck's tracks when you have tracking snow, or just to hunt if you are still waiting for snow.

"Don't work those places too hard, though. If you are working that place for a few days and it's not happening, get out and go to the next place.

"Look for places where the bucks are leaving a lot of sign, because they are obviously spending a lot of time there. Look for natural travel corridors where a buck coming down off the mountain is just naturally going to go. Pay attention to where a buck is taking you when you are tracking him. If a buck takes you through a place more than once, or if more than one buck takes you through the same place, there is a reason. That's a place you will want to remember.

"Look for the saddles in the mountain tops, they like to cross there. Also, look for the doe concentrations. Does will attract bucks any time in the hunting season."

Lane Benoit at a buck scrape. Bryce M. Towsley photo.

Learn to Read Antler Sign

"For years I have concentrated on the big tracks of big-bodied deer, but I have noticed that some of the best-racked bucks are smaller deer. These 170-pound or 180-pound or, even in a good area, 200-pound bucks are deer that I used to pass up. But I don't anymore. I'll follow the track for a while to see if I can get a handle on how good his rack is. If I think it's a small rack, I'll quit the track, but if he is a big-racked buck, I'll try to kill him.

"Look where his antlers are catching the brush when he is traveling through. Look where he has gone under a log and where his antlers have hit. If you follow him long enough, you will see where he has put his nose on the ground to feed and usually you can find where his antlers have hit the snow. This is a great indicator of how big he is. Even if the track indicates he is not a huge buck, if the rack is big, I'll go get him. I think that's one reason my racks are averaging bigger in recent years."

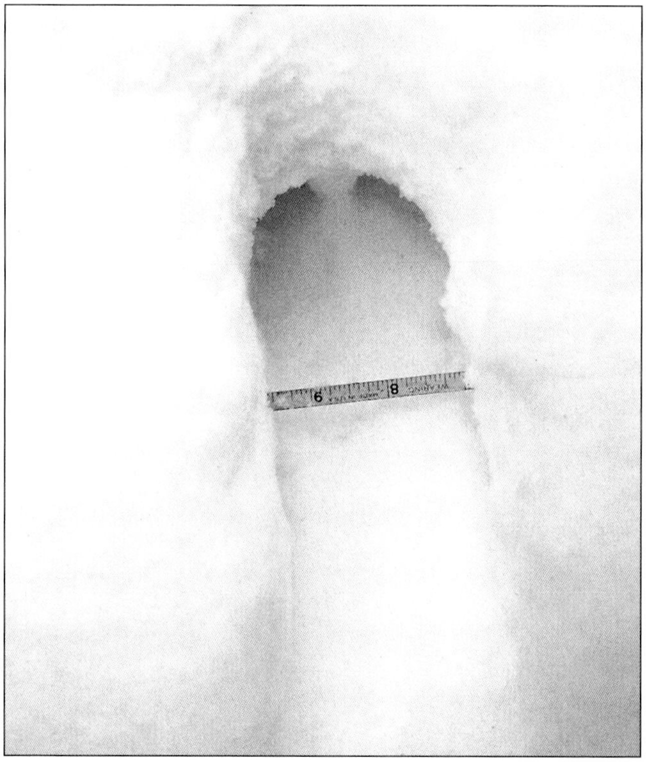

This is a buck track from a deer weighing about 200 pounds. Bryce M. Towsley photo.

Learn to Vary Your Speed According to the Sign

"One of the most important things you can learn is when to vary your speed—when to go fast and when to slow down. You need to learn to read the sign.

"The best indication is when a buck is feeding and meandering and getting ready to lie down. In the North Country, they like to feed on the 'Old Man's Beard.' (This is a green/gray lichen (*Usnea barbata*) that grows on the North Country tree limbs, usually hanging on softwood trees and looking like a stunted version of the Spanish moss common to the South.) They seem to like eating this just before they lie down, sort of like dessert. If he has been eating Old Man's Beard, he is usually bedded down within 200 yards.

"Some of the key places where you will find deer are those protected from the wind, but be careful when you are in those locations. Also, any time you track a buck into a bunch of deer, he has probably slowed down looking for a hot doe. It's time to slow down too.

"But on the other hand, the biggest mistake most hunters make is to go too slow on the track and they never catch up with the buck. You can't shoot at him if you don't see him. I like to move fast most of the time. I would rather bump him a time or two than I would to follow all day without seeing him."

Work Harder Than Other Hunters

"Human nature is to hunt where it is easy for you. We all try to take the easy way out, and the deer know this. The deer simply move into the areas that are a lot of work to get to because they know most hunters will not follow. The best advice I can offer to find big bucks is to work harder than the other hunters and go to places they will not.

"I like to hunt in the thickest stuff I can find. That's where the bucks will be during most of the day."

Keep Your Eyes Open

"Don't just look where the track is going. The buck will not usually be in that direction. They tend to be off to one side or the other of the track. When they bed down, they almost always fishhook to one side or the other of the trail. Watch for the most likely places as you are tracking and make sure you stop and look those places over. Whenever you jump a buck, backtrack him and go back to where you should have seen the buck. Reenact your screw-up to see what you did wrong. This will also give the buck some time to calm down a little. Lots of times, they will only run a little way before they stop and find a good place to look back to see what you are. If you don't follow right away, he will calm down. Use the time to learn what you did wrong, and you kill two birds with one stone."

Lane Benoit moves fast on a buck track in Ontario 2002.

Bryce M. Towsley photo.

Lane Benoit shooting at a buck. Bryce M. Towsley photo.

Keep Movement to a Minimum

"Be careful about making too many movements in the woods. Keep all your movements to a minimum. Blend with your surroundings. Be careful about stepping out into an opening if you think you are close to a buck. Lots of times they will go to an open area and stop to look back. If you step out, they are gone. Look for a stump or a blowdown you can get up on and look out across these open areas before you step out into them.

"Sometimes, if you think the buck is waiting for you, blowing a grunt call can make him move enough to see him.

"Don't be afraid to do something different, to change your routine. Don't become one-dimensional."

Listen to the Locals

"When you are in a new hunting area and you meet a local hunter, talk to him for a while. Or at least shut up, and let him talk. Most guys want to brag on their areas and their success and he will tell you a lot about the area. I will go to their camps if invited and I can see what they have for deer in the area. If they have lots of big racks they have shot over many years, I know it's a great place

Lane Benoit on the track of a buck in Ontario 2002.

Bryce M. Towsley photo.

to hunt. But if all they have are little scrub bucks, I might be wasting my time."

Hunt Where They Are

"If you are going to shoot big bucks, you have to hunt where they are. That means you need to move. Most hunters get familiar with an area that they like and they hate to move. But they don't get big bucks that way. I had a friend once who had hunted a place for 13 years without shooting a buck, but he wouldn't move because he liked the area. 'What the hell are you doing?' I asked him. 'Get the hell out of there and go someplace else.' But he liked it because he knew the land and he didn't get lost. He was so scared of getting lost that he wouldn't move to where there were some big bucks."

Practice Shooting All Year

"One key thing that a lot of hunters ignore is, how fast can you get on that deer and shoot him? Practice shooting all year long. I shoot a lot all the time. I put up full-size deer targets and practice at all ranges. I practice close-range point shooting, just like with a shotgun. Sometimes you have to snap off a shot very fast, and if you learn to point-shoot without aiming, you can be quick. When you jump a buck at close range and you only see him for one jump, it can make the difference between not shooting and getting the buck.

"If you don't shoot, you will miss 100 percent of the time. Don't worry about missing and don't wait for the perfect shot. Shoot at every opportunity and shoot a lot. You can't get them if you don't shoot. Ammo is cheap compared to the rest of it.

"I fit my gun to me with my hunting clothes on. The gun should line up perfectly when you snap it to your shoulder. You should be looking right down the sights, not searching for them. Modify the stock until it fits you like a fine shotgun. For example, I had to cut the stock off on my rifle because it was too long for me. (I joked that he used a dull chain saw to do that, a claim Lane didn't deny.)

"I don't care how they look as much as I do how well they fit me and how good they shoot," he said.

A lot of bucks hanging on his wall can testify that his rifle shoots a lot better than it looks.

CHAPTER THREE

Shane

At 47 years of age, Shane is the youngest of the Benoit Brothers. He is also the family deer hunting historian and the unofficial "business manager" of the Benoit Brothers. He is the driving force behind the business side of the operation, which includes selling books and videos as well as coordinating their seminar appearances.

In "real life" Shane is the supervisor for the Vermont District Six State Highway Garage in Middlesex, Vermont, which means he is responsible for keeping the roads plowed and ice-free during Vermont's legendary winters and for maintaining them during the rest of the year. (Except of course during deer season; then it's somebody else's problem!) Shane oversees a crew of 14, which in the summer may swell to 30 or more.

He is an avid golfer with a handicap of 12 and during the summer he can usually be found on the links. He used to compete at skeet shooting and at horseshoe pitching, and has trophies he won from doing both. He has been married to Donna for 28 years and they have three daughters.

Shane was responsible for much of the Benoit contribution to the first book, *Big Bucks the Benoit Way,* and without his help the book never would have been done. The same might well be said for this book too, as Shane is my liaison with the Benoit family and is the person I worked closest with when compiling this material. He is good natured, easy going, and fun to hunt with. Shane is the Benoit with whom I have spent the most time in the woods, as well as in business and literary dealings, and is the one I probably know best.

He is kind-hearted and generous. He often hunted with his father, Larry, sacrificing his hunting while trying to help his aging dad get his buck.

Shane is a slower and more methodical tracker than either Lanny or Lane was. He is always thinking ahead about what the bucks are doing and planning accordingly. He has a great eye for detail in the woods and notices many subtle things about any track he is following. That not only helps him stay with the same buck, but these little things also help him to form a mental picture of that buck and his personality. It all adds up to a total package that is a great aid when tracking, particularly when it's combined with Shane's inherent patience. Time and again I have watched him sort out tracks that I thought were a lost cause. He does that because of skill, patience, and a bulldog determination to stick with it to the bitter end.

Shane and I spent a lot of time together in 2002 while hunting in Ontario and in New Hampshire. When there was a break in the action, I asked him to tell me about some of his best hunting stories.

Shane Benoit. Bryce M. Towsley photo.

Shane acts as the unofficial "business manager" of the Benoit Brothers.

Bryce M. Towsley photo.

Shane Benoit clowning for the cameras. Bryce M. Towsley photo.

GHOST BUCK

"My first experience with a grunt call was in 1999, while hunting in New Hampshire. I had never used one and didn't have a clue how to work it, but I had Mark Schoff with me as a cameraman and he was experienced in hunting with a grunt call. It was getting late in the afternoon when we found this place that had been logged pretty heavily. They had left a strip of woods that formed a natural travel corridor, and we were standing by that when I laughed and told Mark, 'Why don't you blow on that tooter a little bit?' I didn't expect anything to happen, but after he called, we heard a branch snap a ways out from us. It was one of those cold, still days when you can hear sounds for a long way and the deer was quite a distance from us.

"'Hey,' I said, 'I think I hear one coming, but with my luck it will probably be just a spike horn.'

"We could see the buck off in the distance, hidden by the brush and trees. Mark zoomed in with the camera lens and he could see it a lot better than I could. He started counting the points, 'One, two, three, four, five, six ... jeeze—eight, no wait—I think it's a ten.'

"The buck was on one side of that strip of woods and we were on the other. It was dark in there because of all the black spruce trees, but we could see the buck coming closer to us. We were thinking we could draw him across that woods to where we could shoot him, but he wouldn't come in. We could see him moving around over there, going back and forth and just hammering a spruce tree with his antlers. He wasn't all that far from us, but it was dark because of the timber and the failing light, as daylight was fading fast. Mark could see the buck fine with the camera, but it was just too dark for me to shoot with my peep sight. I probably could have shot him with a scope, but we weren't using them back then. The buck was behind this small spruce tree that I could see waving back and forth as he rubbed his horns on it. Twice he came out to where I could see the sights, and both times, just as I was squeezing the trigger on him, he moved and just disappeared.

"He kept snorting and blowing at us and pounding that tree. You could tell he wanted to fight, but he wanted us to come to him. He just wasn't going to come across that strip of woods. Finally it got too dark and we had to leave. That was my first experience with grunt calls and it sure convinced me.

"Mark had to leave to go back to Vermont the next day, so I was on my own. It was drizzly and dark, just the kind of day those big bucks like. I rode around for a while looking for tracks, but I couldn't find any buck tracks big enough. I knew where a crossing was up on a ridge because I had trailed a buck through there a few days before. He took me through this saddle that a lot of deer were using to cross the top of the mountain. It would have been a great place to sit in a stand—or to locate a track. The day I tracked the buck through there, the deer were running parallel to the road rather than crossing it, so I guessed that's what they were doing this day as well.

"Early in the afternoon I parked the truck and headed up the mountain. I hadn't gone more than 400 yards before I cut a big buck track heading up. I like tracks that are heading up the mountain because that is almost always a buck that is going to bed. That sure was the case with this one because I hadn't followed him for more than 15 minutes before he was feeding. He meandered around feeding for a while through an old clearcut, eating the buds from the new growth and berry bushes. Then suddenly he turned and headed up the mountain. I knew then he was headed for bed. Along the way, he continued feeding on 'Old Man's Beard.' (This is a green/gray lichen [*Usnea barbata*] that grows on the North Country tree limbs, usually hanging on softwood trees. It looks a little like the Spanish moss that grows on trees in the South.) I could see where he had plucked it off the trees and could see where he dropped some on the snow. Then we came to a spruce tree that had blown down recently and he had picked one whole side clean. We moved on up the mountain and got into some hardwood whips and mixed spruce. They had thinned it there when they logged, but they had left a lot of standing timber.

Shane Benoit checks the trail of a New Hampshire buck that headed down a steep bank to a river. Bryce M. Towsley photo.

"It was drizzling rain and foggy and impossible to see very far. I came through a wall of spruces that were just thick enough so you couldn't see through it. I had seen his

Shane's "Ghost Buck" weighed more than 200 pounds. Larry Benoit photo.

tracks go into them and I was pretty sure he was in there. I just crept ahead in the 'death creep,' taking half steps and moving slow, picking the woods apart with my eyes. I knew he had to be there someplace. All of a sudden, I could smell him. I got a good whiff of that buck smell and knew he had to be close. I slowed down even more because I didn't want to break any branches or make any mistakes. I was keeping my eyes constantly moving, looking for any clue of him. My nerves were tensed up and ready for him to bolt out of there any time. I could see where his tracks were going and so I kept my eyes sweeping about 180 degrees, with the track as the center. I missed him the first time I looked and when I swept back the next time to where there were a bunch of short spruce trees, he rose up out of his bed. I guess those trees were just tall enough to hide him when he was bedded. As he stood up, he looked like a ghost rising out of the fog. Even though he was only about forty yards from me, he was hard to see, almost as if he lacked substance. He knew something was there, but he wasn't sure what it was. It was so foggy that all I could tell was that he was a buck, but not much more. It was a leap of faith when I pulled the trigger, but he was a nice 8-point that weighed over 200 pounds.

"That was my first New Hampshire buck. With him, I had now taken a buck over 200 pounds in all three northern New England states: New Hampshire, Vermont and Maine."

MUSK OX BUCK

"The very next year we were back in that same area, and it was another wet, rainy, foggy day. I had missed a big buck the day before and was back looking for him, but I guess I had run him right out of the county.

Shane Benoit's rifle and cartridge belt on log in Ontario 2002. Bryce M. Towsley photo.

"It was so late in the day when I found him that I normally wouldn't have started on the track, but I was driving down an old logging road and he ran across in front of me. I could see he was good and I knew he was close, so I took the track. He had a little track that I would never even have followed if I hadn't seen that great big rack. It was a big, wide 10-point buck that was massive and gnarly, and the minute I saw it, I didn't care what size his feet were.

"He had been roaming all night and half the day and he was tired, so I knew he wanted to lie down. A storm was coming in hard and we were walking right into it the entire time. The sleet and rain were falling fast and the wind was driving it so that it was hitting me in the face and stinging like it was made of diamonds.

"I only followed him an hour and a half before I got the shot. He was bedded down behind a blown-down tree that looked like a snow-covered tee-pee. I had trees and brush in the way and just couldn't see him. I had apparently looked right over him the first time I swept my eyes past where he was bedded. But then I caught the movement as he stood up from his bed. He didn't wait around to see what I was; instead he jumped and took off without a bit of hesitation. I thought he was going one way and I took a couple of steps to the side to get a clear shot. But he turned and went a different way, so I had to step back before I could shoot. I got one shot off at him when he went through the next opening, but I missed.

"I trailed that buck until I couldn't trail him any more. It was stormy and dark, but I stayed with him until it was impossible to see tracks. I barely had enough time to get out of the woods, and it was pretty dark by the time I got back to the road. I was still a long way from the truck when I finally did find the road.

"It was just too late in the day. If I had found him earlier in the morning I think I could have gotten him, but darkness beat me on that one.

"The next day, I tracked one buck in the morning, but he was going through some thick cover that told me he didn't have much for a rack, so I left him to grow another year. A bit later I ended up picking up a different track crossing the road. This time, he was a good buck,

Shane and his "Musk Ox Buck." Larry Benoit photo.

and he was with a doe. I knew they weren't going very far because right from the start she was just feeding and puttering around. They moved into this area that was full of whips and berry bushes. He wasn't feeding like she was; I suppose he had other things on his mind because it looked like he was just keeping her in sight. They traveled into this old cut that had a lot of browse, mushrooms, and fiddlehead ferns. Actually, the ferns had died off by deer season, but there is something they like to dig up and eat where they grow.

"I trailed them out into this select cut while the fog was rolling in and out, so that visibility came and went like something out of an old movie. During one of the 'went' times, I was standing at the edge of the bowl, looking up a logging road. I could see what I thought looked like a deer. Pretty soon, the fog rolled out a little more and I could see it was the doe standing there looking at me. Apparently I had stopped at just the right time and she had not caught me moving, but she was suspicious. She was bobbing her head and stomping her foot, and I stood motionless for about 15 minutes. I still hadn't seen the buck, but I knew where he was because she kept looking at him. The problem was that he was in a little gully that was just deep enough so I couldn't see him.

"I kept waiting, but after a while my feet were starting to get really cold in those thin rubber boots we wear. Then another 15 minutes went by and suddenly she whirled and ran away up the bank. I got ready and out he came. I missed him with the first shot and hit him in the ass with the next. He was running away and it was the only shot I had. That shot turned him around so I could shoot at his ribs. I hit him twice more through the ribs. By then, he was about 125 yards from me.

"His rack was pretty messed up, especially on the left side. I didn't realize that he had such a goofy rack and we joked back at camp that they looked like musk ox horns. I guess I did the deer herd a favor by taking him out of the gene pool.

"Anytime you have this situation, the buck will have his attention riveted on the doe and won't be looking around much. He is worried that she will wander off and he is afraid to take his eyes off her. The best scenario is for her to walk off because he will walk after her and you will have a decent shot. But in this case she ran off and when that happens the buck will run after her, so you have to be ready to shoot fast."

RAINY-DAY BUCK

"There was one buck that I tracked on bare ground up in Maine in 1983 that took two days for me to get. I found his track crossing this road and running into a big softwood swamp. That swamp is gone today; they cut it all down.

"I had actually shot at the buck the year before, but I missed him. Lanny and I tracked him on the snow the last day of the season. We jumped him, but I didn't have

Shane's "Rainy Day Buck" weighed 230 pounds.

Larry Benoit photo.

much of a shot."

"I went back in '83 and I found his tracks going down into that swamp. I didn't have enough time to follow him that day, but I did go down this road that ran to a big pond to see if he had come out and crossed the road and to check for scrape lines along the pond. I always go to the edges of ponds to look for sign because they act as a barrier to deer movement and force them to run parallel to the shoreline. This concentrates the deer movement and is usually a great place to look for scrapes, rubs, and big tracks. By the looks of the sign, I didn't think he had come out of there. It was late by then and I had to go, but I told the boys back at camp that night that I was going to get him in the morning.

"The next morning dawned to a drizzly, rainy day, which I love because it keeps your scent down and makes things quiet to move in. But it was still bare ground, which is tough tracking under any conditions. I found the buck's tracks and he headed down into the swamp on that nice, wet, thick moss where I could follow his tracks almost like we had snow. But before I started on the track, I drove down that road to the lake to make sure he hadn't come out of there. The old tracks showed me that it was his routine to cross that road when he left. The rain had softened the

Northern woods where the saddles on the mountain tops are a good place to look for deer. Benoit Brothers photo.

logging road up to mud enough so I would have seen his tracks pretty easily. I didn't find any, so I figured he was still in there. When I got to the pond, I checked his scrape line and he hadn't freshened any of them up, so he had to be in the thick stuff, just hanging around. It clearly was his favorite spot, and because it was, it's where he ended up dying.

"Bucks tend to have a favorite spot that they keep gravitating to again and again. I don't know if they were born there or what, but they always have a place that they will come back to time and time again. They will bed down, rest, feed, and hang around. Sometimes it's for just a few hours; other times, it's for a few days. Maybe they have more than one of these places; I am not sure. But they all have several things in common: They will have good cover, plenty of feed, and protection from the wind. Another common thing they have is that when I find a buck using one, it is often the place where that buck will die. They are easy bucks to get because they always come back.

"There is some kind of a waxy-leaf type of clover (or at least it looks like clover, but I am not sure what it's called) that they feed on. This buck was feeding heavily on it all the way into this place. From that, I guessed that he was headed in there to bed down for the day.

"There was a light, misty rain falling and the moss-covered ground was soaked with water. He was a big, heavy buck and he left a clear track that was easy to follow. I was just moving along very slowly on the track, trying to pick the woods apart with my eyes. Then all of a sudden I could smell him. That told me he had probably stood up or was standing up. You don't usually smell a buck when he is bedded down. Sometimes you can, as I did in the Ghost Buck story, but it's rare. Usually when you smell a buck, he is on his feet.

Shane's "100-Yard-Dash Buck" taken in 1989 was a 10-pointer weighing 224 pounds. Benoit Brothers photo.

"It was misty and foggy enough so it was hard to see, but I spotted a log that just didn't look right. I held my rifle to my shoulder and was ready as I stepped around to the side a bit for a better view. When you do that and deer are close, you want to keep all your movements very slow. Don't move your hands around and make sure anything else that moves is extremely slow. Anyway, I peeked around this tree and there he was standing like a statue and looking right at me. I could see he was a good buck and, like I said, my rifle was already in position. I think all he saw was a flash and it was over. That buck weighed 230 pounds."

100-YARD-DASH BUCK

"Back in 1989 I was hunting in Maine with Pop. I let my dad out on this buck early in the morning and he followed the track most of the day without getting a shot. I took off to look for a buck track of my own to follow, but never could find one big enough.

"Later in the day I came back around the mountain I call Pug's Mountain and there was Pop walking down the road. He told me he had given up on the track and it was mine if I wanted to take it. I asked him where he had left it, and he pointed up to a saddle on top of Pug's Mountain and told me it was on the backside in the thick stuff.

"I went up in there and found his tracks pretty quickly. There was about five inches of snow and it was pretty good tracking conditions. I hadn't followed very far before I jumped him up and the chase was on. He took me right over the top of the mountain and through that saddle. As we were going along on the other side of the mountain from where I had started him, I could see lots of his beds, rubs, and tracks. I could tell that he liked to lie down on a small plateau on top of the mountain. He could see anybody coming up the mountain, and with one bound, he could escape down either side.

"We went through one of his bedding areas and near there he hooked up with another big buck. It was getting

Shane Benoit sitting on a ledge on top of a ridge in Ontario. Bryce M. Towsley photo.

late and I only had about an hour or less of shooting time left. They went down the mountain and skirted along the edge of a clearcut that had been logged perhaps 10 years earlier. Then the two bucks split up and his track was swinging back toward where he came from. I stood there for a few minutes, looking at the two tracks and trying to decide which one to follow, finally deciding to stay with his track. I turned to look down it and there he was, standing up on a little hill, looking back at me. As soon as we made eye contact, he bounded out of there, much too fast for a shot. It was only about 50 yards from me, but it was steep and thick. I ran to the top to try to catch him coming down the other side. I was running as fast as I could through the slash, berry bushes, and downed trees, and I had to pick my way around them so it was nearly twice as far to the top as it would have been in a straight line. When I got to the top of that hill, I was looking down through a clearcut area. Pretty soon, I could see him jumping over a downed treetop about 150 yards from me. I was very winded, but I just picked up my gun and snapped off a shot. I nailed him and dropped him in his tracks. Then I dropped my gun and stood there trying to breathe.

"I never would have gotten that buck if I hadn't run to the top of that hill. If I had walked, he would have been long gone. Most times when you run like that, you never see the buck, but once in a while it pays off. In this case the buck had been zigzagging through the clearcut and had actually taken much longer to go that 150 yards than if he had simply run in a straight line. I think he wanted to get back into some cover and got a little confused on the best way to do that. He weighed 224 pounds."

MY FIRST STAND BUCK

"We were hunting in Ontario and were plagued with no snow. Time and again I had found this same buck's track crossing through a deep sag in a power line. I found a place to sit high up on a knob overlooking that sag, where there was a big boulder to hide behind and wait. Now, I am not much on waiting on stand, but I'll do whatever it takes to shoot a big buck. Nothing else was working that year, so I waited.

"Pretty soon I saw a small buck working along the power line about 800 yards away. He was just working one side, then crossing over and working the other side. I think he was looking for any hot does that might have crossed. I actually saw a lot of bucks at this place over the next few days, including a good 8-point and a nice 10-point. But I knew there was a really good buck in there from the tracks, so I kept my finger off the trigger.

"One afternoon I was back sitting there again, watching, when a decent buck came out. I didn't think he was all that great, but the cameraman got pretty excited. I am not used to looking at bucks through binoculars, and they always look better than they are through glass. I also wasn't used to working with cameramen who, as you know, are mostly concerned with getting the kill shot; so they want you to shoot just about every buck you see. Anyway, I got fooled on both counts and to be honest, I probably was an easy target because it had been so tough a season, and I was getting a little nervous about shooting a buck.

"That buck was a long way from us, too far to shoot, and it was starting to get dark. I left my stand and crept up to a little hill that cut the distance about in half. But, even still, it was a very long shot. (Shane's right. I have been to that spot with him and have seen where he shot the deer. Even for an experienced long-range shooter, it was long, but for a guy who is more used to shooting at bucks up close and personal, it was a genuine stretch.)

"I got the buck and that's pretty much the end of it. He wasn't as good as I would have liked and the story is pretty anticlimactic. I suppose it's only important enough to even mention here because it's the only buck I have ever shot while sitting on a stand. It's also the first buck I have shot while using a scope on my rifle. I had a Leupold Vari-X III 1.5–5 scope on my 270 Winchester and that made a big difference on this shot. The moral of the story, if there is one, is that you need to do whatever it takes. If you don't have snow for tracking, then you just have to suck it up and endure the hell of sitting on a stand."

FIRST-DAY CATCH & RELEASE

"The snow came to Ontario the week before I got there in 2001. Even though I knew about it, I couldn't get there any sooner. The first day, I was only hunting a few hours when I picked up a nice buck track. I trailed the buck for about half an hour before I jumped him from his bed. It was steep and thick and there was no way I would have seen him. But I smelled him just before I found his bed, so I knew he wasn't very far in front of me.

"I tracked him up on the ridge top where it was ledge and with fewer trees, but his trail ran over the other side and back down into the thick bottom. I knew he was probably standing there someplace looking at me, but I couldn't see him because the trees and brush were hiding him. Then he started blowing at me, and I remember saying quietly to him, 'Show yourself and I'll fix ya!' He certainly could not have heard me, but he ran off like he did and without me ever seeing so much as a glimpse of him.

"I followed him for maybe another two hours and he took me up over another ridge and back down into the thick stuff. When the track led up on top of the next ridge, I could look down and see Pop standing on a big boulder off in the distance. That buck was headed right his way.

"I followed the buck down into some nasty stuff that was choked up and thick with poplar trees. After a while I could see something black that just didn't look quite right. I stared at it for a while before I realized it was a deer's nose. Then I could see the white patch on his throat and then his eyes, and finally things started coming together and I could see his antlers. He was standing there as still as a marble statue and looking right back at me. He was a good buck, but the rack was smaller than what I would like to shoot on the first day. He was a young buck with big feet, one of those that sometimes fool you, so I let him go. What the heck, it was the first day and I had the rest of the season; I didn't want to shoot a marginal buck that early. Of course, the snow melted the next day and never came back that entire season and tracking was impossible.

"The buck ran off in Pop's direction, but he never saw him. It's probably a good thing because if Pop had shot that

Shane's first stand buck was also the first buck he ever shot with a scoped rifle. Tom Blais photo.

Left:

Shane Benoit on the track in Ontario 2002.

Bryce M. Towsley photo.

Right:

Shane Benoit sits at a bench and glasses across a lake to look for a buck that lives on a peninsula. Bryce M. Towsley photo.

buck, he probably wouldn't have gotten the monster that he did later on that season. The buck he did get scored over 170 B&C and was the best racked buck of his life."

Considering how many huge whitetail bucks that Larry Benoit had shot in his long hunting career, that's saying something.

Shane and I hunted together quite a bit during the 2002 deer season, and one theme that kept coming up again and again was the "favorite spots" that bucks always seem to have. I asked him to elaborate a little on what they are and how they can benefit a deer hunter.

Identify and Locate Favorite Places of Big Bucks

"Every buck will have a place where he is most comfortable," Shane told me. "Sometimes they will have even more than one and those places are apt to be different from one another. You probably have read about a buck's 'sanctuary,' usually in magazine articles about how to hunt bucks when there is a lot of hunting pressure. These are simply one example of a favorite place. That buck may spend a lot more time in those places when the hunting pressure is high, but I'll guarantee he is there a lot anyway just because he likes it and is comfortable there.

"Deer are creatures of habit. Any deer hunter knows that and will exploit that weakness to help him fill his tags. Without a doubt, it's what gets a lot of deer killed. But big bucks are survivors and they know enough when the hunting pressure is high to stay out of sight in daylight hours. We think he is hiding in some mystical place, his 'sanctuary,' as if he's a political refugee, hiding in a church where he is protected from harm by a higher power. But in reality, the place the buck is in is nothing more than a location where he feels comfortable. Certainly a hard-hunted old buck will pick his spot, at least in part, for the security it provides, but he is also there simply because he likes the place. It could be that he likes it because nobody bothers him much, which would explain the connection between favorite places and sanctuary locations when the hunting pressure is high. But whatever the reasons, within any given

A view of the vast country in western Ontario. This is the kind of country the Benoits love to hunt. Bryce M. Towsley

area, he will have a favorite location where he spends a lot of time.

"As trackers, we will not usually be dealing with high hunting pressure and the bucks we are after should not feel too stressed. If there are a lot of hunters in the woods, tracking is usually just time spent chasing a buck through the woods so somebody else can shoot him. It's better to track where there are few, if any, other hunters around to interfere. But even then a smart old buck still knows when he is being hunted. The increased traffic on the roads and more man tracks in the woods provide a clue. If he has been around for a few hunting seasons, he knows those clues represent trouble. He will start spending more time in his favorite place, because not moving in daylight is how he stays alive, and he feels safer there than anyplace else. This is particularly true in the early season, when the rut is not influencing buck behavior as much as it will later on.

"Think about your own home. If you have lived there any length of time, I'll wager that there are places you gravitate to without even thinking about it. For a man, it might be the den, garage, or workshop, but there is always a location where you spend the most time. Simply put, this is your favorite place. It's the place where you are comfortable, happy, and content. Well, a big buck has places like that too, spots where for whatever reason—maybe something known only to him—he likes to hang out.

"A dog or a cat is the same way. If you have pets, then you know that there are certain places they like. The dog may like to lie in the dirt under the front porch and the cat may like it under your wife's sewing table. Regardless of where these places are, they become habitually familiar to these animals. Sure, they will use other places to sleep

Shane Benoit checks the tracks leaving a fresh bed. Bryce M. Towsley photo.

or hang out, but clearly there are certain locations that are their favorites.

"To locate and identify these favorite places for big bucks, look for a lot of their sign. A buck can't move without leaving tracks, so that's the first thing you should concentrate on finding, and tracks are the best way to identify an individual buck. Also look for beds, and during the fall, you will find a lot of rubs and scrapes. He is spending a lot of time here and nature is compelling him to rub trees and make scrapes. He is going to do that wherever he is, and because he is spending so much time in his favorite place, it becomes by default a location with lots and lots of scrapes and rubs. One clue that this is a trophy buck's favorite place is that most, if not all, of the sign you find in there will be made by the same buck and that buck will almost always be a big fella. These big bucks are loners, particularly when the rut is on. He will roam around looking for does, but during the rut, he is not very friendly with other bucks. When he is resting or not looking for does, he usually just wants to be left alone. These old bucks are kind of grumpy, and if he is the dominant buck in the area, the other bucks know enough to not bother him. So as a result, you usually will not find a lot of sign from other bucks in his favorite place.

"The other favorite places for big bucks are often a kind of community gathering place. These are used more in the early hunting season, when the bucks are still in bachelor groups and are hanging out waiting for the fun and festivities to begin. Again, to draw the analogy with men, they are places that bucks like, sort of like a friendly bar, or the hunting club, camp, or just your buddy's garage. It's a place where you can go and hang out with your buddies and act like a man. They are the places that

Shane Benoit standing on a ledge on top of a ridge in Ontario. Bryce M. Towsley photo.

a lot of hunters often call 'staging areas,' although a true staging area is something else. That's where a buck will wait in cover for it to get dark so he can safely approach a feeding area without getting shot."

"Even after the rut is cranked up, a buck will go to these community favorite places often, maybe to pick a fight or maybe just because he is comfortable there. Often when you are tracking a buck, you will pass through these locations. Again, you can identify them by the abundance of buck sign, but now it will have been left by more than one buck. You will usually find very little doe or fawn sign in these locations. This is man country and ladies and babies are not welcome. I suppose the ladies are welcome during the rut, but they avoid these places the rest of the year and by habit they stay out of them during the rut too. There might be several of these locations throughout any given hunting area, and any buck might travel from one to another to check out the action and check in with his buddies.

"These locations are important to hunters for a couple of reasons. Obviously, they are great places to locate a stand, if that's how you like to hunt. These are places where a buck will bed, and you may have also read about not 'invading a buck's bedding area' because you might scare him into moving to Mars or something. But if that's where he is spending all his time, isn't it the place where you should be hunting for him? You can't shoot a buck where he ain't. Even if he is out prowling around looking for does or filling his belly, sooner or later he is going to come back to his favorite place for some rest and relaxation.

Left: This is the track of a big buck. Note the long stride and wide spacing. Bryce M. Towsley photo.

Shane's 2002 buck. Tom Blais photo.

If you are waiting in a tree when he does, he may be resting in your freezer and relaxing on your wall before too long. So tell me, how's he going to move to another planet when he's dead?

"For a tracker like myself, I circle these places to look for his tracks leading in or out. If he is in there, I simply sneak in like the buck is bedded. Very often, I'll shoot the buck in my favorite place, his ribs. If I bump him, then I just take the track and hopefully shoot him later.

"Also, those group favorite places are usually along travel routes. There may be several bucks using them, and often they make it part of their swing to check them out as they travel around looking for some action. They are great places to locate a stand or to find a fresh buck track. What better place to locate a fresh track to follow than where the buck you are after likes to spend his time?

"As you are hunting and scouting, you should be cataloging these places in your mind. They will help you form a better understanding of the travel habits of your buck. If you cut a track—particularly one you recognize—crossing the road and heading into an area you know contains one of these favorite places, you can often save some tracking time by going directly to that place. More often than not, you will find his track there and it will be that much fresher.

"Also, if you are double teaming with another hunter and the track is headed for a known favorite place, particularly one that's on a travel corridor, you can send one hunter to circle ahead and wait for the buck to come through.

"Anytime you know something about a buck, it will help you get him. If that information is about a place where he likes to spend time, there are many ways—some I probably haven't even thought of yet—to use that information to help you let him ride home in your truck."

Use Perpetual Rub and Scrape Areas to Your Advantage

"Bucks also will use the same place to scrape year after year. I know places where the scrapes have been used so much over time that they are dug deep into the ground. Usually these places will have several bucks using them and they continue to be used for generation after generation of bucks. These are, of course, a great place for a treestand. But it's also a great place to find tracks.

"They will do the same thing with some rubs. Certain trees have been rubbed on so much over the years that it kills them. But if they are still standing, the bucks will continue to rub on them. Usually these are on travel routes and often where several trails converge."

Double-Team a Buck

"It's not unusual for a buck that knows you are on his track to get into a thick area and stay there. Usually these places are so thick and brushy that a man can't travel around in them without making some noise. The buck will know where you are all the time from that noise and he will move around and around just ahead of you.

"One great way of dealing with this is to team up with another hunter. I like to use Lanny because he is so fast on the track and is so relentless about it. I send him in on the track while I go to the places the buck likes to travel. These are the places I found while I was chasing him around in there, so I know where they are. Or often you can guess from the way the land is laid out. Then I just wait in ambush.

"You may have to set up more than once, but sooner or later he will either make a mistake and get shot, or he will figure out what you are doing and bail out of that place. Either one is good. If he makes a mistake, you shoot him. If he gets out of Dodge, well, then at least you have him out of that hellhole and into some country where you can hopefully track him a little better. If he has a hot doe with him, which is often the case, sooner or later she will get nervous and panic. The buck is going to try to stay with her, no matter what. He may lag behind because he knows what she is doing is dangerous, or simply because she panicked and bailed out of there and left him behind. But a buck in love is going to think about it for a few minutes and then figure that he should follow her, no matter what the consequences.

"Lanny and I teamed up that way for a buck I shot in 2002. He was just circling around ahead of me in this incredibly thick bottom between two high ridges. I sicced Lanny on him while I started circling the area, looking for his tracks leaving. As is often the case, the doe he was with spooked and busted out of there first. She was just ahead of me and I found her tracks by themselves. All I had to do was wait, knowing he wouldn't let her get away. It almost wasn't fair, because it wasn't long before he felt the stick of a 270 bullet in his ribs. Even late in the season, that buck weighed more than 240 pounds. If I start to feel guilty about tricking him, I just remember all the hours I spent fighting through that brush trying to catch up with him and the guilt goes away."

Leap-Frog Your Way to a Buck

"You can also use a variation on this technique if you know the country well. While one man tracks the buck, the other drives to the next road and waits at a known, or at least a likely, crossing. If you have radios and it's legal to use them, you can stay in touch about what the buck is doing and where he is headed. If not, simply wait for a reasonable amount of time, then drive the roads and look to see if the deer and/or the hunter has crossed. If the deer has, but the hunter has not, you can jump on the track and be that much closer to catching him. The other guy will see your tracks when he gets to the road and can take the truck you left behind around to the next road. If the hunter and the deer have both crossed, you simply drive to the next road and repeat the process."

Carry Spare Keys

"We always have a truck key for each hunter. Having a few spare keys for the truck can save you a lot of trouble. Two or more hunters together can use the truck without worrying about finding a hidden key. Too often you forget to hide the key and it's in somebody's pocket. This almost always happens when you find a big buck track and are all excited about getting started on it. Or worse yet, you only have one key and somebody loses it when you are 40 miles from camp, it's 10 degrees out, and getting dark. When that happens, it's likely to be ugly.

"Everybody having a key also helps if we are hunting together and one hunter gets back to the truck first. He can warm up and/or he can go to look for the other guy who may be walking down a road miles away. With only one key, you may wind up waiting in the cold while your buddy walks all those miles back to the truck. In that case, neither of you will be very happy."

I'll add my own experience to that and suggest that you also stash a key on the outside of the truck. Hide it on the frame underneath with a magnetic key holder or simply wire it to the frame. It's a lifesaver if you ever lock your keys inside the truck, or lose them.

Don't Be Afraid to Explore

"If you are going to find new places, you first need to roam. I like to look for big mountains, but the most important thing is they need to be logging. Logging will open up the country and the new growth will provide some feed for the deer. All these 'wilderness' areas where the environmentalists are keeping everybody from cutting trees just can't support any amount of deer. You need some logging.

"I also look for good wintering grounds, that is, big stands of larger evergreen trees that will provide a canopy for winter deeryards. I also look for water and I really like to see plenty of beaver dams.

"Then, of course, I look for big tracks. You will always need to see big buck tracks before you decide to hunt in a new area. If there are big bucks around, they will cross a road sooner or later. Bucks can't move without leaving tracks and when you find lots of big tracks crossing the roads, you know you have found a good spot.

"You also have to be aware of what the winters have been like. The biggest bucks are susceptible to bad winters because they are so run down from the rut. If the winter comes in early and dumps a lot of snow, it's a bad deal for the bucks. They are in tough shape from the rut and need a few weeks of rest and lots of food to recover. If they move right into the wintering area, they might not survive. Wintering areas are usually overbrowsed and do not have adequate food for the numbers of deer. Most of the deer have been storing fat all fall and can rely on those reserves to get them through the tough times. But a hard rutting buck will have burned most of his reserves during the breeding season and has nothing left in the bank for the bad times. A bad winter that kills a lot of deer will usually wipe out a disproportionate number of mature bucks."

Move Slow on the Track of a Wounded Buck

"If you are tracking a wounded deer, approach him like you are sneaking in on a bedded buck. Bucks are tough and they can run a long way when they are hurt, particularly a gut-shot buck. If you don't bother him, he is going to try to lie down fairly soon after the shot. But if you jump him up from that bed and don't get him, they can run a long way.

"So it is important to catch him in his bed and kill him. For that, you need to move slowly. Most guys move too fast on the track of a wounded buck. They are all excited about having hit him and they charge ahead. But your best approach is to follow the track like you haven't seen the buck and he is lying down. You don't want to jump him up and chase him for another five miles, and they can easily go that far if you get them up and moving.

"I hit one in the foot one time and he didn't go very far before he laid down. He really wasn't hurt all that much, and if I had just blundered into him, I never would have gotten him. But instead I caught him in his bed and put the next bullet a little higher.

"One old wives' tale is that a wounded buck won't go uphill; well, they will. They will go just about anyplace they want to go. Sure, if he is hurt bad, he will try to find an easy route and would rather go downhill than up, but if where he wants to go to is uphill, then that's where he is going to go, and that doesn't mean he is not hit hard.

The Benoits checking a buck track that crossed a northern New Hampshire road. Bryce M. Towsley photo.

"Remember, if he is wounded, you want to spend a lot of your time looking for the deer and not looking at the track."

Listen for His Antlers

"When you are tracking a big buck and are close, often you can hear his antlers hitting the tree branches. You may not hear him walking if the snow is quiet, but if you have good ears, you will hear his horns. Particularly when the antlers are big. You just need to learn what to listen for and remember that when you hear it, you are close."

Find the Does to Find a Buck

"If you have been seeing lots of buck tracks for days, but suddenly they just disappear, that probably means that the breeding has started. In the North Country, the breeding window for the does is very short and when it starts, most of the does are bred in just a few days. The bucks are not about to miss that and when the does are in heat, the bucks are sticking tight with them. Does don't tend to move around much anyway compared to bucks and even less so when they are in heat. Of course, the bucks are no longer traveling looking for does in heat, so the amount of

This is a big buck track from a deer weighing more than 200 pounds. Bryce M. Towsley photo.

tracks you are seeing will drop dramatically. Go find the doe groups and you will find the bucks. The biggest and best bucks will be with the does, but there will also be lots of lesser bucks hanging around on the fringes.

"In the North Country, these deer will often be in isolated and very concentrated pockets and you may think that every deer in the woods has disappeared, but keep looking. When you finally find the deer, you may think you have hit the mother lode."

Above and Left: Shane approaches two more bucks after successfully tracking them. Tom Blais photos.

Above: Shane Benoit exits the tent and heads for his truck. Bryce M. Towsley photo.

CHAPTER FOUR

Historic Changes

THE PASSING OF THE CHECKERED COATS

If there was one thing that could be used to identify the Benoits on sight, it was the checkered green-and-black wool coats they always wore. When Larry first appeared on the cover of *Sports Afield* wearing one back in 1970, it was rare to see such a coat in the deer woods. But within a few years, they were more common in the New England woods than maple trees. It's a shame the Benoits didn't get a royalty on those jackets because they must have helped sell a million of them. Where I live in Vermont, they are as common as dirt and are simply called the Benoit-style jacket.

But the Benoit Brothers don't wear them anymore. One of the big changes with this next generation has been in some of their equipment and the jacket has been leading the charge. Today, they wear a high-tech, waterproof wool jacket in Mossy Oak camouflage with hunter-orange overlays. Instead of the old green wool pants, they have matching camo wool pants. A fledgling, hunting garment company called Beagle Outdoor Wear manufactures these in Vermont. They are on the cutting edge of the "new wool" technology that has all the benefits of wool, but is also water-repellant. As any North Country deer hunter knows, staying dry during the November deer season is a challenge, but the Beagle coats are up to that challenge and beyond. They are covered more extensively in the "Frequently Asked Questions" section of the book, so I won't delve into them too deeply here except for one point.

The Benoits have worked with Beagle to develop and design the ultimate hunting coat for their style of whitetail hunting. The resulting "Benoit Coat" has a very distinctive look and in just two seasons it has replaced the green plaid as the Benoit trademark.

The other primary identifier for the Benoits is their Remington pump-action rifles. No matter if it is the Model 760 or the newer 7600, if there is a Benoit in the woods deer hunting, you can be absolutely sure that it will be a pump-action rifle in his hands. That hasn't changed a bit and I don't anticipate that it ever will. Once again, I am sure they have helped sell a million of those rifles, and without a penny or even so much as a free rifle from Remington. They use them because the rifle works best for their style of hunting and not because of some big-dollar contract.

But the Benoit rifles have undergone a change in the last few years. Those pump rifles have always worn a peep sight with a bead front sight that usually was painted red. Lane hunted exclusively with a peep-sighted rifle, while Lanny and Shane still bring theirs to camp and lug them around in the truck. But in several weeks of hunting with them in 2002, I can't recall those rifles ever making it into the woods. The guns Shane and Lanny were hunting with wore scopes.

Shane has a couple of rifles mounted with scopes. Both are 7600 Remington's and both in 270 Winchester. One has a Leupold 1.5–5 Vari-X III that he got some years back on my recommendation. This light, compact scope is bright, clear, and rugged. It features a wide field of view for hunters who like to track and often need to shoot quickly at running bucks. It was the scope that Shane was sighting through when he shot the first deer he took with a scoped gun. (For what it's worth, it is also the scope that I have on the two pump rifles I use most often when I am tracking deer.)

Then a couple of years back, Lanny discovered the Trijicon scopes with their illuminated post-type reticle.

The coats may have changed, but the results are still the same! Tom Blais photos.

Left to right: Lane, Larry, Shane, and Lanny with Larry's 11-point, 250-pound buck taken in the 2001 season. Tom Blais photo.

That post more closely resembles the bead front sight the Benoits were used to seeing and Lanny found that he is more comfortable with it than with the conventional crosshairs used in most hunting scopes. Lanny says that they now have the advantage of optics with a bright, clear image and the ability to keep the target and the sights in clear focus at the same time, while still seeing a somewhat familiar sight picture. Both Lanny and Shane are currently using rifles with Trijicon scopes. Aging eyes may have forced them to this, but after they started hunting with optics, they realized that a scope sight provides more benefit than downside on any deer rifle.

In further recognizing the value of optics—particularly with middle-aged eyes and because they are

Lanny shooting a scoped rifle. Tom Blais photo.

now hunting in some Western areas with more open land—they also are starting to carry and use binoculars, something no Benoit has ever done before to my knowledge. This past year, I witnessed the "boys" using a spotting scope to locate game and to check out the country. Shane even has a laser rangefinder!

This is all a giant leap for a family of hunters who have long prided themselves on simplicity of equipment and stubborn resistance to any changes. But changes in hunting areas and changes in hunting styles have demanded changes in equipment. Also, changes in the generations have brought new attitudes to deer hunting and, like any good predator with a need to remain successful, they have recognized and embraced the need for these changes.

Another big change has been in their ammo. For eons the Benoits have always used Remington Core-Lokt round-nose factory ammo in their pump guns, and in their peep-sighted rifles, they still do. But when they started hunting in the

Photo of Trijicon reticle. This is the reticle as seen in the Benoits' Trijicon scopes.

Photo By Trijicon.

Opposite:
Hornady Light Magnum 270 Winchester & 30-06 Springfield boxes with cartridges. The Benoits use 270 Winchester and 30-06 Springfield rifles.

Bryce M. Towsley photo.

Below:
Loading a Remington 7600 clip with Hornady ammo.

Bryce M. Towsley photo.

West and getting longer shots, they decided first to add a scope and then to try some pointed bullets for the added long-range energy retention and flatter trajectories those bullets could provide. Lanny bought some of Hornady's Light Magnum ammo in 270 Winchester, which are loaded with 130-grain Hornady SST bullets to a muzzle velocity of 3215 fps. Lanny and Landon shot some through their chronograph and liked the increased velocity of the light magnum technology. Then they all shot some bucks and were very impressed with the SST bullets and the quick, sure kills they were getting with them. Today, everybody except Lane used this cutting-edge factory ammo with pointed, plastic-tipped bullets and extra velocity.

In the deer-hunting world, these changes are historic. I almost expect that as with the Kennedy assassination, years from now hunters will sit in deer camps and discuss where they were the day they first heard that the Benoits had scopes on their guns and pointed bullets in their magazines.

CAMP MOBILITY

One big secret to the Benoit's success in consistently shooting big bucks year after year is their mobility. No one area can sustain a continued big buck harvest forever and still keep the quality high. The key is in recognizing when you have taken most of the best bucks out of an area and then moving on to different hunting grounds. This not only keeps the hunter in fertile hunting grounds with fresh supplies of good bucks, but it also allows the old area to rest for a few years and gives it time to grow a new crop of trophy bucks.

Another factor in finding productive areas is in locating hunting grounds that are remote enough so that there are not a lot of other hunters. That usually means that lodging is not available close by. If the hunting grounds are within an easy drive from a motel or lodge, then chances are good it's seeing a lot of hunters' trucks and tracks.

Remaining mobile precludes any sort of a permanent deer camp. If you have a permanent building, you will tend to stay hunting near it even after the best bucks have clearly been shot out. Most hunters have seen that happen in deer camps that are long past their glory days yet continue to attract the same hunters year after year. They talk about how great the hunting used to be and complain about how bad it is now, usually blaming the state's deer management program. Every now and then, one of the gang will shoot a decent buck and it will fire everybody up and get them thinking that the great hunting is coming back. But the reality is that they probably will never again see the days when several of the camp members could shoot good bucks in a single season. That's simply because the bucks are no longer there in the numbers needed to sustain that kind of harvest. To be called any sort of a "good" hunting ground for trophy deer, you need lots of big bucks so that a majority of the best hunters are able to be successful year after year. What is happening at these camps is that the occasional buck that does grow up enough to become a trophy is finally meeting his destiny with one of the hunters. The problem is that he might well be the only good buck in the area they hunt. Yet the hunters keep returning year after year because that's where their "deer camp" is, and so by default, that's where they hunt. It's a never-ending, self-perpetuating cycle that results in frustrated deer hunters with few trophy bucks, and the cause can be traced to the permanent building.

Inside the tent camp in Ontario 2002. Bryce M. Towsley photo.

Above:
A typical Benoit tent camp.
Lane Benoit photo.

Left: For years the Benoits used old school buses converted into campers to keep their camp mobile.
Benoit Brothers photo.

The stove in the Benoit tent camp. Bryce M. Towsley photo.

The secret to staying in great trophy country is found in a mobile camp. For years, the Benoits used old school buses they converted into campers. When it was time to move on to a new location, they just tied everything down, started the motors, and headed out to better grounds.

In recent years, however, they are hunting in places that are simply too far away to drive those old buses. On top of that, they also are traveling with a larger group than in years past. They have cameramen, writers, friends and friends of friends, groupies, and all sorts of other people hunting with them. The buses and most campers are simply not big enough for that large an entourage. A camper is big, heavy, and expensive to transport halfway across the continent for a hunt. Not to mention they are also expensive to buy and maintain.

The Benoits have found the solution in something else. It's something mountain hunters have been using in all kinds of weather for years: the outfitter tent. When folded up, they are small and light enough to pack on a horse, so bringing them in a truck is no problem at all. When set up, they are big enough to provide much more room than any camper and they can provide plenty of warm shelter from the winter elements. These camps can be set up completely in less than a day, but even more important, an outfitter tent is affordable.

The tent they have been using the past few years belongs to their friend and cameraman, Craig Jaques. It's a huge 20x20 outfitter's tent that also has a large attached kitchen tent in the front of the main tent. They pick a camping spot ahead of time, either the year before or when they are looking over the country to check out the

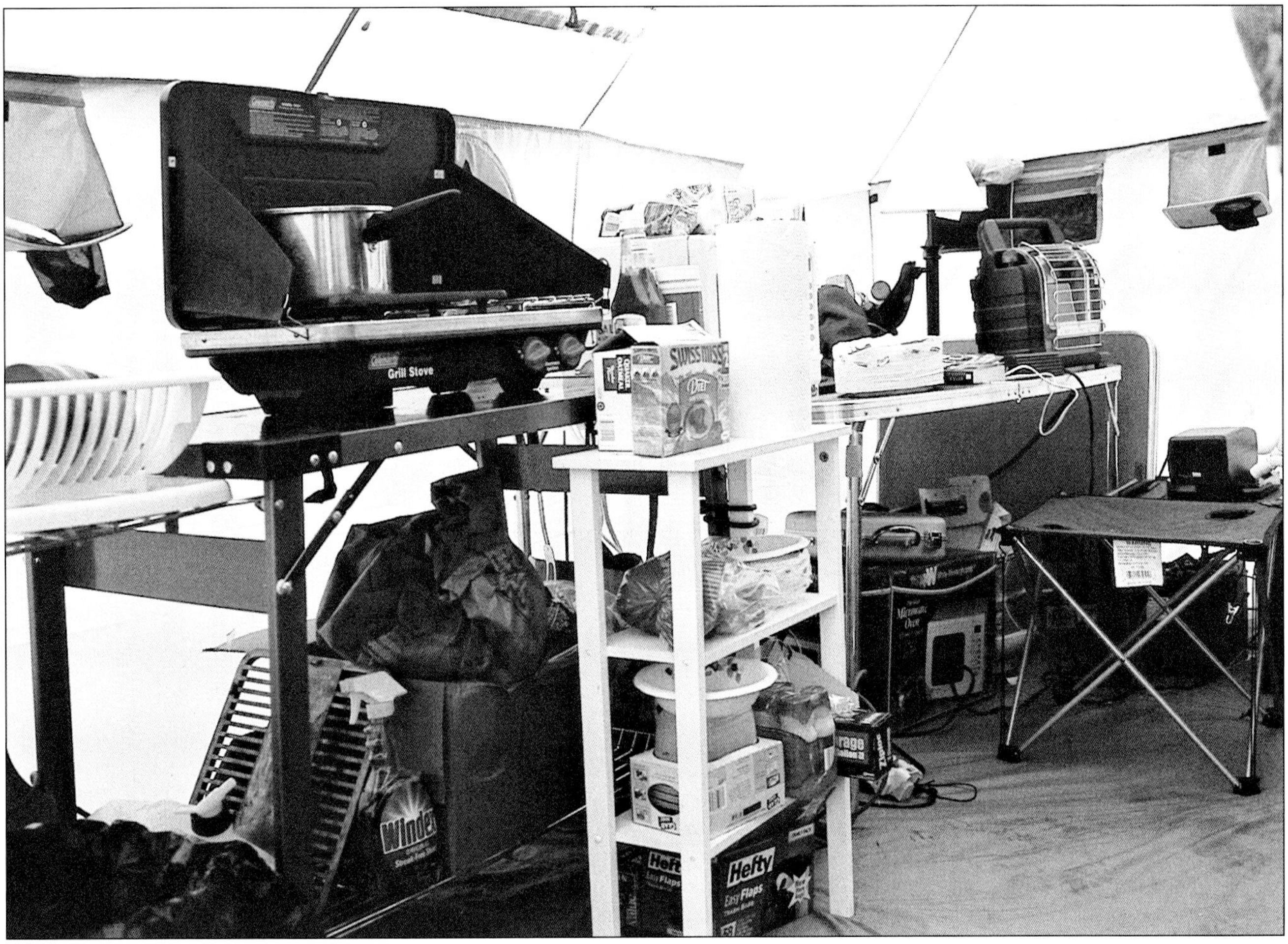

Inside Towsley's tent camp in Ontario 2002. Bryce M. Towsley photo.

possibilities before the season. Then Craig and a buddy head to the hunting area a day or two before the hunting season and set everything up.

This tent is heated with a big wood stove made from a 55-gallon oil drum and the light is from propane gas-lights installed along the ceiling. They have a kitchen set up with a propane cooking stove and they haul water in 5-gallon jugs. The bathroom is a canvas outhouse or simply a tree in the woods. It's a Spartan life, but it works. The Benoits are focused on deer hunting, so they are in camp only to sleep and eat and for that they find this arrangement perfect.

This big tent is a wonderful arrangement for large groups of hunters, but it's a bit much to manage for a small group of two or three hunters. I have my own smaller version of camp that is great for one or two people and can handle three if you don't mind being a little crowded. The difference is that I like my comforts a little more. I have discussed this at length with Shane and he agrees that mine is a great set-up for a couple of guys hunting the Benoit way.

I used my tent while hunting with the Benoits and camped beside them so that I could have a quiet place to work on this book. I also have used it in New England for deer hunting, including during some pretty severe winter storms. My son Nathan and I rode out one Vermont nor'easter that shut down the state for a day and kept the woods free from hunters. The wind howled and it turned from driving rain to stinging sleet and then to snow that piled a foot in just a few hours. Yet we were dry and comfortable inside the tent.

Like a lot of my gear, my tent is from Cabela's. It's their 12x12 Deluxe Alaknak II. (They also make a smaller version, as well as a 12x20 model for large groups.) One or two people can set up this tent very quickly, and it features a sewn-in floor and shelves that fold down from the walls. I added the optional floor liner for extra protection and to help keep things clean. The floor has a zip-out portion for use with a wood stove and the roof has a vent hole above that for the stovepipe. I also added the optional extra roof panel for added protection against any damage from sparks. By next hunting season, I plan to add the attached vestibule that is offered as an accessory and move the cooking area out to it to keep the smoke and odors away from the main tent.

For heat, I use a sheepherder's stove, also from Cabela's. Mine is the packer's model, which is a small 8½ inches by 23 inches. It's the one thing I would change, as it is a little too small when it gets bitter cold. It heats the tent fine as long as you are tending it, but it is not large enough to keep it warm through the night.

I use a Mr. Heater propane heater to take the chill off in the mornings. Outfitter tents are relatively easy to heat, but they don't retain that heat very well. There is not much insulation in those thin fabric walls and they cool off fast. Some quick heat in the morning while the woodstove is cranking up can be a blessing.

I sleep on the NEBO Outfitter XL cot that I also got from Cabela's. This is a big, rugged cot that's large

enough for me to toss and turn all I want. Anybody who has ever slept on a cot in cold weather knows that they need some insulation. Without it, your bottom side gets cold from being suspended up off the ground. So I cover the cot with a 3-inch foam pad I bought years ago. With a huge and incredibly warm Sandstone sleeping bag from NEBO, I think I could sleep through the next ice age in comfort.

I set up a couple of folding tables from Coleman and added a Coleman propane stove/grill. For light, I use propane lanterns, with one suspended on a hook from the center pole of the tent. I bought a flowerpot hanger from the local hardware store and used hose clamps to attach it to the tent's center pole. It's perfect to hang a lantern from. Each of the propane appliances is supplied from its own 20-pound tank.

I don't see any reason to suffer unnecessarily, so I have also added a small microwave oven, a toaster, and several electric lights. I power these, as well as charge my computer batteries and handle any other power needs, with an EU2000 Honda generator. This little wonder is small, portable, and very quiet. Better still, it sips gas like a refined lady sips champagne. Put it in the woods 50 feet or so from the tent, run an extension cord and you barely notice it's out there.

I keep a deep-cycle marine battery in the tent, hooked to a 110 inverter. I can use this to power a table lamp if I have to get up in the night. It's far better than

Lanny says that the "riper" he gets, the more deer he sees. But, my guess is it's an excuse to avoid using this frozen shower more than hunting strategy. Bryce M. Towsley photo.

Left opposite: Bryce M. Towsley's Cabela's tent in Ontario. Bryce M. Towsley photo.

EU2000 Honda generator. Bryce M. Towsley photo.

a flashlight and much easier and faster than lighting a lantern. I simply recharge the battery each day with the Honda generator.

My wife bought me an inexpensive portable clothes rack at one of the "marts," which I use to hang and dry my wet stuff each night. I also have a small set of electric boot driers that I plug into the generator to make sure my footwear is dry in the morning.

To sit on, there are several folding canvas chairs that came from the same "mart" and a collapsible table of the same make for all the comforts of home. Those folding chairs pack up quickly and fit in a cylindrical nylon case for carrying and they double for use on the deer stand. They are easy to carry for a short distance and are far more comfortable than sitting on the ground. Add a few coolers for food and drinks, a garbage can and the camp is complete.

Perhaps the most important piece of equipment is the Portable Environmental Toilet that I also got from Cabela's. This inexpensive little outhouse comes with a tent and a folding "toilet." Simply dig a hole and set them both up over it. When you are done, take it down, fill in the hole and there are no problems with pollution. The little tent is easily warmed with a small propane heater, and if it's really cold, you can bring the toilet inside the big heated tent. For use inside, the toilet uses special waste collection bags with a powder that turns all liquids into a gel to prevent spillage.

I also have a Cabela's portable Shower Shelter, which is a small tent with a "solar shower." It was fine until it got below freezing. After that, it didn't get much use! This entire camp, along with all my gear, fits easily in my 12-foot cargo trailer, or even in the back of my pickup truck. With it, any deer hunter can be mobile from year to year and, if need be, even from week to week. It takes less than half a day to set up or tear down. The only major adjustment anyone would have to make would be to the size of the tent, depending on how many hunters you wish to accommodate, and except for the generator (which has a suggested retail price of $1079.95 and is worth every penny), I think the entire package is less than $1500.00.

Filming the Benoits has added a whole new dimension to the way they hunt. Tom Blais photo.

Cameraman Tom Blais with a nice buck. Tom Blais photo.

Shane and camerman Tom Blais with one of the many bucks killed on camera. Tom Blais photo.

IMMORTALITY THROUGH FILM

"We are going to make a hunting video with the Benoits," the young man told me with all sincerity while I tried to hide my skepticism. I am a lousy actor and I could see in his eyes that I was failing, so I just wished him luck and moved on.

In my business, I am constantly meeting guys who are going to become rich and famous making hunting videos. Most I never see again, and even though I check the standings in the Fortune 500, I don't find their names among the newly rich either.

It hasn't happened for a while now; I suppose because most outfitters have learned some bitter lessons, but for a time it was common. I can't remember how many camps I have been in where there were a couple of guys who got video cameras for Christmas, scammed the outfitter out of a free hunt, and then quit their day jobs for the bright lights of stardom. It seemed that for a while half the hunting population was making a video. I figured this guy was just another in that long string of "wannabes."

I have done enough video and television work to know how difficult it is even under the best of conditions. I am also a friend to many of the big-name guys who have made it in that extremely tough and competitive business. They are all talented, passionate, committed, and extremely hard-working. None of them is rich. If they all took time to figure the dollars per hour they actually make at the video business, the suicide rate in this country would probably take an upward spike, the likes of which hasn't been seen since the market crashed in '29.

Then there is the difficulty factor. There are lots of reasons why almost all the deer hunting segments you see are filmed from treestands. Even at that, it's incredibly difficult to make any kind of deer hunting video, and all but impossible to produce a good video. It's done only a few times every year. But for each successful deer

Lanny and cameraman Tom Blais after another successful tracking job. Photo by Tom Blais.

hunting tape, there are uncounted failures. That's if you take the easy route and film from treestands. Tracking deer with the Benoits? Never happens.

I had recently published a book about the Benoits, so I knew a lot about them and about the way they hunt. I didn't think it was humanly possible to make a video about how they hunt whitetails.

Just as I figured, that guy didn't last. But his partner did. Tom Blais may have achieved the impossible. Not only did he complete that hunting video with the Benoits, but he has also recently completed a second video. The most amazing thing to witness, though, is how he has managed to "tame" the Benoits and achieve their almost total cooperation in front of the camera. They are so focused and so committed to deer hunting I didn't think anything could divert them from that path, not even long enough to film as they did it. My guess was that most cameramen wouldn't last a day with these guys and in truth most don't make it much longer. Somehow Tom managed to make it all work and now, 4 years later, he is still filming them. I figured there had to be some secrets buried in his head, so I asked him to sit down and talk.

"So tell me," I said with a smirk, "about how much fun it is to film the Benoits."

"Actually, I like it," he said with a sincerity that this time seemed well placed, "because it's challenging. I enjoy tracking and did it a lot before I met them. I consider myself a 'conditions' hunter; that is, I'll adapt to the prevailing conditions. I use treestands, rattling horns, and grunt calls. But when the conditions are right, I like to track.

"I have worked in the outdoor filming business, both for television and in producing videos, and I saw this as a challenge. I think Lanny summed it up well when he pointed out that sitting on a stand is boring other than the few minutes when the deer actually shows up. But when you are tracking, you are excited all day long. I wanted to capture that in a video.

"I had tried filming tracking in Montana when I lived out there, but my partner didn't believe in it and he would never be ready. We would jump the buck and he would have the lens cap on or some other mistake. Then he would take that as a sign that it couldn't be done and want to quit. But I saw it differently. I thought the problem was in his belief that it could never work. He didn't believe that tracking would work to kill big bucks and he didn't think filming it was possible. I always believed in tracking and that a tracking video could be done by somebody committed to completing it. I decided that when I was filming the Benoits, I was part of the hunt. I was a hunter, a predator, only instead of a rifle, I wanted to 'kill' that buck with my camera, and that has made all the difference. If I didn't have that mindset, I wouldn't be ready when we found the deer and I would miss the shot.

"It's mostly mental anyway, whether it's tracking bucks or filming the Benoits tracking bucks. Sure, you need to be in good physical condition to film these guys. You are carrying a lot of weight and you have to go at their pace no matter what. But it's more mental, and for most people, the mind will quit long before the body. You have to believe in this kind of hunting and you have to have a positive mental attitude. The Benoits are carrying a seven-pound rifle, two or three candy bars, and a bottle of water. The cameraman is carrying all his own food and water, but he also has a 12-pound camera, extra lenses, film, and several very heavy spare batteries. Plus, I carry a still camera. It all adds up to 30 pounds or more. Then I have to keep up with the Benoits because they are not going to wait. They can't; if they have to wait, they will never catch the buck. On top of that, I have to deal with wet snow and poor weather that are conspiring to keep the cameras from working.

"Obviously, I can't film all of them at the same time, so I hire guys to work with us. We have filmed 12 buck kills with the Benoits in 4 years, eight of them were filmed by me. That's because I want it the most. We actually have trouble keeping cameramen who can handle this hunting. I have been through four different cameramen in 4 years. One guy just quit in the middle of a hunt. He went to town, rented a car, and drove for 3 days to get home. They all want to do it when I hire them, but most don't last. It's just too tough to hunt with the Benoits.

"I believe that we are doing something totally unique in this industry with these videos. When you think about it, the Benoits are freaks. I don't mean that in a derogatory way, but as an illustration of the extreme way they hunt deer and how dedicated they are to it. I suppose I am a freak, too, because I like following them around and filming while they do it. To film them, you need to be a hardcore deer hunter as well as a hardcore cameraman. Then you have to be willing to film rather than shoot the bucks you find. Most guys simply can't put that all together.

"It's important that you are able to see the buck as quickly as they can and to get that camera on the deer very fast, even faster than they can get their rifles on it. Of course, you can't always do that, but it's important that you are trying all the time.

"Again, the hardest part is developing the mental toughness this takes, and to be able to handle the strain of trying to make this all work. It's not unusual to go a week without even filming a deer and that wears you out mentally. It's even tougher when you have spent that week and finally get a deer in front of you and it's dead before you can react, so you have nothing on film. Sure, at times I wanted to quit, but I wanted to make it work more.

"With the Benoits, it was hard to train them not to shoot the bucks until we had them on camera. We would spend days and days tracking bucks and then all of a sudden, there he is, and 'bang-bang,' the deer is on the ground before I could even get the camera turned on. I tried keeping the camera on standby, but in that

Friend and cameraman Craig Jaques shares the campfire with Larry Benoit. Benoit Brothers photo.

cold weather the batteries didn't last and nobody can carry enough spares. It takes about 8 seconds for the camera to turn on, and even at that I had to convince them to wait until I had the buck in the viewfinder before they shot. For years, they simply killed the buck as soon as they saw him, now I was asking them to wait. Sometimes that even meant the buck would get away, and that goes against everything they have done and believed their entire lives. My job was to train them to accept a huge and dramatic change in their hunting style and in their potential for success.

"They are very competitive guys and now they are trying to outdo each other with the best footage, so it's really coming together. It's no longer just about which of the Benoits is shooting the best buck; it's about which one is shooting the best buck with the best video

Artwork on the stock of Lanny Benoit's Remington 7600. Bryce M. Towsley photo.

footage! You saw yourself this year how they would pass up good bucks because there wasn't a cameraman along to record it. They thrive on challenge and I think that it has energized the Benoits because this is a new and difficult challenge that adds a new dimension to their hunting experience.

"I am looking to create 'reality' deer hunting and it's a little different from what most deer hunting videos are all about. Sort of like the difference between a sitcom and the reality shows. It might not be as polished, but it's a lot more honest.

"But it's also been a two-way street. In 4 years of hunting with the Benoits, I have earned a PhD in deer tracking. It's like taking golf lessons from Tiger Woods to spend all that time hunting with the Benoits. I can't begin to tell you how much they have taught me. We 'freaks' have been good for each other!"

Lane Benoit in Ontario 2002. Bryce M. Towsley photo.

Left to right: Shane, Larry, Lane, and Lanny with the bucks they took in 2001. Benoit Brothers photo.

A Benoit Brothers Scrapbook

Lanny admires one of his many bucks he has taken by tracking. Tom Blais photo.

BEAGLE

Opposite:
Lane and the buck he took during the 2001 season. Tom Blais photo.

At left:
Shane poses with his 2002 8-pointer. Tom Blais photo.

Below:
Lanny and cameraman Tom Blais with a nice North Country whitetail. Tom Blais photo.

Above: Tom Blais poses with Lane and the buck Lane took in 2002—a real monster! Tom Blais photo.

Opposite left:
Shane admires the first buck he has taken from a stand. Tom Blais photo.

Opposite right:
Tom Blais next to a "shaggy" rub and a pair of sheds from a very nice buck. Tom Blais photo.

Opposite lower right:
Lane had a great season in 2002. The buck on the left is his Canadian monster, while the other buck was taken in Vermont. Lane Benoit photo.

Above: Lanny shows his happy face after putting down this monster. Tom Blais photo.

Another successful tracking job for Lanny resulted in this long-tined buck. Benoit Brothers photo.

After the kill, the real work begins! Benoit Brothers photo.

Another nice buck results in another broad smile from Lanny. Tom Blais photo.

There's no better feeling than walking up to a trophy buck after a long day of tracking! Tom Blais photo.

Shane starts the drag while Larry looks on. Tom Blais photo.

Counterclockwise:
Shane and another North Country trophy buck.
Tom Blais photo.

Bucks like this one can make the drag a little more enjoyable! Tom Blais photo.

The Benoit Brothers and their bucks after a successful hunt in 2002. Tom Blais photo.

Another buck falls to the patient hunting tactics of Shane.
Lane Benoit photo.

The buck pole can get pretty crowded in any Benoit hunting camp! Tom Blais photo.

The buck pole on Larry Benoit's front porch after a successful hunt. Benoit Brothers photo.

Lanny gives thanks for younger brothers as Shane starts the drag to the truck. Tom Blais photo.

Left:
Larry and the boys pose with their bucks taken during the 2000 season.
Tom Blais photo.

Sometimes it's necessary to "double-team" a stubborn buck in order to get him. Lanny and Shane do it quite often.
Tom Blais photo.

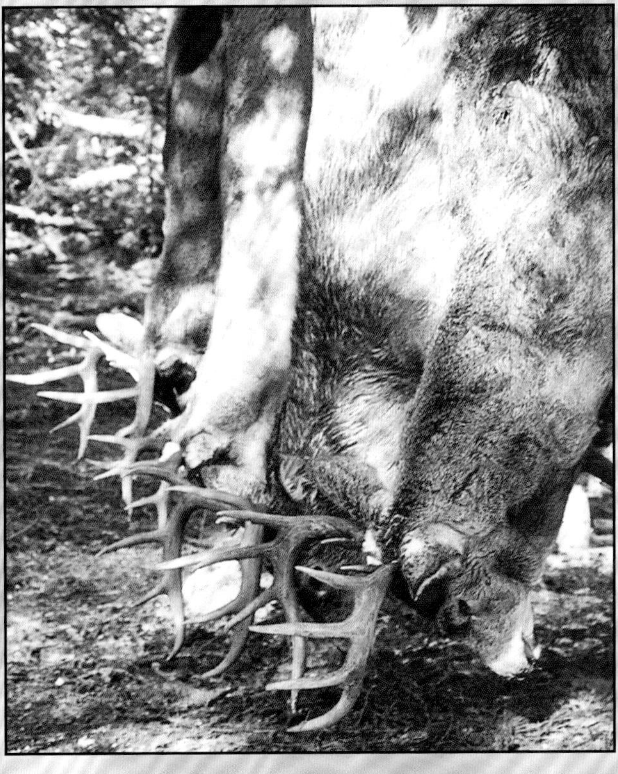

The buck pole during the 2000 season was impressive indeed.
Tom Blais photo.

Sometimes you need to go to extraordinary measures to retrieve the trophy! Benoit Brothers photo.

Below middle:
The buck pole on Larry's porch after another successful season of tracking by the Benoits.
Benoit Brothers photo.

Below left:
Dave Coker with a monster buck taken in 2002. Dave Coker photo.

Above:
Craig Jaques with a big Ontario whitetail.
Craig Jaques photo.

Lane glasses from a high ridge overlooking a beaver meadow in Ontario. Bryce M. Towsley photo.

A metal deer head inlaid into the stock of Lane's rifle. Bryce M. Towsley photo.

Below:
Lanny looks under some brush for a buck he's been tracking. Bryce M. Towsley photo.

A sign on the back trail in northern New Hampshire.
Bryce M. Towsley photo.

Lane laughs it up during the 2002 Ontario hunt.
Bryce M. Towsley photo.

Below: Inside the Benoit tent camp in Ontario during the 2002 season. Bryce M. Towsley photo.

Lanny "holding court" before beginning a hunt in New Hampshire in 2002.
Bryce M. Towsley photo.

Getting stuck is part of exploring new country.
Bryce M. Towsley photo.

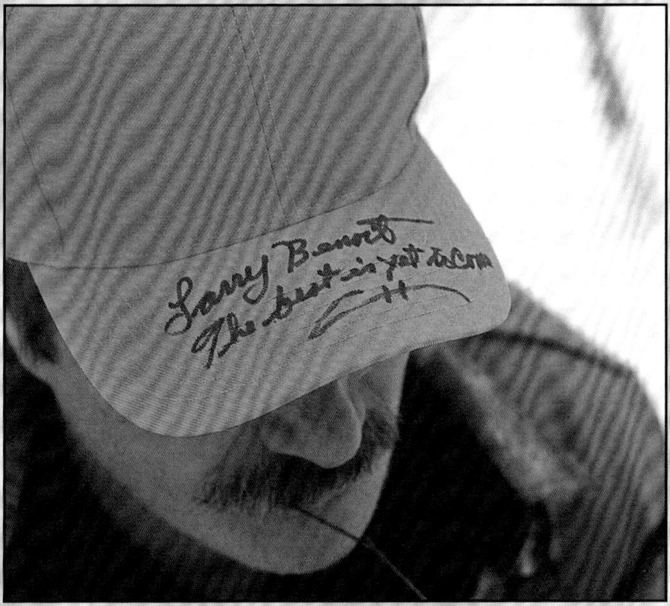

Craig Jaques wearing a hat inscribed by Larry Benoit, a legendary deer tracker. Bryce M. Towsley photo.

A cartridge belt hung over a truck seat. Bryce M. Towsley photo.

Left:
Lane heads out on a track in Ontario.
Bryce M. Towsley photo.

Above:
A single 270 Winchester cartridge stuck in a hole in the dash of Casper—ready for quick use.
Bryce M. Towsley photo.

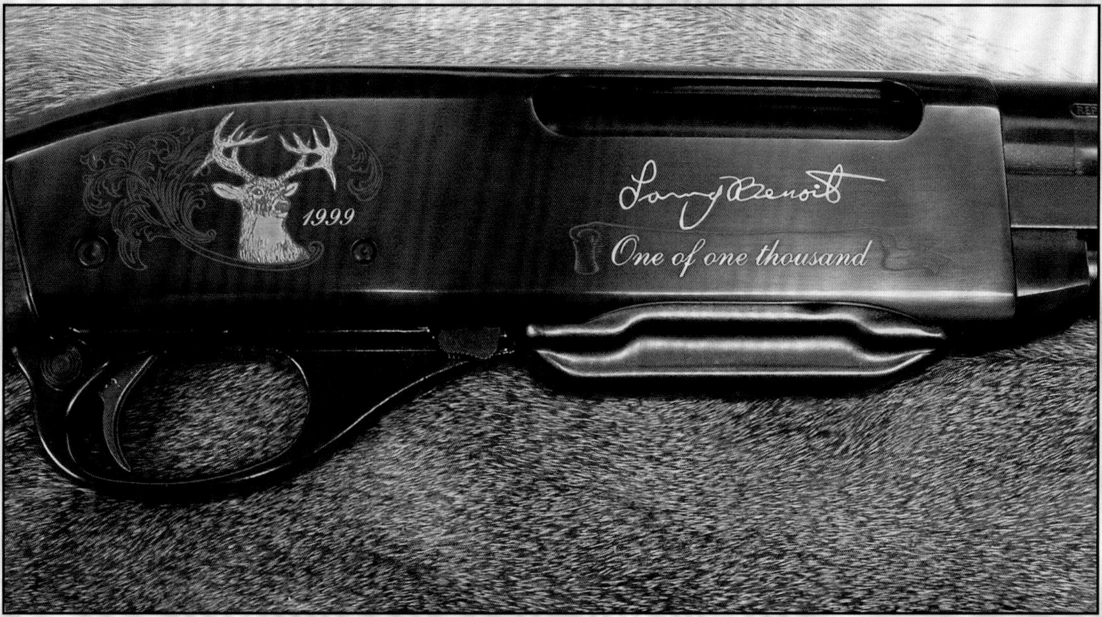

Left:
Larry Benoit's signature a Model 7600 produced by Remington in 1999.
Bryce M. Towsley photo.

Shane's cartridge belt on an Ontario log—the tools of the tracker. Bryce M. Towsley photo.

Left: Vermont license plate for a hard-core deer hunter. Bryce M. Towsley photo.

HOW THEY DO IT

CHAPTER FIVE

Twenty Common Mistakes Trackers Make

Nobody likes to admit they make mistakes and I think this trait is particularly strong in deer trackers. The independent streak that is necessary to be good at this type of deer hunting suppresses any inherent willingness to admit that we might screw up on occasion. The old joke goes, "I never make mistakes. Once I thought I did, but it turns out I was wrong."

But the truth is that deer trackers, like any hunters, will make mistakes. In fact, tracking is more susceptible to mistakes than most other styles of trophy whitetail hunting because it is active hunting. It's far easier to sit on a stand and wait for the deer to wander by than it is to be out moving and actively chasing the buck mistake-free.

The Benoits have learned about the common mistakes over the years by making most of them themselves at one time or another or by listening to what the thousands of other hunters they talk with are saying.

I asked Lanny, Lane, Shane, and Tom Blais to compile a list of the most common mistakes that hunters make while tracking deer. Then I grilled them on how to correct those mistakes. It turned out that a few of them were also in my field of expertise and so I added some of my own solutions into the mix. Here in no particular order are the most common mistakes that deer trackers make and some ideas on how to correct them.

1: Walking with Their Heads Down Too Much

There is a strong tendency to watch the track rather than looking for the deer. A lot of hunters get mesmerized by the track or are so afraid they will lose it that they don't take their eyes off it. They walk along with their heads down and the result usually is bumping the buck without getting a shot. Remember the main point here is not to follow the track, but to shoot the buck and to do that you must see him. Whitetails as a

Instead of keeping your head down watching the track . . .

rule don't stand around posing and waiting to receive a bullet, so you must be constantly scanning the land ahead of you looking for any evidence of the buck.

Don't look for a "calendar" buck standing broadside in the open, as wild deer rarely do that. Instead, look for movement. That's the easiest way to spot a buck. But hope and pray that the movement is simply the buck going about the business of being a deer and not because he has seen you first. Watch also for horizontal lines in the vertical forest and for parts of the deer rather than the whole deer. Look for pieces of antler, the shape of an ear, the white around his eye, or even his wet and shiny nose. Look for the shape of his tail (when it's in the resting position; if you see the underside you already blew it!). Look for patches of hide, as deer hair is a different texture than tree bark. Look for his legs. Look for anything that appears out of place. Sometimes on a cold day you will even see his breath as he exhales. It creates movement from a stationary buck.

Most of the time when you are following the trail, use your peripheral vision to see the track. Of course, sometimes you will need to look hard at the track to sort it out, but most of the time, when it's clear and evident, you should only glance at it now and then while keeping track of it out of the corner of your eye. Keep your eyes constantly sweeping back and forth, watching for the deer. At times you may wish to glance down quickly at the track to confirm that everything is still "on track" so to speak, and of course there are times when you must watch the track exclusively to sort out a problem. The majority of the time, however, your eyes should be up and looking for deer. Try to look at the track as far ahead as possible, which allows you to walk to that point without checking the ground again. Anytime you can, you should be forcing yourself to watch for deer rather than looking at the ground. If you lose the track once in a while so that you have to stop and sort things out, often by back tracking, then you are probably balancing it just about right.

. . . keep it up with your eyes constantly sweeping back and forth, watching for the buck.

Bryce M. Towsley photos.

2: Moving at the Wrong Speed

Tracking the buck at the wrong speed is a very common mistake. Most hunters simply move too slow and will never catch up with the buck. Remember he has four legs to your two; he is in much better physical condition than you and on terrain he is familiar with walking every day. He also has a head start (otherwise he wouldn't be in front of you!). You can't "sneak along" and expect to ever catch a traveling buck.

The key is in reading the sign and knowing when to move fast and when to slow down. If the buck is very

close and bedded down, you want to slow down to the "death creep" before you blunder into him and spook off any chance for a shot. But if the buck is traveling, you have to move fast on the track or you will never see him.

Lanny takes a much different approach in that he rarely varies his pace; he simply keeps up a fast, ground-eating walk on the track. Sometimes he shoots the deer the first time he catches up with it, but just as often he bumps the buck. Sometimes he bumps the same buck as many as ten or more times in a day, but he almost always shoots them sooner or later.

Lane, too, liked to move fast. "Sometimes I like to get them up and moving," he told me while we were hunting in Ontario in 2002. "If they are bedded in a good place it's hard to sneak up on them, so rather than waste the time trying, I just walk along at a fast pace on the track and get them out of there and hopefully into a place I can see and shoot them."

The key with this approach is to move as fast as you can *while you still look for the deer.* The mistake that a lot of

Lanny Benoit on the track of a buck. Bryce M. Towsley photo.

Landon Benoit is moving fast on this buck's trail. Bryce M. Towsley photo.

younger trackers make is to mistake aggression for skill. They move so fast on the trail they are unable to watch for the buck. As a result they often fail to see the deer before he is presenting the "moon" salute. Walk fast, but keep your eyes sweeping ahead for the deer. Never concentrate so much on the track or on how fast you can go that you fail to pick the terrain ahead apart with your eyes. After all, the primary point of all this is to actually see the buck long enough to shoot him.

3: Fear of Getting Lost

Getting lost isn't all that bad. I do it all the time! Just bring a space blanket, some matches, and lots of granola bars. But even I will admit that not getting lost is way better.

Successfully hunting big bucks by tracking requires complete and total focus and concentration. Tracking is most effective in big country, and if you are worried about getting lost all the time you cannot concentrate on deer hunting. To be a successful whitetail tracker you must first learn to be comfortable in the woods. You have to be confident in your abilities to not get lost and secure in the knowledge that even if you do it's no big deal.

One great way to develop these skills is to walk the big woods during the off-season. Spend some time traveling deep into the woods and off the trails when you are not hunting. Any time is fine, but if you go after the hunting season and practice tracking bucks you will also build your tracking skills. If the snow is not too deep and the deer haven't headed for the winter yards, you may make it your goal to take a photograph of the buck. But even just hiking and exploring any time of year is a great way to learn "woods skills," such as how to walk quietly or how to use the terrain to your advantage, while at the same time learning to be comfortable when you are far from the roads. It may also help you locate a few big bucks to hunt next fall.

Develop a familiarity with the big woods and that will lead to a comfortable association with them. The

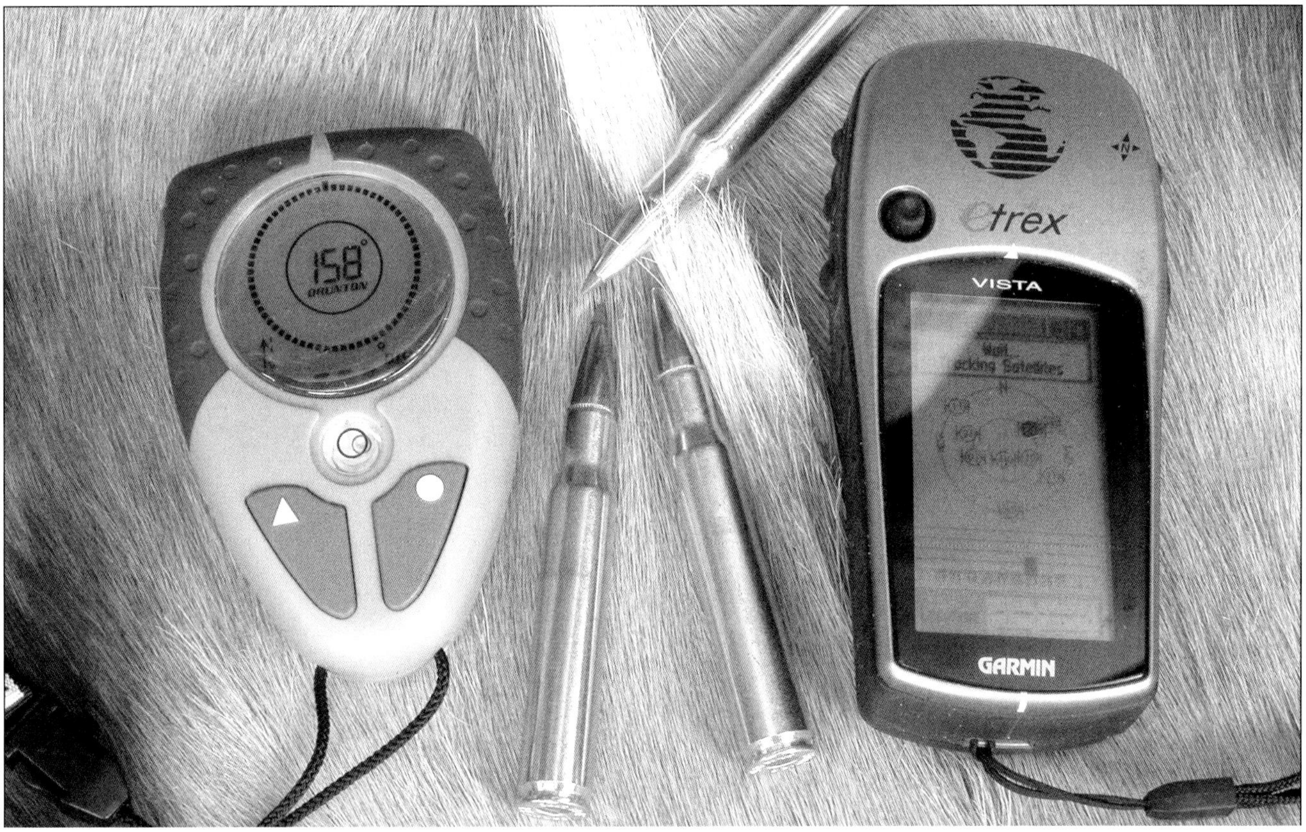

Brunton electronic digital compass and Garmin Etrex GPS. GPS has changed big woods navigation and has all but eliminated the fear of getting lost. Bryce M. Towsley photo.

more time you spend deep in the woods, the less intimidating they become.

It's pretty rare today to have a block of woods where whitetails live that is so large that you can't walk out of it in any direction in several hours' time. A man in a hurry can cover about 3 or 4 miles an hour in the woods. In 5 hours that is at least 15 miles, and it's pretty rare today to find any whitetail woods that stretch on for that distance without crossing a road or a trail. It may mean a long hike, but both of these will lead you to civilization sooner or later, so getting "lost" is something you will probably have to work pretty hard at to succeed. You may have an uncomfortable night, but if you use your head, you really can't get "lost."

Don't worry about spending the night. It's no different than spending the day in the woods, except it is darker and perhaps a bit colder. You don't have any problems in the daylight and don't expect to die, so why expect problems at night? Nothing really changes at night. There are no "wild animals" that pose a serious threat; besides, don't you have a gun with you? In the unlikely event you get "lost" and have to spend the night, just find some shelter, build a fire, and stay put until daylight. Keep your head and you will be fine. Probably cold, hungry, and tired, but fine. After all, men have been living in the woods for eons without a house or electricity or a hot tub and they survived. Do you think the mountain men had a pop up camper to sleep in every night? They just slept on the ground where they were.

The problem with modern hunters is they feel they "must" get back to camp every night, no matter what. They spend the day worrying about that and hunt accordingly. A buck doesn't worry about getting lost, and if you do, he will leave you in the dust.

Once you have accepted that, even if you do get lost, it will be nothing more than an inconvenience, so you can concentrate on hunting. You will also discover that getting lost is all but unheard of if you pay attention to the woods and the land. In the past a compass, knowledge of the land, and an observant mind was usually enough and few woodsmen got truly lost.

Today we have affordable and accurate GPS systems that will fit in your shirt pocket. They will pinpoint your location and give you a direction and distance to get to any point on the map that you have entered. No serious big woods deer hunter should be without one. The important thing is to first learn how to operate it before the hunting season and then to use it while you are hunting. It will do you no good if you don't know where you need to go. Unless you enter the waypoints it can only tell you where you are, not where you need to go. Actually that's not completely true, as some models today have built-in maps that are detailed enough to tell you how to find the nearest road or landmark. But for the best use of your GPS, always enter the location of your truck when you leave it to hunt. Do this even if you think you are only going to be traveling a short distance on land you know. You simply can't predict what the day will bring, and if you become distracted by a track and suddenly find yourself miles from the truck with a snowstorm moving

The Benoits favor the use of a pin-on compass.

Bryce M. Towsley photo.

in, it is too late. Make it a habit to always enter the location into the GPS and to take a compass reading every time you leave the truck.

Anytime you make a major direction change or encounter a choke point that must be used in your return such as a river crossing, mark a waypoint. Or if you are really worried, buy a GPS with a "backtrack" feature and leave it on. It will lay a trail of electronic breadcrumbs that you can follow back to your truck.

You should always bring a spare set of batteries and you still must always have a good compass. Like any technology, a GPS can fail or it can be broken or lost. Electronics or any other technology is never a substitute for good woods skills. Always pay attention to the land you are traveling through and the direction you are traveling. Take care not to become so distracted by the track that you fail to notice these things. Always have a compass for backup. More importantly, make sure you know how to use the compass as well as how to navigate through the woods without it.

Learn to be a woodsman first, and then learn to use a GPS later. Use it to help keep you focused on deer hunting and free from fear of getting lost, but don't bet your life entirely on it. The only thing you can ever count on completely is yourself. With that in mind, go out and buy a good GPS.

It takes a while to learn how to operate a GPS and even longer to develop a trust in it, but once you learn how wonderful this invention can be, you will be able to travel into the deepest woods with complete confidence. For the directionally challenged hunter, the GPS is the greatest invention since smokeless powder. It allows you to keep your mind focused on deer hunting and that alone will dramatically improve your odds of success.

4: Giving Up

There are reasons why the Benoits are so successful at tracking and shooting big whitetail bucks. First is confidence in what they are doing. Every time they take a buck track they truly believe they will kill that deer. They believe in what they are doing, they have great confidence in their ability to do it well, and they always expect nothing less than success. After all, what's the point of tracking a buck if you don't expect to shoot him? Without that expectation you cannot maintain the mental focus necessary to succeed and so lack of confidence becomes a self-fulfilling prophecy.

Another big factor for the Benoits is a mental and physical toughness that keeps them going for as long as it takes. Many hunters can develop the physical conditioning and toughness necessary, but the mental aspect is something altogether different. You must not allow yourself to get discouraged or to start thinking that you can't shoot this or any other buck. The moment you allow doubt to poke its nose under the tent of your mind, you are finished. No matter how bad things are going, suck it

Lanny and Shane Benoit are tired after a long day of tracking and dragging.
Tom Blais photo.

Right:
Many deer have distinctive hoof characteristics that allow you to distinguish their tracks from others.
Tom Blais photo.

Opposite page:
Note one side of this deer's hoof is shorter than the other. This makes for a distinctive- looking track and helps to identify the deer you are tracking.
Tom Blais photo.

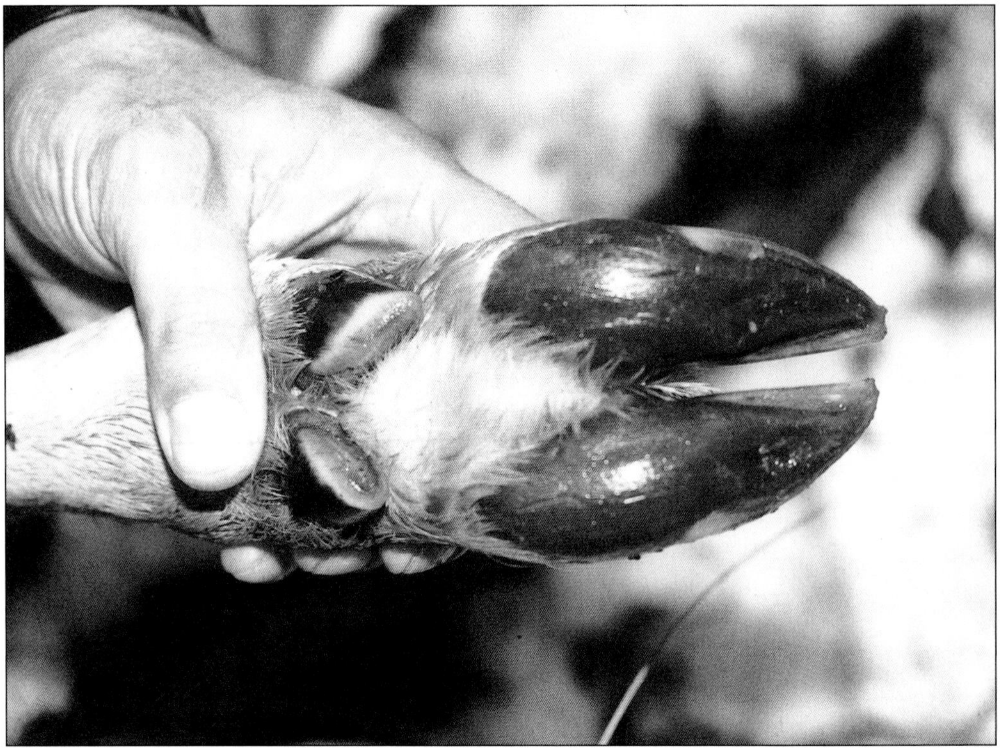

up, believe you will kill this buck, and keep going.

This applies as well to the mental weariness that comes from hunting hard day after day without success. Many hunters start to get homesick after just a few days. They start to miss their family, their dog, their television set, and after several days of hard hunting without success, they start to think about reasons to give up and go home. This will result in failure. Remember that you have allotted a certain number of days to deer hunting. They have been planned for that activity for a long time and nothing short of a true emergency should deter you from using those days as you planned. You knew it would be hard when you started, but then you were determined to see it through. Don't talk yourself into quitting; instead talk yourself into succeeding.

The Benoits often hunt an area for as much as a month at a time. There are many days when things don't go their way. Days when the weather is crappy and they are wet and cold. There are always times when it's raining for the third or even sixth day in a row and bucks are as scarce as honest politicians. Days when they don't feel good, days when their bones ache and their muscles shriek with pain. There are days when they miss their families and worry about their jobs. Like anybody else who is human, there are lots of days when they want to quit, pack the truck, and head for home. But every night when they lie down to sleep, they genuinely believe that tomorrow they will kill a big buck. And with that thought, they rise into the cold, gray dawn and set out to find another track, confident that this is the day they will shoot a big buck.

To be as successful as they are at shooting big whitetail bucks, you must develop that same attitude and toughness. You need to be physically tough, but you also need a mental toughness that keeps you hunting as well as keeping you going on the track.

Finally, the Benoits are successful for the same reason as most other extremely successful hunters. They simply are willing to do things that most other hunters are not.

Jim Shockey is one of the most successful hunters I know. Jim has taken all the North American big game species with a muzzleloader and most of them make the record book. He has also taken several outstanding whitetail bucks. I think he summed it up well when he was telling me about some of his solo hunts deep into the Canadian mountains. These are backpack hunts where every ounce counts. They often last for weeks at a time, but Jim brings very little equipment into this harsh

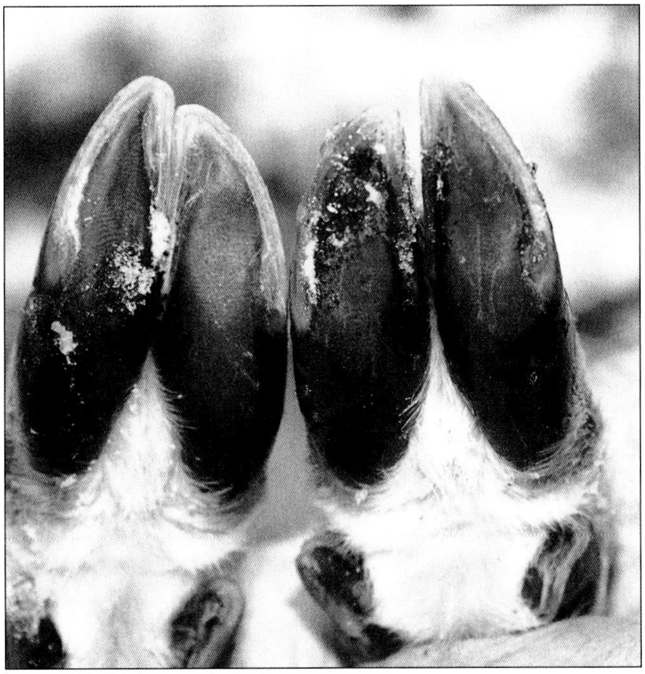

environment. This keeps him mobile and able to pursue the game without the umbilical of a camp holding him back. But at times he suffers a great deal for that choice.

"The human body is tough and can take a lot of punishment," he said. "It may not be comfortable and in fact at times it hurts like hell, but unless you make a big mistake, you won't die. You just suck it up and keep going until you reach your goals."

Most people will not endure that kind of pain. They like their comforts and when it starts to get difficult or painful they quit. Those hunters will never be successful at tracking trophy whitetail bucks. The Benoits will suck up both the physical pain that is part of any difficult hunt and the mental pain that is probably a bigger factor with most hunters and keep going until they succeed. Like a lot of important things in life, it all comes down to how much you want it and what you are willing to do to get it. The Benoits simply are willing to do a lot more than most hunters. If the buck goes into rough country, they go in after him. If he crosses a river, they cross the river—even if it means stripping off their boots and clothes and wading across barefoot and naked. Whatever it takes.

Many hunters lose confidence in their chances of success or they get cold, tired, hungry, or afraid of becoming lost. They get discouraged because they have jumped the buck or because he is headed into rough country or has crossed a cold river, or for whatever reason they can conjure up to justify quitting the track. This hunter digs until he finds a reason he can live with to justify in his mind abandoning the hunt, and then he quits the track and leaves. At that point, failure is an absolute certainty. Hunters who are successful time and again at shooting big bucks don't quit. They don't quit the track and they don't quit the hunt. They stay focused on the goal and keep going when others turn back, and as a result they shoot big bucks.

It's not "luck" and it's not voodoo, it is simply a willingness to do whatever it takes and a deep stubbornness to keep trying and to keep going, no matter what.

5: Losing the Track

Sometimes losing the track is unavoidable. If you move into an area with little or no snow, it becomes hard to follow what isn't there. But many hunters lose the track when they should not.

Actually every tracker, even the Benoits, will "lose the track" quite often. It's part of tracking bucks. The important thing is to find it again. Remember, the buck had to go somewhere, and unless he learned to fly, to get there he had to leave tracks.

If you are watching for the deer and keeping your head up rather than looking at the track, you will lose the track often. Usually it's simply a case of stopping and looking around or maybe backtracking yourself a little until you locate it again. It's important to be careful to never walk in the track for this reason. If you have obliterated the trail with your footprints, you can't go back and find what's not there.

Often the trail will be lost when the buck passes through an area with lots of other deer tracks. This is why it's important to first be following an exceptionally large buck so that the track will be noticeably larger than all the other tracks. A big track is recognizable when it's mixed with other deer tracks. Sure, there could be another big buck making tracks, but it's not likely and even if you do find another track that's as large or larger, you might consider taking that one. The Benoits switch deer all the time. The new track has the advantage of being available and it may well be fresher. Or you can simply continue looking for the buck you were following previously, if you can even tell the difference.

Every track has a personality and on a buck's trail you should concentrate early on learning what it is. It may be the shape of the hoof, the length of the stride, the way the buck places his feet, something unusual about the footprint or a combination of some or all of these factors. If you learn to identify this buck's track, you will be able to tell when you find it again.

During November in the big woods of the North, deer tend to congregate in pockets. This will often result in sections of woods with lots of deer tracks, which can make following a specific track confusing. If the buck has entered an area that has a lot of deer activity and a multitude of tracks that obscure his, then simply back off and circle that area until you find his track leaving. It's important to recognize the buck's track "signature" so that you can identify the track you find as the one you had been following.

If you make a complete circle and don't find where this buck has left the area, then at least you know where he is. Go to where you lost the track and try to think like a buck. Look at the terrain ahead and think about where this buck would go. If you have been trailing him long enough then you have a good idea of how he moves, the places he likes and the places he does not. You should be able to make a good guess about where he would go. Continue to do this as you watch carefully for both his track and for the deer. If you exit the active area and cut your own tracks from where you circled without finding him, circle again to see if you bumped him out. If not, you obviously didn't choose correctly about his route. Try again. Sooner or later you will find him or his tracks. If it's the buck, shoot him. If it's the track, you are back in business.

Keep at it, and sometime in the future you can expect to have the "shoot him" option on the table.

6: Lack of Confidence

Tracking is about 30 percent physical and 70 percent mental. A hunter in great physical shape can have an advantage, but if he lacks the mindset, he will fail. You must expect to shoot a buck every time you take a track. You must have confidence that it will happen and that you have the ability to make it happen or you will not be giving the 100 percent effort and focus needed for success.

This is a big problem for hunters who are new to tracking and have not experienced success. They don't really believe it can work because they haven't seen it work yet and so they lack confidence.

One of my favorite ways to hunt deer is to rattle antlers. Over the years I have rattled in hundreds of bucks in dozens of locations and I know it will work. But that was not always the case. The first few times I tried it I felt like a damn fool banging those horns against each other. For years I had been taught that a deer hunter is quiet in the woods and making a racket went against every instinct. I was always half-hearted in my attempts and failure followed. Pretty soon I started to think like so many other hunters who believe horn rattling would not work anyplace except maybe Texas. But I kept trying. Not often, but once in a while, just to keep proving to myself that I was right. One time I was bow hunting from a treestand and

Confidence in their hunting techniques plays a huge role in the Benoit Brothers' success. Tom Blais photo.

when I finished my rattling sequence I casually hung the antlers on a tree limb confident nothing would show up. But as I turned back around, I could see a buck not far from the base of my tree, standing with his head up and watching me. He ran off and I said a bad word. I eventually got that buck, but it took a long time and a lot of work. But the lesson stuck. Now when I rattle horns, I expect to see a buck every time. Of course, I don't actually see one every time, but when I do, he rarely surprises me.

It's the same thing with tracking. If you don't believe in what you are doing, you will probably fail. But if you have great confidence in tracking as a way to shoot good bucks, you will work harder, stay focused, and eventually succeed.

Self-help seminars often focus on "believing" in your abilities and they are right about that. You must believe that you are indeed good enough to do this. There is nothing magic about tracking big bucks, and the Benoits are not really any different than you and me except for experience and perhaps confidence. Like any hunter they make mistakes. They spook bucks they fail to see. They still break a stick at the wrong time and they miss a shot every now and then. But they truly believe in what they are doing and have great confidence in their abilities. If they make a mistake, they simply keep going and put it behind them.

Believe that success will happen, visualize that success in your mind, and never lose confidence. Big bucks will follow.

7: Being Too Fussy about Conditions

Many hunters will not track unless the conditions are perfect. They will instead sit in a stand, still-hunt, or not hunt at all on the days when the snow is "bad." That results in a lot of days when they are not tracking bucks because perfect conditions are simply not all that common.

If there is snow on the ground, you can probably track a buck. Consider, too, that if there is snow that will show a track you can follow, there is no other hunting method with as great a chance for big buck success as tracking. And there is no other hunting style that offers the excitement, thrill, and challenge that tracking does, so why would you want to hunt any other way? Sitting on a stand is defined as hours and hours of boredom mixed with a few minutes of excitement. (Kind of like baseball, isn't it?) One hunter I know defines sitting in a stand during a successful deer season as 30 seconds of adrenalin-filled thrills packed into 10 days. Tracking is interactive hunting as opposed to the "passive" hunting style of sitting on a stand. When you are tracking, you have a big whitetail buck in front of you all the time. You are actively taking the hunt to him and an encounter between you and the deer can happen at any moment. If you truly are a tracker and have the confidence that you will succeed, then you are on an adrenalin-filled rush all day long.

Want to tell me again how sitting on a stand is better than that?

Lanny on the trail of a New Hampshire buck.

Bryce M. Towsley photo.

Lanny Benoit in New Hampshire. Bryce M. Towsley photo.

Don't let conditions stop you from tracking. If you have snow, spend your hunting time tracking. For example, one common problem is "crunchy" snow that makes walking noisy. That is snow that was wet when it partially melted on a warm day, before the temperature turned colder and froze the snow. This results in noisy walking conditions and most hunters will not attempt tracking. In 2002, crunchy snow was the norm for most of the season. A lot of hunters wouldn't even think about tracking, but the Benoits had a great season. They all shot outstanding trophy bucks. Lane's had the best rack of any buck in his life.

"Most of the time the buck is going to hear you, no matter what the conditions," Lanny says. "Their hearing is so good that you can't sneak up on them very often anyway. The sound of crunchy snow will not carry as far as you think so the buck will be relatively close to you when he is first aware of the noise. The buck usually doesn't know what is making that sound and he might think it's a moose or another deer. If he doesn't know you are behind him, he will usually wait for confirmation of what you are—either by sight or scent. By waiting before he runs, he is giving you a chance to shoot him. The secret is not to give him a lot of time to think about it. If you pussyfoot around trying to sneak up on him, he will hear you coming for a long time. That gives him too much time to think about it and he will become nervous and run away. But if you keep moving in a fast and steady walk, by the time he hears the noise you will be close. He may instinctively wait without thinking about it too much and you will see him and get a shot. You may not get him the first time you encounter him, or even the second or third, but sooner or later he will hold long enough for you to shoot him. I know it doesn't sound like it will work, but trust me, it will."

If you doubt that last statement, consider that in that noisy 2002 season Lanny shot four bucks, three by tracking in crunchy snow. They were all big and one was exceptional. Even more astonishing is that he had a cameraman with him on every one of the bucks. Every single kill was filmed and there were two sets of boots crunching in the snow!

Lane Benoit in Ontario 2002. Bryce M. Towsley photo.

8: Not Taking the Shot

Probably more trophy bucks than we would care to count are alive today because of hesitation on the hunter's part in taking the shot. This applies to all aspects of deer hunting, but none more than tracking.

Television shows, videos, magazine articles, and books all have us convinced that we have to wait for the perfect broadside shot at a standing buck. But that's about as common when tracking as PETA members who are serious deer hunters.

When you see a trophy buck, take the first available shot. If you wait for a better one, the odds are just as good that you will not get any shot. One thing that separates a great hunter from the rest of the huddled masses is the ability to judge a situation and act decisively and quickly. Most of the truly great hunters I have been in the field with (and that list, of course, includes the Benoits) are very quick to spot game, judge the situation, and get the shot on its way. They don't hesitate, they are confident in what they are doing, and they do it decisively. They are also, to a man, excellent shots. That's not something any of them was born with, but it's a skill gained in practice—lots of shooting and lots of hunting.

Part of what makes the Benoits successful is a willingness to take a shot other than one that is "perfect." They can recognize a killing or disabling shot quickly and do not hesitate to take it when they do. You must take the first killing shot available. If he is quartering away from you, shoot for the off shoulder so that the bullet passes through his chest. If all you can see is the buck's head looking at you, shoot for the white throat patch under his chin. If he is facing away from you, shoot him in the butt.

That last sentence is sure to be controversial, but very often that's the only shot you will get when you are tracking bucks. We Americans don't take that shot be-

Lanny Benoit in Ontario 2002. Bryce M. Towsley photo.

cause we consider it somehow "unethical." I fail to understand why that is, because if you are using a powerful enough gun with proper bullets, it is a very deadly shot. If the critter dies in a fast and humane way, how are you being "unethical?" Yes, it will usually spoil some meat. But how much meat will you have if you don't get the deer? Isn't it better to sacrifice a little meat and have the rest than not get the buck at all? But for some reason most deer hunters have a psychological resistance to taking this shot.

I have fallen into this trap myself and paid a price. Like most American hunters, I have been conditioned to believe a rear-end shot is a poor one and somehow "dishonest" to good sportsmanship. Intellectually, I know better and I recognize that in some places, particularly Africa, it is considered a "good" place to put your bullet. In August of 2001 I was hunting in Natal, South Africa. My Zulu tracker and I found ourselves looking at the south end of a very good nyala that was pointing north. My rifle was chambered for a custom wildcat cartridge that I designed called the 358 Ultra Mag Towsley (UMT). It's a very powerful cartridge that drives a 250-grain bullet to 3100 fps. It is suitable for hunting just about anything that walks except perhaps elephant and it was certainly more than enough gun for the mule-deer-size nyala. But I wasn't thinking about that, I just couldn't get past that mental block about taking a rear-end shot, so I waited. I didn't make a conscious decision not to shoot him there, but rather years of conditioning caused me to never even give it consideration. Finally, the nyala turned a little and showed me some neck. It was an easy shot, except the bullet hit a branch, which deflected it enough to miss. The Professional Hunter, Deon Cillers, later chided me for not taking the first shot presented. "You have plenty of gun to penetrate into the vitals and that is a deadly shot. You should have taken it," he said. I just shook my head and muttered my agreement.

I later took another nyala, a very good bull, but

243 Win.,7mm-08, 30-06 Springfield, 270 Win. and 35 Whelen. The larger "30-06" class cartridges are a better choice for tracking big northern bucks. Bryce M. Towsley photo.

smaller than that first one. My friend Peter Lajoie wound up shooting the bull I missed, and it turned out to be an exceptionally good trophy that placed well into the record books.

The point is that you should always take the first good shot presented and do it without hesitation. You should be using a cartridge that is powerful enough along with a bullet that will penetrate deep enough to reach the vitals of any buck from any angle.

Learn whitetail anatomy and learn to judge how to put a bullet through the heart and/or lungs from any angle. Then don't hesitate to do it. You are going to get a lot more opportunity for odd angle shots on bucks while tracking than you ever will for perfect broadside presentations.

Any buck you can track will be easier to track with a bullet through him, so even if you muff the shot a little you will still get the buck. If you can track him down and shoot at him when he is healthy, it will be even easier to do if he is wounded. That's not to suggest that you should ever take a shot with the intent to wound a deer. Rather, every shot should be intended to be a killing shot. However, it should be taken from any angle with the confidence in knowing that if you hit him you will get that buck.

Just make sure you have a rifle that is powerful enough and that you are using a heavy-for-caliber, deep-penetrating, and high-quality bullet. Smaller deer cartridges may be more than adequate for hunting from stands, but they are not a good choice for tracking deer. Rather, as the Benoits have done, choose cartridges in the 270 Winchester and 30-06 Springfield class as the minimum you should consider for tracking. Also stay away from lightweight, rapidly expanding bullets that are often favored by deer hunters who always shoot for the ribs. They might provide dramatic kills when hunting from a stand where a broadside shot is almost assured, but they do that because they expand and fragment very quickly. This limits penetration and may cause the bullet to not reach the vitals when the buck is big and the shot angle less than perfect. Don't be fooled by the argument that is often made in hunting magazines that a bullet should stay in a deer and expend all its energy. That's a flawed argument, as energy doesn't kill deer, tissue damage does.

Wound channels are relative to energy transfer and the frontal area of the bullet. Consider how it would look if the animal were a homogenous material, like ballistic gelatin. As a bullet first contacts, the wound channel is bullet diameter. Then as it penetrates, the wound diameter will grow relative to the energy transferred and the contact damage caused by the expanding bullet diameter and shape. If the bullet is going to stay in the game and velocity slows as energy levels drop, the wound channel diameter will again begin to taper smaller until it reaches current bullet diameter at the point where the bullet stops. This results in a misshapen, football-shaped wound channel with a large maximum diameter. Fine, if it's in the right place, but if it ends short of vital tissue, problems arise. Consider, too, that bullets that tear apart and fragment will have an even shorter wound channel.

With a premium bullet design and adequate initial energy, the bullet exits with energy remaining. The resulting wound channel has a minimally decreasing profile and will remain near the maximum diameter all the way to the exit. So what if the bullet exits with remaining energy? The important thing is that it created a sufficient wound channel completely through the target. Even though that wound channel diameter may be less at its peak diameter than one created by a bullet that dumps all its energy and fails to exit, the wound channel is much longer and has a better chance of passing through something vital. It probably also has more total area because of its length.

The results may not be as spectacular as a double lung hit with a bullet that tears itself apart, dumps its energy in a short wound channel, and fails to exit, but it is much more predictable, reliable, and consistent. These are far more desirable traits for an ethical hunter than dramatic impact results with a high failure potential.

In that light, you can almost never go wrong by buying the best ammo. I have also read in magazines that using the high-quality bullets designed for deep penetration can be a mistake for deer hunting. That may have been true at one time, but today's hunting bullets have evolved and now perform well over a much wider range of conditions. I have shot a lot of game with most of the premium bullets loaded in factory loads, and I disagree with any statement that they will not expand on deer. Today's best hunting bullets work well over a wide variety of conditions and on a diversity of game, and I will say without reservation that they are never a mistake for deer hunting.

For deer trackers who are hunting only the biggest and toughest deer and who must often take shots from less than perfect angles, bullet performance is extremely important. The clear choice is to pick a good controlled expansion bullet that will retain all or most of its weight and penetrate deep. This bullet will almost always shoot all the way through the buck and create an exit hole. As a result, you should have a good blood trail to follow, and if you put the bullet in the right place, that blood trail will end at a dead buck. But it's important to remember that a bullet is only as good as the cartridge propelling it, so it's crucial to also follow Robert Ruark's advice and "use enough gun."

Don't be afraid to miss. Everybody misses and I am fond of saying that any hunter who claims he has never missed either hasn't hunted much or is a damn liar. I have hunted with some of the best shots in the world and they miss sometimes. Even the Benoits miss sometimes. A lot of that is because they are not afraid to shoot. Their philosophy is "if you don't shoot, you can't get them" and so they shoot a lot. They take the shots many other hunters will not. Sometimes they miss, but usually they don't. The one true thing is that if you don't shoot you will not get that buck.

When I first started hunting nearly 40 years ago my grandfather gave me some advice I have never forgotten. He said, "Even if you think you hit that buck good, if he is still on his feet, or if he is down but has his head up, keep shooting. A few extra bullet holes are nothing compared to losing a wounded buck." I have always remembered that advice and I know it has saved me from anguish and disappointment more than once. When I began hanging around with the Benoits during deer season, I soon noticed they subscribe to the same philosophy. They don't stand around admiring the first shot. If the buck is in sight and not down, they keep shooting until he is, or until the gun is empty.

Finally, there is the question of running shots. I am not sure what has happened to deer hunters, but there has been a profound change in thinking on this subject over the past couple of decades. Our grandfathers thought nothing of shooting at running deer. They were trackers and still-hunters and often that was the only shot they had. They understood that a man who knows how to shoot is deadly in this situation and saw no "ethical" question to debate. Many of today's hunters, however, won't even consider the question on the table for debate. Some of the most venomous and nasty letters I have ever received from readers were in response to a shooting article I did for a major gun magazine on how to hit running game. I was called many names, including an unsafe, slob hunter and others we can't print here and wouldn't if I could.

I suppose the prevailing change in hunting tactics to where most whitetails are ambushed from a stand has played a big role. In this case, often the hunter can wait in hiding for a perfect shot, as the deer is unaware of his intention to make venison out of him. So, too, have over-zealous hunter education instructors who are not looking at the big picture and maybe don't understand the many aspects of hunting all that well anyway. I am sure there are other factors as well, but it's undeniable that somehow we have created a generation of deer hunters who think that any shot at a moving deer is slob hunting. They can believe as they wish, but it's certain these guys don't have much of a future as trackers.

The reality is that if you are tracking deer you are going to have to take occasional running shots if you want to kill big bucks. Learn how to do that, practice a lot and develop an ability to shoot well. Then take the shot with complete confidence because there is nothing unethical about it if you can do it.

9: Hunting the Wrong Location

No matter who the expert presenting it may be, in just about every big-buck, hunting seminar I have attended I think I have heard the same thing from somebody in the audience.

"Sure, you are shooting all those big bucks in the great places you hunt, but let's see you come to where I hunt and shoot one."

If you think about it, this is not only a foolish challenge, but it's also being made by a foolish hunter. The first point is obvious. Chances are that the reason he or anybody else can't kill big bucks where he hunts is because there probably aren't any! Trophy hunting is pointless at that location. The reason the guy is foolish is because he is hunting there and seems to be proud that he is.

Any trophy hunter knows that to shoot a big whitetail buck you must hunt where they live. The best bet is to hunt where lots of them live. If you are hunting where there are very few or no trophy bucks, move! How much more obvious can it be? Yet thousands and thousands of hunters fail to shoot a good buck every year simply because they continue to hunt in lousy places.

You cannot consistently track and shoot trophy bucks on crowded public lands. That's not to say you can't kill big bucks on land that is open to the public; the Benoits only hunt on open public access land and they shoot big bucks all the time. But you can't hunt on crowded public land and expect success. To find trophy bucks you must remove yourself from the huddled masses. First of all, most of the bucks on land with lots of hunting pressure are killed the first year they have legal antlers, so very few ever grow old enough to attain trophy status. Even if you found a track, there is a good chance you will just chase the buck past some pilgrim's stand and he will benefit from all your hard work.

Tracking trophy bucks works best in remote areas. The places that are so large and desolate that many other hunters are intimidated into staying away and where you can find room to avoid those few hunters who do venture there. Also, consider the places with low deer densities. Stand hunters tend to avoid these locations because they don't contain a lot of deer sign. But you only need one buck, if it's the right buck. The lack of hunting pressure and the vast country in which to hide will allow bucks to grow old. These bucks may have learned how to avoid the few stand or still-hunters that show up, but a buck can't hide from a tracker.

The key point is not to keep hunting in the same poor area expecting a different result. If you don't find tracks from big bucks where you are hunting, move until you do. If you have shot a few good bucks from your area and the sign indicates that you have "shot it out" of trophy bucks, move. Give the bucks that are left some time to grow up and plan to come back in a few years. The key to finding big bucks year after year is to keep finding new country. That's one part of Lanny's success. He possesses a rambling spirit and he is constantly exploring new country where other hunters can't or won't go. As a result, he finds lots of big buck tracks.

Don't get hung up on one buck, either. Scout out

as many big bucks as you can. If you are not having any luck with hunting one, try another one. Be flexible and mobile.

10: Not Covering Enough Ground

This common mistake kind of ties into the last point. Most hunters think in terms of a few hundred acres or at best a couple of square miles. Even in big woods, they tend to go back again and again to the same places. You have to get rid of that kind of thinking. Big bucks are too scarce a commodity and in big country they tend to be spread out. Think in terms of hundreds of square miles or more. If you are not finding bucks in one place, move on. Don't ever become a "home body" and get hung up on one or two places.

11: Not Spending Enough Time Hunting

The Benoits hunt for 6 or 8 weeks every fall. It takes time to locate big bucks and to learn their travel patterns. Then there is the weather to deal with. If you don't have snow or the weather is warm enough to shut down deer activity, there is nothing you can do but wait. You keep hunting of course, but in reality it's waiting. You may even shoot a big buck while you wait, but any true tracker is only doing the best he can while he waits for the snow. Sometimes that results in a used deer tag pinned to a big buck, but it's not the same. A tracker wants to track.

Even when conditions are perfect it sometimes takes a while to kill a big buck. Tracking trophy bucks is hard and it takes time. It's not supposed to be easy; if it were then everybody would do it and it wouldn't be worth a damn. Kind of like golf, if you ask me.

To be a serious trophy hunter you need to devote a lot of time. Instead of one week of vacation, take two. Or three, if you can. I can remember Larry saying that he had quit a lot of jobs because they wouldn't give him deer season off. Most people think that's foolish, but most people are not Benoits. There are several differences, but the most noted one is that most people do not shoot the number of huge trophy whitetail bucks that they do. To the Benoit family the most important thing in life is tracking trophy bucks. They make certain they have the time to do that every fall. Sure it extracts a price at times, but nothing in life that's important comes without sacrifice.

Of course, not everybody is going to quit their jobs to deer hunt (although, like the Benoits, I think these people may have their priorities misplaced) and most won't even use all their vacation days. But you can maximize the time you do have to hunt. Make every minute count and hunt dawn to dark. You don't need to go back to camp for lunch and you don't need to "meet up" with your buddies to see how they are doing. Both waste time and cause you to focus on something other than the hunt. If you are worried about a planned rendezvous time, you will not give your full attention to the track and you may leave the woods when you should have kept tracking.

With every minute you spend in deer country, your odds of success go up. Stay in the woods all day, every day and stay focused on hunting.

12: They Don't Practice Shooting Enough

How sad it is to spend hours or days tracking a big buck, to put yourself through that gut-wrenching labor and to finally see the buck, only to miss because you can't shoot.

The bullet is the only physical connection you have with the deer and everything you do comes down to that tiny metal pellet. The shot is the final chapter, and if it fails, all the work, time, money, blood, sweat, and tears will have been wasted. The shot is also one of the most controllable aspects of the hunt. While many factors are left to luck, you can improve your shooting skills enough to sway the odds on the outcome of the hunt in your favor.

Everybody thinks they are a great shot, but most are not. Firing a couple of shots at a target before the season is not enough to make you a good shot. I have met, shot with and watched the best shooters in the world and the one common theme is they all practice—a lot. No one was born with the natural ability to be an outstanding rifle shot. Sure, some people have more natural talent than others, but nobody is great without practice.

The Benoits shoot all the time. They shoot in the

off-season, but to stay sharp, they also shoot during deer hunting season as well. In Maine, where hunting is not allowed on Sunday, they often spend part of the day practicing shooting. It's not uncommon for them to practice shooting during lunch on a slow hunting day. They bring lots of ammo to camp with them and they recognize that it's best utilized when it's expended. I have often seen them go to town for more ammo. They recognize that it's a consumable commodity and that they can always get more.

You will probably never shoot enough to wear out a modern deer rifle, so don't think you are hurting your rifle in any way. Consider too that the cost of ammo is low when compared to the cost of hunting. If you spend thousands of dollars on your hunt, but are too cheap to spend a couple of hundred on practice ammo, then maybe you deserve to miss.

When the opportunity to shoot a big buck presents itself you must act instinctively with your rifle. You don't have time to think or to fumble with the safety. It takes hundreds and perhaps thousands of rounds of shooting to get where the act of shooting is conditioned into your muscle memory as an automatic reflex.

Ninety percent of rifle shooting is mental. The rest, of course, is physical, but to think you can master one without the other is pure folly. Sure, your muscles support the rifle and that's physical. But the key is in holding it in a way that allows you to hit your target. That part is mental. You must use your brain to control the rifle, emotions, thoughts and your body. That's a lot tougher than simply holding an 8-pound rifle.

In teaching the basics of shooting, most instructors will try to make the trigger release and the shot firing a surprise to the shooter. That's a good technique as far as it goes. It sets the stage for the mental aspect of good shooting, but to be a truly good shot you must take it beyond that point. This is particularly true when field shooting at game. The best shooters, particularly the best game shots, know exactly when the trigger will break and the rifle will fire. It takes a lot of focused shooting practice to achieve that skill level.

Every year at the range I can count on hearing some guy who is having a bad day say, "I can't hit paper, but I am deadly on game." That's baloney. Good shooting is good shooting, regardless of what the bullets are hitting. He is only saying that because usually there is no witness to his misses on deer, only his successes. To learn to shoot well you must punch some paper so you can see

Bryce M. Towsley in Ontario 2002.

Bryce M. Towsley photo.

the bullet hole locations and assess what is happening.

While most of us will never achieve the control level of an Olympic champion, it is desirable to reach a point where you are in control of the rifle and the shot. You will know you are approaching this point when you start to "call" the shots. If you make a poor shot, you will know instantly where the bullet went and why without looking. A check of the target should confirm what your brain saw and the bullet will likely have struck where you called that it would.

You can't will yourself to this point and you have to arrive at your own pace. Practice the technique that has the gun firing as a surprise enough and one day you will realize that it's not a surprise any more, that you know exactly when the rifle will fire. You can't force it, so don't try. Just keep practicing until it happens on its own. You will find that your shooting has improved through this and by then you should be shooting very well.

It is only after you have arrived at this point of rifle/trigger control when shooting from any position that you will truly become a good game shot.

Then you can learn to hit running deer. The ethical questions of shooting at unwounded, but running game have recently been the subject of debate in the hunting world. But with all our modern day hand wringing and apologetic guilt aside, we must admit that the reality is what generations of hunters before us knew and accepted: That an accomplished rifleman who knows what he is doing can take many running shots with good confidence and a clear conscience. Many of the big bucks the Benoits have taken have been running. It's a simple fact of life that shooting running deer is part of tracking. In that light, the most sensible approach would be to learn and practice for the shot that may make the difference between the buck of a lifetime and bitter disappointment.

Most aspects of rifle shooting require a methodical, reasoned, thinking approach. Shooting well with a rifle is a fixed mechanical process that requires the shooter to think about what he is doing and every step must be executed in a precise manner. Try that on running game and you'll be so frustrated that you'll be feeling like a trophy hunter at an animal rights convention.

Shooting well at running game requires a more esoteric approach and the use of a different part of your brain. I remember well many years ago when a shotgun shooting coach was becoming visibly agitated with my insistence on using "rifle shooting" techniques for sporting clays. I was "aiming" the shotgun rather than pointing it and I was trying to think the shot through, just as I did when shooting a rifle. As a result, I kept missing. I'll never forget how he snarled at me, "You have the greatest computer on earth sitting on your shoulders, but you won't let it work!"

Once I understood that shotgun shooting required that I allow a different part of my brain to function, I started breaking targets. That same coach happened to be watching me shoot trap at the Wolfe Creek Olympic shooting center near Atlanta many years later. I was having a good day and afterward he stopped me to offer congratulations.

"You were one of my most frustrating students," he said. "Those damn rifles just about ruined you. It was a trial for both of us, but I can see you finally learned how to shoot at moving targets."

Sure it was shotgun shooting, but shooting at running game with a rifle requires a similar technique. You must learn to let your "computer" work its magic. When you put your hand on a hot stove, you don't stop and think, "this is hot, and I should take my hand off." Instead you yank your hand away without thinking about it. It's that part of your brain making you take your hand off the stove that you need to use when shooting at running deer. The difficulty is that for all your rifle shooting life you have used the more logical part of your brain, that part that might say, "this is hot, I should remove my hand," if you had not already reacted. Making the transition is not easy, but it can be learned.

It's like in martial arts; if you must think about your next move, it's already too late to make it. The move must be automatic and controlled by the same subconscious part of your mind that moves your hand off the stove. It doesn't matter if it's martial arts or shooting at moving targets, it doesn't just happen, and it takes hours and hours of practice. Practice builds muscle memory and conditions your mind and body to what the move should be. Rather than logically thinking about each step, you must develop the ability to let your mind go into a "Zen"-like state so that the unconscious part, again, the part that moves your hand from the stove, is doing the shooting.

You must, of course, still be aware of the sight position, trigger control, and all the thousand other things that make for good shooting, but turn off the thinking part of your mind and let that all run on automatic pilot.

You should have done enough shooting by now that the trigger control and sight picture are automatic and you don't need to think about them. If you have done that much shooting, then you have built muscle memory through repeating the process over and over and your body knows what to do. Shooting well requires lots of burned powder. You must practice until you are able to fire your rifle as an extension of your body. Only then is it wise to practice on moving targets. Once you start, it will take a lot more burned powder before you can hit them well. I have seen men like Lanny Benoit and others who are good enough to shoot clay pigeons out of the air with a rifle. But they didn't get there overnight; it took practice and lots of it.

Lanny Benoit shooting at an aerial can of soda. Shane Benoit tossing. Bryce M. Towsley photo.

I used to spend a lot of my winters hunting coyotes with hound dogs. One cold, clear morning I was sitting on a powerline that was a favorite escape route, waiting for the dogs to strike, when a big coyote just happened to come wandering by and sat down to look at me. At 250 yards a coyote that is sitting and facing you is not a very big target and I missed. By the time I racked another shell into my Model 700 243, he had the afterburners kicked in and was heading for the safety of the woods. The next shot was behind him. I worked the bolt again and without thinking I allowed my subconscious mind to take over. The third shot went off without me realizing that I pulled the trigger and the 85-grain Sierra took out both his lungs while he was just 5 feet short of his escape.

I can't tell you how fast he was running, the exact angle or distance or how far I led him, but I could have told you when the trigger sear broke that he was dead. I knew the shot was good before the bullet left the barrel. It's that wonderful computer perched on my neck being allowed to work its magic.

When I made my first western hunt in Montana many years ago I didn't know a thing about how it all worked. One bitter cold morning there was a big mule deer buck running up the far side of a wide canyon. It was a very long shot, further than I had ever attempted to shoot at game at that time and at my first shot he kicked his back feet up like a mule.

"You got him, stop shooting," said the guide. But I never believed in stopping until they were down. Besides, I saw the bullet strike the snow behind him and I knew it was too far back. I shot twice more and the 7mm Remington Magnum was empty. I was digging in my pockets for more ammo when the guide, who was still looking though the spotting scope, commented, "Nice shooting, he's down."

It turns out that the first shot went through the spot on his rear leg between the tendon and bone that you would cut to put the gambrel in to hang a deer. It caused no real damage, but the sting made him kick. However, the next two bullets hit his lungs.

Somebody asked me where I was holding for those shots, and before I could tell them, I had to remember back to the mental picture of where the crosshairs were when the gun went off. They asked how I knew to hold there and I couldn't answer, except that in thinking back I realized after seeing the first shot hit the snow my mind made the necessary adjustments for the next two shots.

The most commonly suggested way to practice shooting at moving targets is to put a piece of plywood in the center of an old tire and have somebody roll it down a hill for you. It helps if the terrain is a little rough so that the tire bounces unpredictably as it rolls. When the plywood gets shot up you can staple paper over it so you can see your bullet holes (or lack of them!)

Make sure you have a safe place to do this with a good backstop and that the tire is well away from your buddy who is rolling it before you start shooting. We use a flag that the tire must pass before we can shoot. Actually, the best way is to have several tires so that you can shoot at more than one before collecting them to bring back to the top of the hill. A 4-wheeler is pretty handy for that chore.

In a moderate wind, releasing balloons and shooting at them as they skid along the ground is good practice, just make sure you clean up after.

Lanny likes to practice by shooting apples or soda cans out of the air. I have seen him do it and he will go a long time between misses. During a practice session on a slow day of hunting, he shot up all my sodas without a miss. It was something to see, but I didn't have anything to drink for the rest of the afternoon.

As you become better, try shooting at clay pigeons either thrown from a hand trap or with a small automatic trap. Start with the target going away from you, and then as you get better have somebody throw them from various angles. (Again, only where there is a solid, safe backdrop. Rifle bullets can be dangerous for a very long distance.)

It's not easy and you won't break them all or even a majority of them. But if you reach a level of proficiency where you are breaking almost as many as you are missing of these little targets, a buck's chest is going to look pretty big in your sights.

There are three basic techniques for shooting at running game. Swing through, sustained lead, and point shooting. Although you will use the point shooting method most often when tracking whitetail bucks, it's a good idea to learn and practice them all.

Swing Through

With this method the hunter starts with the rifle behind the running target. By swinging the gun faster than the game is moving, the sights will pass by the target and when the forward lead is correct the shooter fires the rifle. The timing requires anticipating when the lead will be correct and shooting a little before that to allow for shooter lag time as well as the lock time for the rifle.

The rifle is kept moving the entire time, until well after the shot and follow through. If you stop moving the rifle when the sight picture looks right, you will shoot behind the target. You must keep the gun moving and fire without hesitation when the sights are at the correct amount of lead. Hesitation in pulling the trigger will usually cause you to shoot in front of the target, as the gun will swing past the correct lead before firing. Stopping the rifle will cause you to shoot behind the target.

I find this to be the most difficult method and I rarely use it in the field. The few times I have were when my sub-conscience realized that there wasn't time for a sustained lead shot and just took over. Any computer, even your brain, is only as good as the data fed into it, so practice this method to build memory so when the time comes you do need to use it, you can maybe make it work.

Sustained Lead

The gun is moved with the target at the same perceived speed. The proper lead is attained and retained while the rifle is kept moving through the shot and follow through.

This is my preferred method for long range shooting at moving targets. I think it is easier to maintain a constant lead than to shoot during the very short instant when the lead is correct when using the swing through or point shooting style of shooting. It's how I hit that coyote, and even though I didn't know what it was called at the time, I also used it on my first mule deer.

Point Shooting

The best method for shooting running deer in the woods where the distance is usually short is called point shooting. To do this you shoot with a stationary rifle at a spot ahead of the target where you think the animal will be when the bullet arrives. Generally this is done by throwing the rifle to your shoulder as you focus your vision on the spot and shoot as soon as the rifle hits the right place and the sights look correct. You are predicting where the target will be at a point in the future that will coincide with the bullet's arrival and are aiming at that spot. For this to work correctly, the hunter must fire the instant the sights look right. Any hesitation at all will cause you to shoot behind the animal.

Where to aim is dependent on a lot of factors. But with a modern high velocity rifle like a 30-06 and when the shots are relatively close—50 yards or less—usually the aiming point is just ahead of where the bullet will hit the deer. So aim at the deer's shoulder and you can expect to hit the shoulder or the ribs just behind the shoulder. Many hunters make the mistake of adding too much lead and they shoot in front of the buck. Of course, as the distance to the deer grows longer, so too should the lead until at some point it will become necessary to extend the lead to the point where the sights are no longer on the buck. I can't tell you how much without knowing exactly how far the deer is from you, how fast he is running, what the angle is and the velocity of the bullet. Even then I would need to feed all that information into my computer to get the exact lead. But, if you shoot that rifle a lot at practice targets and then let your own computer do the work, the one in your head will automatically set the correct lead. All you have to do is trust it.

Another tip that Shane adds is that when a buck is bounding, there is a slight moment when his front feet hit the ground and he is "bunching up" to prepare for the next leap, that his shoulder is almost stationary. If you time the shot for that moment, it's a lot easier to hit the deer. It's the same concept that many trick shooters use to hit an object that is thrown into the air. The object will rise until gravity overcomes the energy that is propelling it and then it will begin to drop to the ground. When the object makes the transition from moving up to dropping down there is a short, split second when it is stationary. If you time your shot for that moment, it's a lot easier to hit the target. The same with a bounding buck. If you time the shot for when his front feet hit the ground, you have a better chance of hitting where you want.

Point shooting works well when shooting at close targets, particularly in thick brush. It helps a great deal to have a rifle that fits you correctly and hits your shoulder with the sights lined up perfectly with your eye. Without a perfect fit, your eye needs to search for the sights. Even if it's only momentary, it will take enough time to likely cause a miss. Despite some "conventional" wisdom, most serious riflemen recognize that a low power scope is far superior to iron sights of any kind for this situation. Even the Benoits are starting to believe that, as Lanny and Shane are now using scopes on their deer rifles.

Gramp's Advice

A variation on this method is how my grandfather first taught me to hit running deer. It is the same style usually employed by the Benoits.

"It's thick here where we hunt, with lots of trees," Gramp said. "If you try to swing your rifle with the deer, you will hit a tree almost every time. To hit a running buck in this country, pick an opening in the woods a little bit ahead of him and point your gun at where you think he will be as he comes through. Watch the sights, but keep looking for the buck with the corner of your eye. When he enters your sight picture, pull the trigger. If you miss, don't chase him with your rifle, shooting trees and wasting all your bullets, get on the next opening, hold the rifle still and do it all again.

"You will kill a lot more running bucks this way when the brush is thick and the deer is close to you. Focus on the sights, you still have to aim, but let your brain figure the lead. Don't try to think about it too much, your eyes and head know how to make it work."

Safety

There is an inherent danger in shooting at running game in that the shooter tends to focus on the animal and block out the rest of his surroundings. When the target is moving and the rifle is moving with it, this can be very dangerous, particularly when you are double-teaming on the track with a buddy.

It is far too easy to shoot your hunting partner as you swing the gun, failing to notice that he is standing in the path. This is a common scenario for hunting accidents. The hunter is following a fleeing deer and just as he pulls the trigger his hunting partner's head appears in the scope. Both are focusing on the same deer and never even notice until it's too late.

It's also easy to block out the background behind the fleeing target and to swing the gun into an unsafe direction. With today's increasing urbanization of hunting areas, even areas in which you may be tracking a buck, this is even more critical. Even if no damage is done and no one gets hurt, the sport of hunting has another black eye.

Always remain fully aware of what you are doing, where everybody else is and what lies in the direction you are moving the rifle muzzle. Never let your focus on the shot become so complete that you fail to realize where the muzzle of your rifle is pointing at all times. So what if it means that the animal gets away from you? There is no deer worth the risk of shooting somebody. Just get back on the track and you'll get another chance.

The power of destruction from a modern rifle bullet is catastrophic, particularly at close range. Once that bullet leaves the barrel you can never take it back. Make sure it doesn't become a nightmare. Never let the moment allow you to forget safety; pay attention at all times.

Learning to Use A Scope

Like the Benoits, a lot of hunters are starting to realize that aging eyes and peep sights are not the best mix. The obvious solution is to use a scope. But if you are not experienced with one, without practice you will be frustrated trying to shoot at running deer.

In 1968 I spent my summer vacation bailing hay on a local farm. I saved every penny I was paid for that sticky labor, and on Halloween night Gramp took me to the general store in town to pick up my new Remington Model 788 243 Winchester. As he helped me get it ready for hunting season, he advised me on how I could learn to hit running deer with my new rifle.

"Now don't think you can just go out and be able to hit the first running buck you shoot at, nobody is born a good shot. You need to practice with your rifle. There are some differences there too; the bullet from your new 243 is going twice as fast as my old 45-70. When the buck is close, it doesn't make much difference, but it does make some. You need to learn that. Also, you have that fancy new scope on your rifle while I use a peep sight. The way you shoot the deer is pretty much the same, but you need to train your eyes to use that scope.

"Take your empty rifle out in the woods with you when you are walking around (today we call it "scouting"). Follow flushing partridge (grouse), rabbits, deer, squirrels, birds, and whatever else you can find. Right now you are swinging the rifle with them. You are not shooting at them, only trying to learn how to use the scope. Keep practicing until you can follow a flushing partridge or a running rabbit without losing sight of him in your scope.

"Make damn sure that gun is empty, then start to practice shooting at them by dry firing. Pick an opening ahead of them, just like I told you. Dry fire the gun, it won't hurt your rifle any. After a while it will begin to come together in your head and your brain will know when to pull the trigger.

"Then get somebody to roll an old tire with plywood in the center down a hill and try to hit the middle of the plywood. Do it in the woods if you can where you have some trees to get in your way, and you'll see what I am talking about. It's not the same as a buck charging through the brush, but it's the best we can do and any practice helps you to get better.

"Remember, deer season is short and those bucks are

smart, you may only get a chance at a buck once in a while, try not to screw it up by not bothering to practice. Even still, you are going to miss some bucks before you figure it all out and even a few more after you do. Don't let it get you down too much; instead use the pain of missing to make you want to get better. Missing a few good bucks will remind you to keep trying and keep practicing."

13: Buck Fever

I don't care who you are or how long you have hunted, if the sight of a big buck that you want to shoot doesn't excite you, then you need to quit hunting. That kind of excitement can cause you to miss, or not even shoot. It's called buck fever and most everybody has experienced it sometime in his life.

I remember years ago, back when he was still in junior high school, my little brother Scott came home from deer hunting one day, near tears and looking for me. It turns out he shot at a buck up in the woods we knew locally as "Sherwin's." I guess "shot at" is an understatement; he emptied the old Marlin lever action 38-55. A buddy who was hunting close by said it sounded like a Gatling gun fighting off an Indian attack.

"He was huge!" Scott exclaimed. "I couldn't have missed him! He was right on top of me, just standing there looking around and acting all confused."

Daylight found us standing by a pile of empty brass. We looked for hours, following clear tracks in the snow, but there was no evidence he put a bullet anywhere near the deer.

"Where were you aiming?" I asked.

"I don't know."

"You don't remember?"

"I remember fine, I just don't know."

"Did you even look at the sights?"

"I don't think so."

"What were you doing while you were shooting?"

"Mostly shaking."

It was as classic a case of buck fever as I have witnessed, and trust me, I have seen a few.

It can happen to the best of us. You work day after day to shoot a deer. It's something you want more than anything else in life and it seems like it's never going to happen. Nothing you can do will force it to happen. You can't buy a deer and sometimes hard work isn't enough to earn one. It's frustrating because you simply don't know what else you can do. You keep working at it day after day while the hollow pain in the pit of your stomach keeps snickering to your brain that you will never shoot another deer. Then without warning he's there in front of you and it's time.

Suddenly your arms won't stop shaking, your knees won't support your weight and it's getting really hard to breathe. You planned for the moment, worked it all out in your mind a thousand times, but now your brain isn't responding. You can't think, you can't breathe, your peripheral vision has deserted you, and nothing is working right. Everything on your gun has moved and it's all in the wrong place and it looks like he is going to get away.

Think it can't ever happen to you? Don't bet on it.

So how do you beat "Buck Fever"?

That's a question that hunters have been wrestling with since they were chucking stone-headed spears. The very best thing I know is to do a lot of hunting. Experience seems to help more than anything else. Beyond that, there are a few things you can do to prepare.

Be ready, know your equipment, and have confidence in your ability. An awful lot of bucks are still alive because the hunter started second guessing himself about the shot. Even more owe their lives to hunters who couldn't find the safety. Know your gun and believe in your ability and that knowledge. You get there by shooting a lot before the season, practicing for the one shot that will count.

When I first see a deer I want to shoot, I usually start to shake and my respiration rate shoots though the roof, but I have taught myself to mentally calm down enough to make the shot. When it's time to shoot, regardless if it is 10 seconds after I first see the deer or 10 minutes, I can usually get my mind and body into a "zone" where I calm down, bring my heart rate and breathing to a manageable level, and mentally concentrate on shooting. I forget how much I want the deer or how big his antlers are, I just concentrate on the shot. After the shooting is over I might fall apart again, but I can usually hold it off long enough.

Being around a lot of deer helps, but not a lot. There is a big difference between a deer you want to shoot and those you are simply looking at. Hanging around deer you truly want to shoot is the key.

One more thing that I think helped me a lot was competitive shooting. There were times when I wanted to win a match as badly as I ever wanted any buck. Inevitably, those were the times when I lost.

Lanny, Lane, and Shane were all competitive shooters and they all agreed that learning to deal with the pressure of competition has helped in controlling buck fever.

You need to learn how to control your emotions, to focus only on shooting, to concentrate only on the shot at hand, and not to worry about anything else. You can't do this with casual practice, it has to count for a lot and be something you want so badly it hurts. If you can't do it with deer, do it in some form of competition that matters—even if it's a bet with your buddy that you can't afford to lose.

Make sure there are lots of people watching, as the pressure of doing it in front of a lot of people will often manifest itself in symptoms that mimic buck fever almost exactly. Nobody wants to look bad in front of other people and it's for that very reason that we often do. The pressure of performing in front of people you want to impress will teach you a lot about handling buck fever. Or it will humiliate you until you stay locked in your room, curled in the fetal position and sucking your thumb.

Finally, visualizing the shot in your mind over and over before you ever see the deer will help. Athletes use this technique to prepare, so can hunters. In your mind, see yourself shooting a buck. Make him a big one, so if the real buck that shows up is huge you are ready for that too. Walk through it in your mind's eye step by step and do it again and again. By the time it really happens, you will be "experienced" enough to do it right.

One more thing about buck fever. It signifies the importance we place on hunting and indicates what it means not only to our hearts, but also to our souls. If we didn't care, if it was easy, it wouldn't be worth much. Buck fever is a reminder of that.

Like Shane said, "I hope it never stops. The day I don't start breathing fast at the sight of a big buck, I'll quit hunting."

14: Being Out of Shape

Tracking big bucks through the snow day after day is hard. Too many hunters underestimate just how hard and they burn out and fail. You may think you are in great shape, but you will probably learn you are not when you start tracking. It not only requires that you be in good physical shape, but that you have developed a lot of stamina and endurance. Each day can be tough, but to do it again the next day and the next and so on is often more than most hunters, even hunters in good shape, can take.

Tracking trophy whitetail bucks takes strong physical conditioning as well as mental conditioning. It also takes the ability to ignore pain and fatigue and to keep going. As one of my hunting pals, Tony Kinton, called it on a tough caribou hunt, "the willingness and drive to keep on keeping on."

Walking in the woods with deep snow requires a different set of muscles than simply walking on a paved road. Sure, you can build your fitness by walking and jogging, but you should also spend time in the woods. Hike hard through the woods and stay off the groomed trails. Force yourself to travel in rough country so that you condition the right muscles.

Conditioning helps to diminish the possibility of a season-ending injury such as a pulled muscle or twisted joint. Don't think that you can sit at a desk all year and then hunt hard. Even if you work out at the gym you need to condition for the woods.

The Benoits are not in particularly good shape in the common use of that term. They probably won't enter and certainly won't win any road races, but they are well conditioned for walking in the woods. Because they have a lot of time to hunt, they also start out slow and build their conditioning as the season progresses. If you don't have the luxury of several weeks of hunting, you need to work on conditioning before the hunting season.

15: Not Hunting Because of the Weather

The one undeniable truth about late autumn in the North Country is that it's a time of change. Among the most unpredictable of these changes will be the weather. Autumn is the time of transition and is always a volatile period, particularly late fall when most of the deer hunting is going on. You can be certain that during any deer season, sooner or later you will need to deal with some nasty weather. Many hunters will use that as an excuse to stay in camp and complain. In that scenario there are two things for certain. The first is that no matter how much you bitch about the weather, you will never shoot a trophy buck sitting at the camp table with a cup of coffee in your hand. Second—the deer are still in the woods.

Nobody likes to be out in bad weather, but you shouldn't let that keep you from hunting. If you dress correctly, you can remain relatively comfortable in any weather and the only possible chance you have of shooting a trophy buck that day is if you go hunting.

Actually, some of the best days to hunt are when it's stormy. When the rut is on and unless it's approaching hurricane status, the bucks are usually still on the move and in fact may actually increase their activity levels. The falling rain or snow will help to hide your movements and muffle your noise, particularly if there is a little wind too.

Very severe weather, a hard rain or snow and/or high winds, will usually cause the deer activity to drop considerably. But they are still out there; it's where they live and they have no place else to go. Look for the deer in sheltered areas and consider that they will almost always be bedded down. Use the weather to cover your approach, move slow, and always keep your eyes moving.

Once you have him gutted you can head to the comfort of the camp table in good conscience and with nothing to complain about.

16: Moving Their Hands Too Much

This is one of Shane's pet peeves.

When you are tracking a buck you should keep your movements smooth, fluid, and deliberate. Any fast movement will attract attention from the deer much sooner than a slow fluid movement. Most hunters remember that with their body and head movements, but forget when they move their hands. We are used to rapid movement with our hands and do it in the woods unconsciously. This alerts the deer. Remember to keep your hand movements to a minimum and to keep them slow.

17: Wrong Type of Boots and Clothes

Many hunters overdress for tracking. They soon get overheated, sweaty, and dehydrated. Then they quit. Dress for walking because that's what tracking is, lots of walking. If you think you are dressed about right, chances are you have on too many clothes. If you think you will freeze to death when you step out of the truck, you are probably just right.

Also, many hunters have the wrong boots. Boots that are too heavy will tire you out fast when you are walking a lot. They are also too warm and hard to walk quietly in through the woods because they are stiff, bulky, and heavy. The Benoits use uninsulated rubber boots that in my mind are better for summertime gardening than deer hunting in the snow, but it's hard to argue with their success. Most hunters will probably do better with a compromise of a little insulation, but still a thin, lightweight rubber boot.

One important aspect of the boot is the sole. It must provide good traction for walking on snow covered, rough country. Without that you will be fighting the footing all day and getting tired and distracted. You may also fall and become injured. The sole still must be thin enough to allow you to "feel" where you are stepping. When the buck is close and you are in the "death creep," you want to be able to feel if you are stepping on a stick before you do. That allows you to withdraw your foot and to step elsewhere.

18: Making Too Much Noise

When I was grilling the Benoits about common mistakes, this was Shane's "dig" at me. My feet get cold easily. I frostbit them years ago and they have been cold ever since. When shooting photos for this book,

Lanny Benoit speaking at a seminar. Bryce M. Towsley photo.

we were not moving as fast as we normally would be when tracking and my feet got cold in my thin rubber boots. So I switched to felt-lined packs.

It was fine until we were tracking a buck for real and I had the cameras in my backpack and my rifle in my hands. I don't know how many dirty looks I got that day for making noise, but it's when I developed my deer-tracking motto: "Leave no stick unbroken."

I continued that theme a few days later with Lane to the point where he was looking at me in disgust more than he was watching the track. (To tell the truth, by the end of the day I might have been messing with him a little and breaking branches on purpose. A man's got to have a little fun.)

But, they have a point. Many hunters fail to realize just how quiet you must be in the final approach. If the buck is bedded, you cannot break any sticks or make any noise in the last 100 yards or so or you probably will not see him. Also, when tracking, you can never be certain when the "final approach" actually is because you can come upon the buck at any time, so you must be as quiet as possible all the time.

Learn to move quietly. It's an acquired skill and it takes practice, but anybody can do it—even me.

19: Scouting Incorrectly

One of the great things about tracking bucks is that you can actually take a track literally within minutes of finding it for the first time and have a good chance at killing the buck. It is one of the few methods of hunting trophy whitetails that can work without pre-scouting the hunting area.

However, tracking, like most types of deer hunting, is most effective when you scout first. The key to shooting big bucks the Benoit way is in locating a lot of big whitetail bucks, learning the land, and knowing what the bucks are doing and where they are traveling. Scouting is how you learn these things.

With any deer hunting it's important to scout first and hunt second. The Benoits do their scouting while they hunt, but make no mistake, they do scout. Certainly if they find a huge buck track right out of the gate the first morning of hunting they will take the trail and maybe kill the deer. They recognize that sometimes you have to accept

Shane Benoit smells snow from the edge of a scrape to see how "fresh" it is. Bryce M. Towsley photo.

Four-wheeling is important to getting into back country where big bucks live. Bryce M. Towsley photo.

what is given you and none of the Benoits would be foolish enough to turn down a "gimme" on a huge buck, even if it's early in the hunt. But that would not be their first choice.

Their preferred way for the hunt to progress is to spend the first several days or even a week learning about the bucks in their hunting area. Once they have a clear picture of how many bucks are around, how big the bucks are, and where they like to travel, they decide on hunting strategy. What is amazing is that once they have arrived at this point and decide to "get serious" about shooting a buck, the game pole fills up incredibly fast. The success looks easy on the surface, but it is predicated on the days and days of scouting they do first.

Most hunters are in so big a hurry to "get hunting" that they shortchange the scouting process. They think they are wasting valuable hunting time by scouting, but it's a false economy. That thinking will actually have hunters using time inefficiently and burning up the hunting season accomplishing nothing. They slap up a stand the first place they find that looks good, or they take the first good track they find no matter where it's headed. This wastes time and effort. It is far better to hunt with a plan and to make sure that plan includes some intelligent scouting. It's better to take time early in your hunt to learn about the bucks in your area. The intelligent hunter will sacrifice some hunting time to map out what he is dealing with and then plan a strategy to hunt the smart way. You will always kill more trophy bucks with your brains than you can with your legs.

The Benoits do all their scouting after they arrive in deer camp for the hunt. They might start where they found big bucks in the past year's hunting season to see if they are still around. After they check out all the good bucks they didn't get last year, they will then branch out to find new country and fresh buck sign.

"Casper" in the lead. Bryce M. Towsley photo.

In the Benoit way of thinking, the scouting process is the fun part; exploring new places and locating big buck sign is all part of the adventure, and as Lanny says, "The goal is to have an adventure each time we go out the door." The kill is the climax, the end of the hunt, and with it the adventure is over for another year. They are never in a hurry for that to happen.

Another mistake most hunters make is they don't have the proper skills or equipment to locate big bucks in wilderness areas. You need a truck that you are not afraid to trash a little and a willingness to go where "no man has gone before."

Big bucks get road wise very quickly. They recognize that the increased truck traffic that comes to the back roads when deer season opens signifies something dangerous. It's not long before they start to avoid the roads. This can keep them from crossing the roads, even at night, and pretty soon you stop finding tracks.

When scouting big bucks in large, wilderness country you have to cover a lot of ground. You must get into places where the big bucks are located or to where they have "relocated" if hunting and vehicle pressure have pushed them back from the roads. Those places are for the most part where other hunters will not go and getting there can be hard on a vehicle. The best approach for a serious trophy hunter is to have a vehicle that is primarily dedicated to hunting. Set it up for "four-wheeling" use and equip it with tire chains, a good jack, towing straps, a come-a-long, and even a winch. Also make sure it's a vehicle you don't mind crashing through brush, fording a deep river, or getting stuck in the mud. Your wife's new $40,000.00 SUV might not be the best choice.

Perhaps the best-known Benoit vehicle is Lanny's white Chevy Suburban he calls "Casper, the friendly Suburban." Lanny likes to name all his vehicles and this one is called Casper because it's white and because it looks pretty damn friendly after a twenty-mile hike. Made famous in the first Benoit video, this rig is in a lot of ways the "ultimate scouting machine."

Lanny is a motor-head who loves the "four-wheeling"

as much as any part of deer hunting. He likes nothing better than to take Casper into new country holding big bucks that have been undisturbed by other deer hunters. Sure he gets stuck a lot, but that's part of it too, and is actually a way to gauge your scouting efforts. If you are not getting stuck often, then you are not trying to go to places the other hunters will not enter. If you take the cautious approach and stick to the roads and trails you know you can get through, then you are just like the rest of the "Orange Hoard" out deer hunting and you will have trouble finding big buck tracks.

Just remember that if you do get stuck, you are on your own and can't count on any help in getting out. Make sure you are prepared to extract your own vehicle because AAA doesn't make calls to that part of the world.

Burn a little shoe leather (or in this case "boot rubber") scouting as well. Sometimes you need to go to places where you can't drive and where others are not willing to hike. Again, you will need to cover lots of country so plan on walking, not hunting. Of course you should have your rifle as there is always a possibility of a random buck sighting, but if you are sneaking along like you are hunting, you can't cover enough ground fast enough. With the low deer densities of most good tracking areas, you are wasting time thinking about still-hunting. Cover the ground, find the track and follow the deer. That's how you kill big bucks in this country, not still-hunting aimlessly through the woods.

Don't overlook inaccessible places that might hold mature bucks like big swamps, high mountaintops, closed roads, and other places that are hard to get to. If a deer can walk there, so can you and these are the kinds of places where a buck can grow old.

It's your job to help him with his retirement plan.

20: Failing to Learn from Their Mistakes

I once read that one definition of insanity is repeating the same action over and over but expecting a different result.

Deer hunters who make the same mistake over and over, but fail to learn from it, are doomed to failure, and quite possibly insanity.

"Time and again I have had hunters tell me the same story," Shane said. "They say, 'I tracked that buck all day and jumped him ten times, but I never saw him well enough to shoot.' That's because they were not learning from their mistakes. The hunter should have realized the first time he jumped the buck without seeing him that he made a mistake. Most likely he had his head down looking at the track or was moving too fast and not looking enough. He failed to see the buck before the buck saw him. He should have learned from that, but judging from the fact that he did it nine more times that day, he obviously did not."

You should be constantly analyzing what is happening and what mistakes you are making. You need to learn from them, find a solution, and make a correction. Only then will you stop making those mistakes and shoot the buck. Always be thinking; always act on what that thinking is telling you. We all make mistakes, but only the successful hunters learn from them.

CHAPTER SIX

Frequently Asked Questions

The Benoit Brothers do several deer hunting seminars every year throughout the Northeast. Those I have attended have been standing-room-only as more and more deer hunters are trying to learn the secrets to their success. What they discover along the way is that these are dynamic, entertaining, and funny guys. Shane acts as a low-key coordinator and does a lot of the product segments, explaining about the clothing, guns, and boots. Lane took to the stage like he took to everything else, full bore and larger than life. With his wild hair, bushy beard, and a bear claw necklace, he cut an imposing figure on stage as he brought his memory for detail and story-telling ability along for what was always a good ride. And finally, Lanny takes over with his low-key, self-deprecating sense of humor. Like all good speakers he never fails to leave them laughing and wanting more.

A large part of each of these seminars is usually made up of a question-and-answer session with all three brothers. While each session usually brings new and thought-provoking questions, as any seminar speaker can tell you, the same questions also keep surfacing time and again. I asked the Benoit Brothers to help me compile a list of the most frequently asked seminar questions and the answers.

How do you tell a buck track from a doe track?

Other than "Where exactly do you hunt?" this is probably the most commonly asked question and one of the most complicated to answer.

In spite of all that's been written about this topic or passed on as conventional deer hunting wisdom, it is very difficult for most hunters to look at average-size tracks and know if a buck or a doe made them. There are lots of subtle things that will show the truth eventually if you follow the track long enough and know what to look for. But to simply look at a single track or even a set of tracks and say for sure "That's a buck," without any other input, is tough for an inexperienced tracker.

But the Benoits are able to identify tracks quickly and almost flawlessly. When pushed to explain how, they always first say, "Years of experience and looking at thousands of deer tracks." When pushed harder on the topic, however, they are able to articulate a few clues.

Even young bucks are built differently than does. They are thicker through the chest and as a result, their track will be wider-spaced from side to side. If you drew an imaginary straight line up the center of the track, a doe's footprints will be close to that line, while a buck's will be spaced away from the center. Bucks usually have more rounded feet that are wider; a doe tends to have pointed, narrow feet. Also, a buck's track usually toes out slightly, even that of a young buck. Of course, if you follow the track you will see other signs that can help in identification. How the track is laid out can tell a tale. Does tend to meander and "putter" around while a buck's track, especially that of an older buck, is usually more purposeful and directional. Scrapes, rubs, and other "buck" sign such as antler marks in the snow are positive identification of what kind of deer made the tracks. But smaller indicators such as the distribution of urine stains can also provide clues. A doe will usually urinate in one spot in the center of the track, between or slightly behind the back feet. This results in a small area of snow that is stained, usually with a single hole melted deep into the snow. A buck will more likely spray and dribble when he urinates. The stain will be ahead of the back feet and cover a larger area. Also, the buck will often spray as he walks along, making "dribble" marks in the snow for several feet.

There is one circumstance, however, when a hunter can be almost certain a track was made by a buck, even at first glance. Size does matter. Big tracks are almost

A sign indicating the direction to head for the next Benoit Brothers deer hunting seminar. Benoit Brothers photo.

Lane Benoit speaking at a seminar.

Bryce M. Towsley photo.

Note the long stride and the staggered spacing of these tracks.
This is a good buck. Bryce M. Towsley photo.

This buck track has a long stride, but is rather narrow in the spacing. This might indicate a young buck. Bryce M. Towsley photo.

always made by a buck.

If your goal is to track and shoot a trophy buck, then the only track you really need to positively identify is that of a big buck. A yearling or a 2½-year-old buck may have feet that are similar in size to and a body weight that is close to that of an adult doe. By simply looking at the track, it's going to be tough to positively identify it as that of a buck unless your tracking skills are near the level of those of the Benoits.

By following the track for a while, you may find clues that will allow you to finally say for sure "That's a buck," but what's the point? Is it a buck you are willing to shoot? If you are serious about tracking trophy bucks, then of course the answer is no. Spending a lot of time following a questionable track to positively identify it as a buck or a doe is wasting time that could be spent looking for a buck that is worthy of your efforts.

Big bucks, however, are different. A mature northern whitetail buck is the biggest deer in the woods. He may weigh twice as much as the average doe and will be half again bigger than younger bucks. He will have big feet and a long stride. He will be wide through the chest so that his front feet will be placed with wider spacing than any other deer. He will be heavy and will cause a

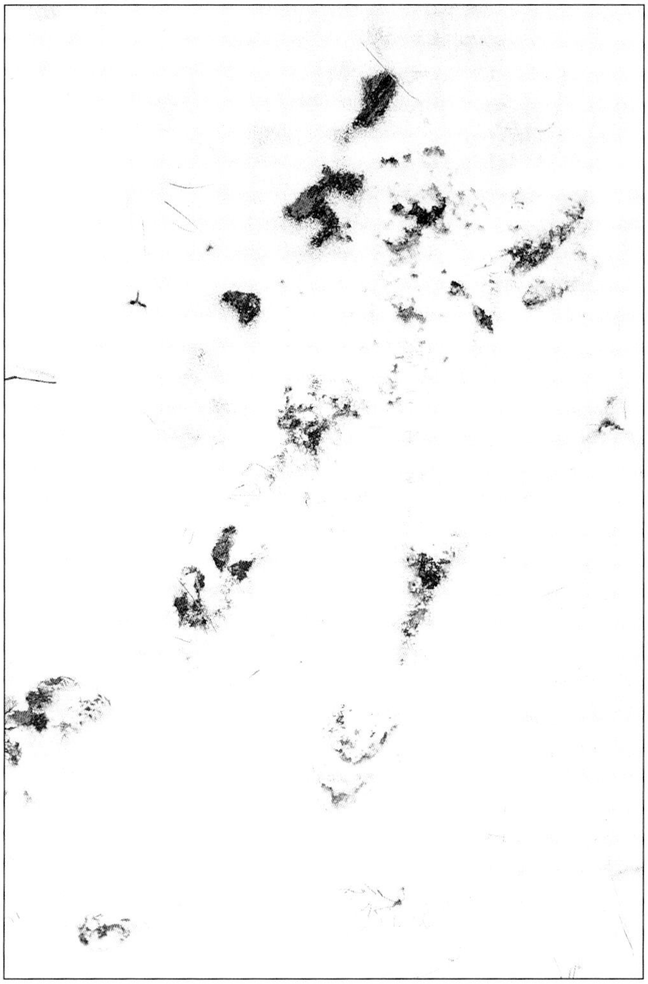

This dribbling urine was left by a buck. Bryce M. Towsley photo.

deeper impression than other deer. This buck's tracks will be different from those made by any other deer, so for a hunter who knows what he is looking at, it will become unquestionably clear the track was left by a trophy animal.

Of course, there are exceptions. Some does can grow pretty big and may have large feet. And some trophy bucks may have small feet or even be small-bodied. While the "Benoit" measure of a trophy has always been in the field-dressed body weight—with 200 pounds as the threshold for trophy status—that's not the case with much of the rest of the deer hunting world. Most hunters judge deer primarily by the antlers. The scoring system used by the Boone and Crockett Club has long been the

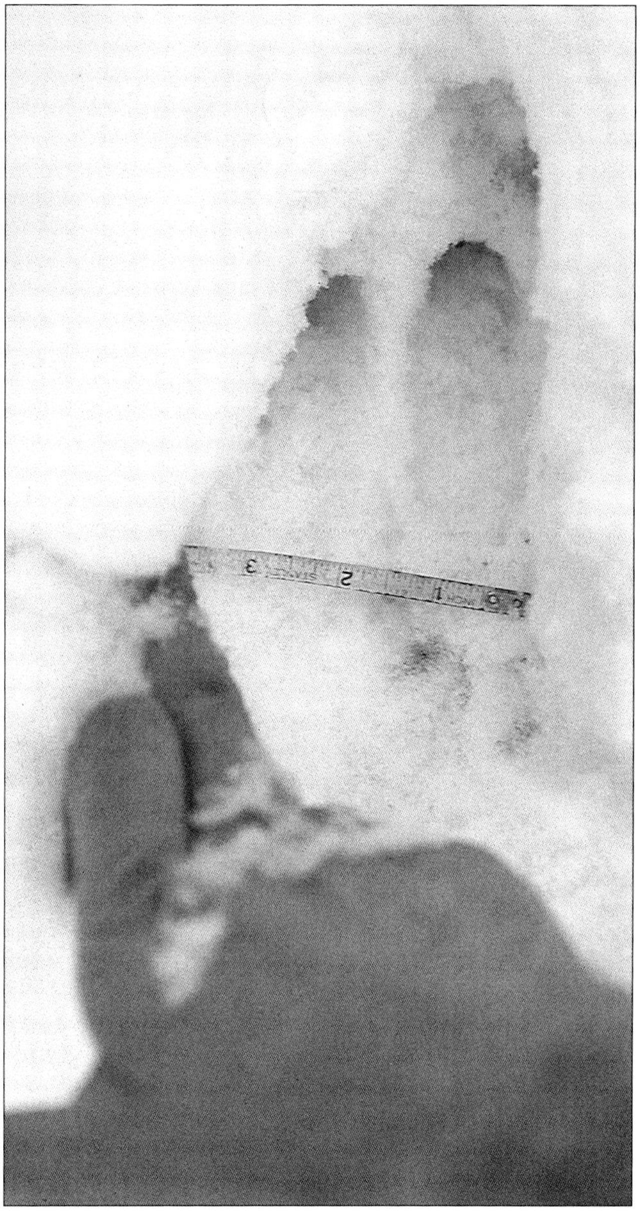

This is a very good buck. Lanny later killed this deer and post-rut he still weighed nearly 250 pounds. Before the rut he might have been close to 300 pounds. Bryce M. Towsley photo.

standard of identifying a buck's trophy quality. While some hunters are concerned with the net score and how it will place in the record book, most talk in terms of the gross score before deductions are applied. This is the raw number from the measurements made to the rack, in effect a total measurement of the buck's antlers. Even those hunters not interested in the perceived immortality

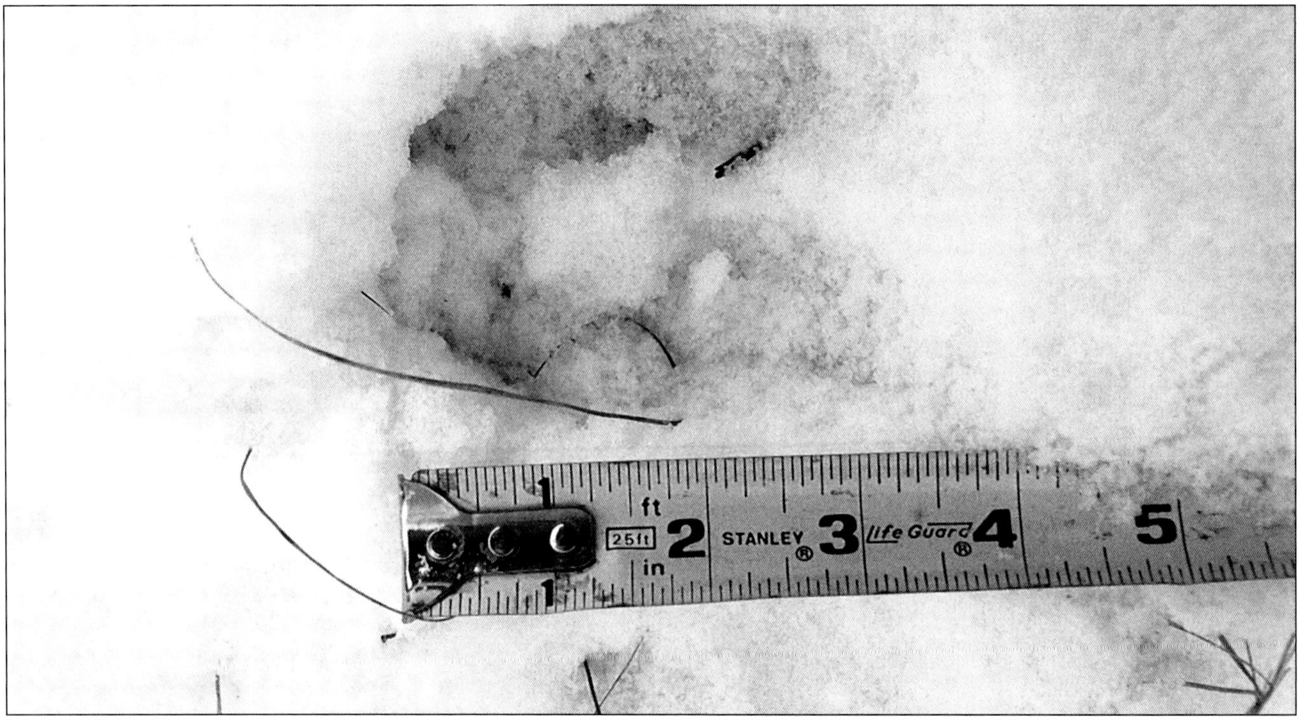

This is a big buck track from a deer weighing more than 200 pounds. Bryce M. Towsley photo.

of having their name in the "book" will use this system of measurement. When deer hunters gather and one speaks of 140-, 150-, or 160-class bucks, they all can form a visual image of how big that buck's antlers are. It has become the standard of deer hunters throughout the whitetail's domain and is now a part of every deer hunter's vocabulary.

I can even see some changes in this with the Benoits. While they still are oriented toward big-bodied deer, they are starting to pay a lot more attention to the size of the antlers. As I sat in a cold tent last November sipping coffee and listening to Shane and Lanny discussing Boone and Crockett scores, I realized I was a witness to a milestone passing in the evolution of Benoit-style deer hunting.

The point is that while trophy bucks will invariably be older, they might not always be the biggest-bodied bucks in the area. Most big-bodied bucks will have big antlers, but not all big-antlered bucks will have big bodies. If your measure of a trophy is true to Northeastern tradition and is body weight only, then nothing has changed. But if you are also looking for the largest antlers in the woods, there are some things you must consider.

Over the years I have interviewed hundreds of hunters who have shot big-antlered bucks. I have written many magazine articles on exceptional bucks that have been taken from various parts of the continent and many common themes have emerged. One is that these unusually large-antlered bucks are often smaller in body size than might be expected for the area in which they live. It's as if they have put all their growing efforts into developing outsize antlers at the expense of growing larger bodies. In the Northeast, for example, where a trophy buck will usually dress out at 220 pounds or more, the exceptionally racked bucks I have investigated are often only 170 or 180 pounds, or about 20 percent lighter.

I have observed that phenomenon throughout the whitetail's world. For example, I just returned from south Texas and a very successful hunting trip. My buck had the largest antlers of the dozen or so that my party took, but he was the smallest-bodied of the bunch, weighing about 20 percent less than the average. It was late in the season and he was pretty well "rutted out" and looking bony. But then, so were all the other bucks, so I

Most of the bucks the Benoits kill are heavy-bodied deer with very respectable racks—trophy deer any way you slice it. Tom Blais photo.

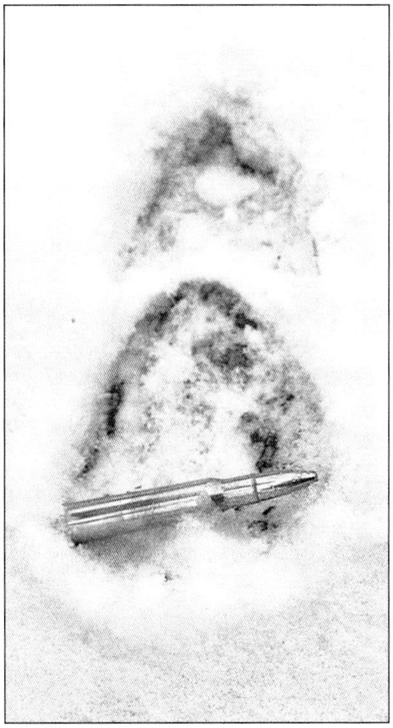

Using a 30-06 cartridge in a deer track to illustrate the width. Bryce M. Towsley photo.

think that cancels out that factor. He was simply smaller than all his contemporaries, but he made up for it by growing bigger bones on his head, which is not unusual, no matter if it's Texas, Maine, Canada, or Kansas.

So how do you know for certain a track was made by a buck? If you base your judgment on the size of the track, how do you be sure that you are not walking away from a trophy buck with small feet? There is only one way to know for sure, and that's to see the buck standing in the tracks. But the other clues can make it pretty certain.

First of all is the size. Any big trophy buck is still going to have a big track when compared to the other deer in the area. The width is as important as the length. As a rule, a wide foot indicates a big buck, and anything over 3 inches wide is usually a mature buck. The Benoits use a cartridge case as a guideline, and a Remington 180-grain round nose 30-06 Springfield round is about 3⅛ inches long. The cartridge case (the brass case without the bullet) for most 30-06 class cartridges such as the 25-06 Remington, 270 Winchester, 280 Remington, 30-06 Springfield, and 35 Whelen measures very close to 2½ inches long.

I measured a lot of tracks in the past year and most of the bucks that were called big enough to track by the Benoits were at least 3 inches wide and the best were closer to 3¼ inches. The tracks that got Lanny acting like a bird dog with a noseful of scent were almost always wider than 3¼ inches. Shane cautions, though, to look at all the information, not just the size. Sometimes big bucks have small feet and sometimes small bucks have big racks.

The track will also be long, but there are some variables in just how long. The type of terrain he lives in can influence the shape of the buck's feet and how long the toes will grow. Usually an older buck will have worn the ends of his toes off, so that the front of the track will be rounded and he will walk with his weight farther back on his foot. Does tend to be pointier-toed and they tend to walk up on their toes more. Length of stride is also another good indicator; a big buck's stride is much longer than that of a doe and he will take longer steps. Some bucks have longer strides than others. For example,

This is a big buck track.

Bryce M. Towsley photo.

in Ontario I noticed that the deer seemed to have unusually long legs. I suspect it's some kind of evolutionary process to adapt them to the deep snow common to the area. A buck's stride might be a bit longer there than in a place where the bucks tend to be shorter and more compact. However, one truth remains constant: in a given area, a big buck will always have a longer stride than a doe.

Another indicator is the width between the tracks. Any buck is much thicker through the chest than a doe and his tracks will be spaced wider. Does tend to walk with their feet in alignment, while a big buck's tracks are more spread out. They may also tend to point their toes out slightly more as they become older and heavier. Don't expect a buck's tracks to be spaced out like the tire tracks from a Dodge truck; they are still deer and a relatively narrow critter. But the spacing will be wider than that of a doe or smaller buck. While it's by inches and not feet, one key to identifying big bucks is in learning to recognize the difference.

A big, mature buck will walk heavy and flat-footed on his hooves, kind of plodding like an overweight man. The track will show that the weight is placed farther back on his foot than with smaller deer, which tend to be up on their toes more. A truly big buck will have a flat-footed-looking track and may show his dewclaws prominently. The old wives tale is that only a buck's dewclaws will show in the track and that's simply not true. However, if they are prominent in the track, they can be part of the total information package that will indicate whether or not a big, heavy buck made the track.

These things will give you enough information to make a judgment on whether the track is worth further investigation. What you discover later will confirm if you are right or wrong. Following the track will provide more information such as how the buck approaches thick cover or trees close to his path. A reluctance to pass through thick brush may indicate a large set of antlers. You may find where he has urinated, which can provide some important clues. If he makes a scrape, rubs a tree, or leaves his antler imprint in the snow, you are pretty much assured it's a buck you are following.

How do you tell how old the track is?

That's a tough one to explain in print, as it requires a lot of experience and a good measure of common sense to judge the age of tracks. Several factors affect how a track ages including temperature, humidity, precipitation, wind, and sunlight. No two situations are exactly alike. Aging tracks accurately is an acquired art that can only come from looking at a lot of tracks under a lot of conditions.

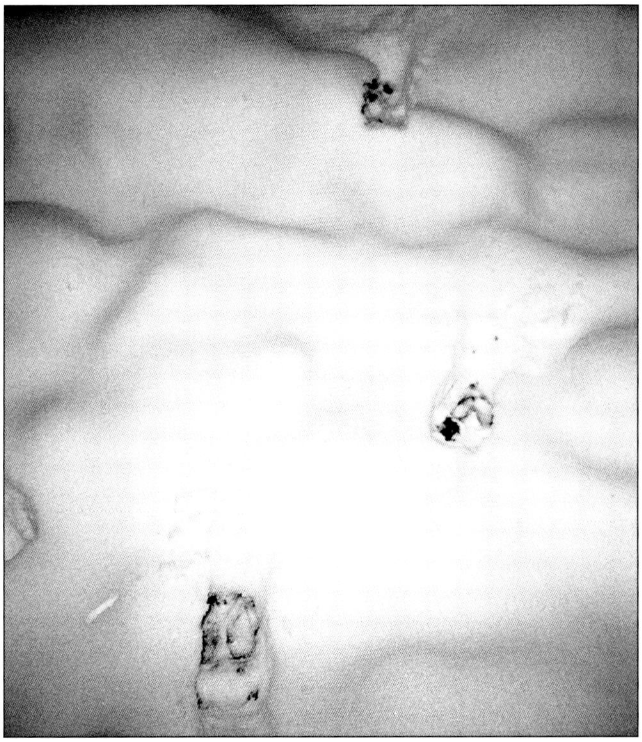

Above and right: Note the long stride and the staggered spacing of these tracks. These are both good bucks. Bryce M. Towsley photos.

Below right: Old deer track in snow. Note the ice in track. Bryce M. Towsley photo.

Obviously, if it is snowing, you can judge the track by how much snow has filled it in. During a hard snow the track can fill in quickly, and even a buck that is just ahead of you can have tracks with snow in them. The key is in recognizing how fast the snow is falling, which can be surprisingly difficult.

Without snow falling, you can be certain that a track was made after the last snow. If that was recently, you have closed the gap, but if it hasn't snowed in several days, that information is not much help.

After that, it becomes more complicated. You must consider the current weather conditions and the conditions for the past several hours. Is the track frozen? Have the sharp definitions melted or eroded? Remember that even in very cold weather the sun and wind can cause a track to melt or erode on the defined edges.

Step beside the track and compare it to your boot

track. Does this deer track look like it was made when the snow conditions were the same as they are now? If the snow when the track was made was wetter, softer, fluffier, icier, or different in any way, then think back to when the snow was like that. Consider that the night is usually much colder than the day and that the first hours of dawn are usually going to be a lot different than later in the day. Before the sun comes up, it's still cold from the night and the snow may be frozen, but as the sun warms the day even slightly, the snow conditions can change rapidly. Remember that snow will melt or change and react to changing conditions much faster than ice will. When a buck steps in the snow, he can cause the snow on the bottom of his track to melt as it compresses or to fill with moisture if the ground underneath is not frozen. In cold conditions this moisture can turn to ice very quickly. Your first clue here is if it has indeed turned to ice yet. If not, the track will of course be fresher than one that has ice in the bottom.

As the day warms, the track will change. Because of the ice that may be in the track and the fact that its depth can cast the bottom in shadow, the track may thaw slower than the surrounding snow and it may remain frozen or ice-filled longer than you might expect. The key is to think about the conditions over the past several hours and even days, and try to relate them to the current condition of the track. Even if the track was made under different snow conditions, that doesn't necessarily mean it's too old to follow, as it may have only been made a few hours ago.

Also, consider what the weather has been doing over the past several hours. If it has been warming fast, the track may appear to age quickly. However, if it was made at dawn by a tired buck heading to bed, it may well be a viable track to follow even if it is several hours old. But if the track is heading downhill, away from the mountaintop bedding areas, there is a good chance that buck is rested and on the prowl. With a head start of several hours, unless he is distracted by a hot doe, you probably are wasting your time trying to catch him.

When the track you are following passes other deer tracks, look carefully at how the snow is moved by their passing. A deer track will roll a bit of snow off to the side, much like a snowplow. This creates tiny ridges of snow or "snow banks" along the edges that you must look carefully to see. Obviously, the track that made the "snow bank" on top of the ridge of the other track is the fresher of the two.

You should always look at all the tracks you encounter when hunting. That includes deer tracks as well as tracks left by other animals. Also, watch the man tracks and even the tracks from your truck. Look at how they appear in the current snow conditions and how they compare to the deer tracks.

Your subconscious brain monitors all of this information and it will be using that information to help form data about how the tracks are aging. If you have examined old tracks as well as fresh ones, that information can help you determine if a track is fresh enough that you have a chance of catching the buck or if following it will be a waste of time.

Do you stay out all night? Camp out and stay with the buck track?

Not on purpose! Shane admits to "camping out" one time when night overran him before he made it back to the truck, and he decided that continuing that quest in the dark would be too dangerous.

My grandfather used to tell of an old woodsman from his youth who would grab a little food and a blanket before heading out the camp door. "I'll see you after I get him," he would say over his shoulder as he headed up the mountain. That man would simply pick up a big buck track and follow it. When darkness overcame him, he would lie down, wrap up in the blanket, and sleep until dawn. Then he would pick up the track again and continue on. He kept this up until he shot the buck.

Many uninformed hunters think that is how the Benoits hunt, but I can assure you the loud snores that fill the camp each night prove it's not true. They always go back to camp at night. Now, sometimes it's pretty late before they get there, but they never "camp" on the track.

Another misconception is that they follow the same buck day after day. While they do that on occasion, that's not the normal scenario. They might go back to the same area the next day and look for his track, but if another buck track looks fresher, they are just as likely to follow that animal. I have hunted with them when they may follow several buck tracks in the same day. If one doesn't work out for whatever reason, they don't hesitate to leave it to find another, more promising track to follow. They caution that getting bogged down on hunting the same deer day after day can often lead to a frustrating and unfulfilled season. Be flexible, be versatile, and be smart. And remember, a camp with a wood stove is much more comfortable than a blanket in the snow.

How do you tell when a buck is going to lie down?

When he brushes his teeth and puts on his pajamas!

Actually, like most things in tracking, it's a combination of several indicators. The first is where the tracks are headed and what time of day it is. If it's morning and the buck is headed into a known bedding area, then it's a good bet he has been on the prowl all night, he is tired, and he is going to lie down. Big bucks like to move high on the mountain to bed, and if a track is heading up, then rest is probably on his agenda. However, if the track is heading away from a bedding area or down off the mountain, then chances are he is rested and back on the prowl. That buck probably won't lie down for several hours and he is going to be hard to catch up with.

Shane says, "Anytime I am hunting, but particularly first thing in the morning, I always like to find a buck that is traveling uphill rather than downhill. As a rule a buck that's going up is looking to feed a little and lie down, but a buck heading downhill is usually headed someplace. Chances are he has rested and is now ready for a walk-about. That's a buck that is going to be hard to catch. But the buck headed uphill is tired and isn't going to be at the top of his game. Not only is he probably going to be easier to catch up with, but he also might not be quite as alert."

Bucks like to eat before lying down, and if you are following a track of a buck you suspect is going to be lying down soon, watch for feeding activity. Often they will meander a bit as they walk to each bit of food. Northern bucks in November are usually going to be nipping at browse, so the evidence of feeding is not going to be greatly apparent to a hunter who is not looking. Don't expect to see pawed-up areas on the ground (although you might, so don't rule them out completely, either). Rather, a rutting buck will nip a bit of browse here and a bit there. The evidence of this is easy to miss if you are not looking. They eat only the small buds on the very ends of branches, and the fresh-cut ends of branches are tiny and not very noticeable.

I was hunting with Shane recently and we had been on the track for a while, when he told me that the buck was starting to feed a little. I admitted that I hadn't noticed. We had been following this buck for hours and as far as I could see, he wasn't doing anything other than laying tracks on the ground. His track was still straight and pointed through the woods like he was late for an appointment. But Shane had noticed that even though he wasn't deviating his path, the buck was grabbing a bit of browse when it was within easy reach. Shane pointed out a few small branch tips that had been nipped off, leaving the characteristic small tab of bark that indicates a whitetail had done the deed. After that, I started watching more and noticed a few myself. Later, the buck started to meander a bit to reach some of the choice tidbits and we knew he was thinking about bed.

I would like to tell you that we got that buck, but my mother taught me not to tell lies. Just because a buck is bedding down doesn't mean you will shoot him. This one passed through a bunch of thick woods that was choked with brush and blowdowns before bedding on a ridge past this thicket. There was simply no way to get through the junk without making some noise (as I told Shane, my focus when tracking deer is to leave no stick unbroken). The buck knew we were headed his way and he vacated his bed long before we arrived.

The point is, we *knew* the buck was going to bed down. We just didn't know what to do with that information. Sometimes it just doesn't work out. We didn't do anything wrong, but rather the buck did everything right. Another day, it might have turned out differently.

The Benoits shoot a lot of bucks in their beds. The secret is to first recognize they are going to bed down and then to sneak quietly enough to shoot them before they wake up and run away. It's not easy, but it can be done. When you begin to do it with some regularity, then you can safely call yourself an accomplished deer tracker.

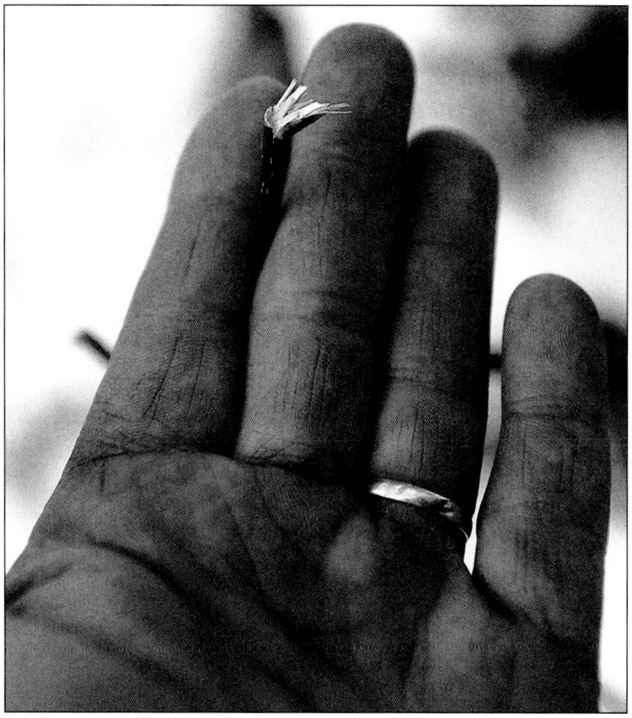

This branch was nipped off by a feeding buck. The buck bedded soon after. Bryce M. Towsley photo.

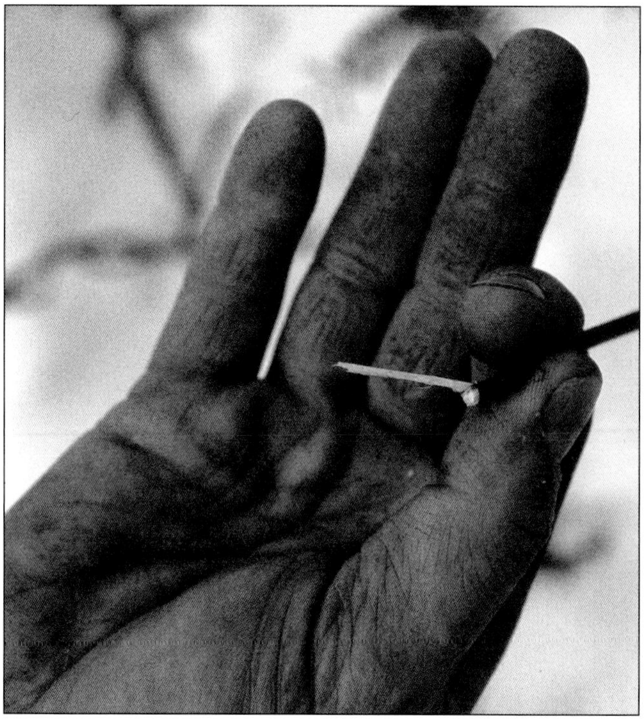

Note the "tab" of bark that is indicative of a deer feeding. Bryce M. Towsley photo.

What's easier, tracking a buck that's alone or with a doe or other deer?

There is something to be said for both circumstances, and both situations can work to the hunter's advantage, or against him. A lone buck has only one nose and one set of ears and eyes, whereas a buck with one or more does has the advantage of all those extra eyes, ears, and noses. The chances of getting busted are much higher. On the other hand, a lone buck is usually on the move or bedded. He can be a hard critter to catch up with as he keeps on the move looking for love, and if he is bedded, his sharp ears and nose make getting close difficult.

However, most deer hunting is during the rut, when the deer are distracted. The buck obviously is distracted by the doe. Any deer hunter knows the advantage provided by that. It's often said that without the rut to make them stupid, we would never shoot a trophy buck. That's probably true, but we need to put it in perspective. A buck only gets lucky with the ladies during a very short (I suppose he would call it "painfully short") period of time once a year. If that were the case with humans, we would make a lot of mistakes too. We already make enough in the pursuit of the opposite sex as it is, imagine if the females could or would only breed with us two or three days out of each year. How would we act? What else would we have on our minds? How adept would we be at surviving and evading somebody trying to shoot us while we were intent on scoring with the ladies? When you look at it like that, a buck that keeps his hide free of bullet holes long enough to achieve trophy status is a pretty sly customer. He doesn't make many mistakes, but if he does, it's a sure bet the rut is the likely cause or at least the catalyst to the cause. So anytime a "hot" doe or a doe that is about to become "hot" is around, it can benefit the hunter.

Does are also distracted during the rut. If they are not ready to breed, they are doing their best to avoid the bucks. Bucks can sense when a doe is close to being ready and will hound her mercilessly. Nearly every deer hunter has seen does running from bucks. This isn't simply playing hard to get; the doe still isn't ready to breed, but the buck sure is. Bucks can be pretty insistent at this

This buck ducked under this fallen tree, which is an indication that it may not have a large set of antlers, but then again it could. This is only one clue—not necessarily the total answer. Bryce M. Towsley photo.

This hair was left on this stub when the buck ducked under this fallen tree, which is an indication that it may not have a large set of antlers. Note also the broken branch above.
Bryce M. Towsley photo.

Opposite page: Note how this buck steps around this tree. This may indicate that he has a wide set of antlers.
Bryce M. Towsley photo.

time, sometimes to the point of injuring or even killing the doe. I once saw three bucks that had a doe trapped against a fence, and I truly believe they would have killed her if I hadn't interrupted them. The best one ended his breeding days forever and that doe was the last thing he saw on earth. I have often wondered what he was thinking at that point. That she was an "angel doe" or that perhaps she was tougher than he thought and maybe he should have left this one alone.

A doe that is trying to stay away from the buck will be distracted and the buck will also be distracted as he chases after her. If she is ready to breed, they are both going to have more on their minds than hunters. Either way, it gives the hunter an edge.

So, the answer is that usually it's easier to track a buck that has a doe with him, but not always.

Is that clear enough?

Larry Benoit took this buck in 2001. Tom Blais photo.

This buck stuck his nose under this log and his antlers hit the snow on both sides. This gives an idea of how wide his antlers are. Bryce M. Towsley photo.

What's the best weather to hunt in?

What's that old saying? "The best day to hunt is any day you can!"

But, given a choice, the best time to track and kill a buck is when there is a gentle rain falling and the ground is covered with about 6 inches of soft, wet, noiseless snow. It's also a very good time when snow is falling, particularly that slow, lazy, big-flaked snow that takes forever to reach the ground. On such days, the air is thick with humidity and no wind disturbs the trees. When the still air is thick with moisture and a gentle calm seems to pervade throughout the woods, a true hunter will find tracking deer is all that matters. The deer seem to be calm, almost serene at times, as if the weather has a tranquilizing effect on them. Scent doesn't travel far and the thick air seems to muffle sound. The wet ground is quiet to step on and anybody who isn't in the woods on that kind of a day has no business calling himself a deer hunter.

How do you tell what a buck is carrying for a rack?

Another view of Larry Benoit's "tight-racked" buck he took in 2001. Tom Blais photo.

The best way to tell the size of the rack on the deer you are tracking is to shoot him and then look it over at your leisure. The second best way is to see the buck. Both are difficult to do on demand.

There are other signs, however, that can provide strong clues as you track the buck. The most common way is to watch where the buck is going. If he is traveling through thick brush rather than around it, he probably isn't carrying much for headgear. A buck that's not spooked will go around thick spots rather than try to muscle his rack through. He will bypass trees that are close together and go around trees that are close to the trail. This last point was a bit hard for me to grasp. I was looking for a buck that made a big sweep away from the offending trees with his track, making a noticeable detour, but the reality is much more subtle. The buck will only make a small step away from the tree so that his rack will clear the tree trunk. I saw it many times without recognizing what I was seeing. Lanny finally pointed it out to me, and it was one of those "slap your forehead" moments. Like so many other things about tracking deer, the reality is subtle and small. But then, noticing the things that others miss is what makes a great deer hunter. In this case, we are talking inches here, rather than feet. The buck simply deviates a small distance from his path so that his head will not hit on the tree. They tend to do this rather than to swing their head out around the tree. Nobody can explain why, but all the Benoits agree they do it and that it's an important tool in identifying what a buck may have for a rack. It's only one step and you need to pay attention to notice, but the larger the deviation, the wider the rack.

I was hunting in Canada with Shane, and he kept commenting that the buck we were following through some of the thickest, nastiest brush I have ever tracked a deer through had a "tight rack," which is Shane-speak for a narrow antler spread. After he mentioned that point several times and I was bleeding from several locations, I finally asked him, "Why are we following it through this hell-hole then?"

"Well," Shane replied. "The bucks right here in this area tend to be tight, so it's probably our only option unless we want to move several miles. Also, if you remember the buck that Pop (Larry) shot not too far from here 2 years ago, it had a tight rack that was only about 14 inches inside spread. It also scored over 174 Boone & Crockett and had a dressed weight of 250 pounds."

I figured he had made his point and I shut up.

A buck that is in snow will usually leave his antler prints sooner or later. When he lowers his head to sniff a track, to eat a mushroom, or to lick a mouthful of snow, he will often hit the surrounding snow with his antlers. Again, it's easy to miss if you are not watching. I was on a track with Lanny when he pointed to a place where the buck had grabbed a bit of low-hanging browse and clearly left his antler tine marks in the snow. We were tracking the buck along the bottom of a steep riverbank, and when he nipped the branch, his antler tines put several holes in the snow on the riverbank. They were off the track to the side and very easy to miss. I would have walked right by without noticing and so would most other hunters. But Lanny doesn't miss much. From that evidence he guessed it was a wide 10-point.

It turns out he was right.

What's the heaviest buck you have shot?

It depends when you ask. If it's right after dragging it out, the answer is the one they just shot. But in terms of actual weight on a scale, it's as follows:

Shane	268 pounds
Lanny	271 pounds
Lane	284 pounds
Landon	225 pounds
Larry	275 pounds

What's the longest time you have spent to get a buck?

It took Shane a full year to get a buck one time. He tracked the buck in 1982 and shot at him, but missed. Then in the 1983 hunting season, he finally got him.

It was a rainy day with good tracking and sneaking conditions. He knew about that buck's favorite spot, his sanctuary, and when he found tracks leading in but none coming out, he knew he had him. After that, it was simply a matter of tracking him to his bed and interrupting his dreams.

The Benoits have all spent several days and even a couple of weeks before finally shooting a buck they had set their sights on. But they try hard not to get hung up on a specific buck. If it's not working out after a few days, they go find another buck, so they rarely spend a lot of time trying to get a specific buck. Most bucks they shoot are taken the day they decide to hunt them—that is, the first time they take his track.

The hours of daylight in the short days of November pretty much set a limit on how many hours they can spend. For a lot of bucks, they have pushed that limit to the borders. It's not uncommon to take a track as soon as it's light enough to follow and to shoot the buck just before it becomes too dark to see tracks. That's a long day, and they still have to get back to the truck.

Why are you using a scope?

"Can't see!" is how Shane usually answers that one. The Benoit Brothers are getting older. Shane is the baby and he is 47 years old. They all have been blessed with remarkable eyesight, but nobody can deny the aging process. Reading glasses are a fact of life for most middle-aged men, as is not being able to see an iron sight clearly. Lanny told how he was seeing two front beads. "I just put the buck between them and most of the time it worked," he said. "Until we started hunting in a new place where we were getting longer shots. It worked fine at 50 yards, but not so good at 250 yards."

"When we started hunting in Canada, we found that there were a lot of opportunities for longer shots," Shane told me. "The area we hunt was burned several years ago and the new timber is still small. It's full of ridges and it's not unusual to top one ridge and see the buck you are tracking on the next one. But they can be pretty far apart, and a peep sight is just not precise enough. Those long shots are one of several reasons and probably the most important one."

Shane and I have a running argument about which type of sight is faster for quick shots at running deer. He still believes deeply in the peep sight for this type of hunting. That's because it's what he has always used and what he is most familiar with and what he trusts. Unlike most

The mark in the snow made by this buck's antler as he fed is easy to see. This allows for judging how wide his rack is.

Bryce M. Towsley photo.

Larry Benoit with a buck he took with his Remington 7600 rifle, which carries a Leupold 1.5–5 Vari-X III scope. Benoit Brothers photo.

deer hunters today, the Benoits didn't grow up shooting with scopes, but rather they transitioned to them late in life. Trust, confidence, and experience are very important to shooting well in any situation. For Shane and the rest of the Benoits, those qualities are found in the comfortable and familiar peep sights.

However, I must respectfully disagree with them on the point. I make my living writing about guns and hunting for some of the largest firearms and hunting magazines in the world. I shoot a lot and I hunt a lot. My first love is whitetail deer hunting and I have been fortunate enough to pursue this great game animal in just about every good place they are hunted. I love adventure and new places, so I have worked hard, and with some luck, I have been able to hunt over a good part of the world. Much of that has been thick cover, and some for dangerous game such as Cape buffalo and Alaskan brown bears, where shooting fast and well is part of staying alive. I also shoot almost every day testing guns, ammo, and sights. As a rule I am among the first in the country to test and hunt with any new cartridge or rifle that is introduced. I have used every type of sight common to hunting and have taken game with them all. Even on my days off, I shoot competitively for recreation. Lately a lot of that competition is with guns equipped with peep or iron sights. These are events that are based on accuracy and speed, so I have a good idea of how well these sights can perform. I have shot with and hunted with some of the very best hunters and shooters in the world and many of them are my friends. Hunting, guns, and shooting are my passions in life, and I believe that a life well lived indulges one's passions.

Tom Blais photo.

I hope this doesn't sound like bragging because I am only trying to establish where my opinions are rooted. It's not often that I will disagree with the Benoits on matters of deer hunting, but this is one of them. I want to make it clear that this is my opinion, not that of the Benoits.

For the Benoits and thousands of other hunters who have always hunted deer with a peep sight, it truly is the best choice for a fast shot or for shooting at running deer. However, for a hunter who has grown up using a scope and is comfortable and familiar with it, or for a shooter who is equally experienced with both types of sights, a properly applied scope sight is faster and more accurate than any iron sight in any and all hunting situations using a rifle.

Open sights require three separate points of focus be dealt with—the rear sight, front sight, and the target. The human eye is not capable of focusing on all three and to shoot well you must keep the front sight in sharp focus. This is very difficult because your mind wants to watch the deer. Peep sights allow you to ignore the rear sight, but you still must focus on the front sight. Other than the obvious problems it creates with trying to aim, this also causes the target to "blur" out. That's fine if you are target shooting, but when you are hunting, it would be better to keep watch of the animal. You want the deer in sharp focus so you can stay attuned to any body language or a change in position.

Scopes, on the other hand, magnify and brighten the image while putting the sights (crosshairs) on the same focal plane as the target, allowing both to stay sharp in your vision. A shooter with a low-power scope will always be a faster and more accurate field shot than the hunter

This red-painted peep sight has been traditional on any "Benoit Rifle." This is Shane Benoit's rifle shown here. Bryce M. Towsley photo.

who insists on using iron sights. That includes deer that are running as well as standing.

Consider that in every form of "speed shooting" competition where they are allowed, the top shooters use optical sights. Usually they are electronic red-dot sights, but it's for the same reason that a scope is best for hunting. The target and sights are all in sharp focus. Plus, there is only one aiming point to consider instead of two, as with iron sights of any kind.

Only a couple of decades ago, another argument against scopes was that they were unreliable and prone to failure in poor weather. I remember back in the early '70s, I had a pair of the old Weaver K-4 scopes mounted on the only two rifles I owned back then. The weather in Vermont's November deer season is consistent only in its inclemency, and it was never a question of if these scopes would fog up, but when. Every December for several years in a row found me at the post office sending one or both of these scopes back to Texas for repairs.

Things have changed, though, and it's been a long time since I have seen an undamaged, quality scope fog up while hunting. This includes the new Weavers, which are now a good scope for the money. Junk is still junk and you get what you pay for, but the quality of most scopes on the market is so much better today that fear of failure is no longer a viable reason to not use a scope.

Yes, they do fog up on the outside of the lens or become obscured by water or snow on nasty days, and that's probably the only legitimate argument against a scope for tracking deer. But then, so do peep sights. I think that on snowy days when I am using a peep-sight-equipped rifle (yes, I do use a peep quite a bit) the peep or front sight

Two-thirds of the Benoit Brothers (Lanny and Shane) agree that a scoped rifle is an advantage in certain situations and they have started using them on a consistent basis. Tom Blais photo.

is filled or covered with snow and useless as often as a scope, or nearly so.

The bottom line is that under almost all hunting conditions, a scope is a superior aiming device, and even the Benoits will agree with *most* of that statement. I am still working on them to convince them of the error of their ways about the rest.

Actually, there have been other changes in their hunting styles, and the longer shots that have resulted are another big reason why the Benoits now have scopes on their guns. Because of several factors, the Benoits are also now hunting from stands on occasion. (Did anybody check to see if Hell has indeed frozen over? Scopes? Hunting from stands? No more green-checked coats? What's next, bolt-action rifles? Warm boots?) Many of these stands are in open areas such as powerlines or old burns with deer trails crossing and again the shots can be long. On long shots, even the Benoits will not argue that a scope sight is the clear choice.

Why the new hunting clothes?

The Benoits are rooted as deeply in tradition as any deer hunters I know, and I know a lot of deer hunters. They do many things the way their father did them, the way his father did them, and the way his father before him did them. They do this for a variety of reasons, not the least of which is because they have always worked and they continue to work. There may be a better way today, but they are big into the personal philosophy of "If it ain't broke, don't fix it." (Rumor has it that a distant Benoit ancestor was still taking big bucks with a stone-headed spear well into the flintlock rifle era. He said that he had always enjoyed great success with the spear and saw no reason to give it up.) As thousands of deer hunters can attest, the old lightweight green-and-black-checked wool jackets they made famous worked extremely well for tracking bucks in the Northwoods. But they had their faults, and the design is a bit dated. Technology has brought us far better alternatives and the Benoits have discovered some of them.

Hunters no longer use flint arrowheads or stone knives because man has used technology to create something better. That's the case with the jackets too; something better has come along. It takes a lot to make the Benoits change anything, but they recognized the superiority of these new Beagle Outdoor Wear wool coats and made the switch.

I'll never forget my first morning of hunting with the Benoits many years ago. It was late season in Maine and the morning was bitter cold. The snow was frozen and crunchy. The bucks were tired of being harassed and had become wary and difficult. The Benoits had been after a good buck, but one man alone and tracking wasn't working because the buck could tell exactly where the hunter was and stayed just ahead of him. So we all took up positions along escape routes, while Lanny took the buck's track. The idea was that the buck would probably try to stay with the hot doe he had holed up with in this thick and protected basin. But he didn't count on Lanny. The man is persistent and when he is on the track, he is relentless. We hoped one of the deer would finally tire of that and bail out of that thick patch of woods with the idea of putting some miles between them and that pesky guy in the green coat. They finally did, but it took a while.

I was there to work on the first book, *Big Bucks the Benoit Way*, and if I was going to write a book about these guys, I was determined to hunt with exactly the same equipment they used. I ordered a Remington 7600 pump-action carbine in 30-06 Springfield and fitted it with a Williams peep sight. I had on light rubber boots and a lightweight checked wool jacket. Although I will admit mine was red—something Larry harassed me about relentlessly—it was the same in every other respect.

I was waiting near the top of a ridge where a bitter wind was blowing hard enough in those cold temperatures to cast the wind chill well below zero. Lanny might have been comfortable hiking through that protected basin, but I thought I was going to die on that desolate hilltop in Maine. In fact, before it was over, I was so cold I was afraid I wouldn't die! Those light wool jackets were great for the hard and constant physical activity while tracking, but they were never made for sitting around on a cold northwoods day.

The Benoits are all getting a bit older and they have slowed down just a little in their hunting style and techniques. They have adapted their hunting to these changes, and if anything, they are shooting more big bucks than ever. But with less activity and slower movement, they have found that a warmer coat was a necessity. They still dress very lightly compared to most deer hunters, but they have stepped up one notch in warmth with these new Beagle Coats.

Also, anybody who has ever hunted in the rain knows another fault of the old-style wool jackets. Wool may stay warm when it's wet, but it will sure soak up a lot of water. If the jacket is wet, then everything underneath is wet and uncomfortable too.

I might mention another problem with these jackets. As I said, mine is red and black checked. Some years ago, the opening day of Vermont's deer season was filled with rain. It was one of those hard-driving, all-day-long, cold downpours that New England is known for in late fall. I had been hunting in Montana the week before, and as airlines are known to do, ours was having problems. My flight was delayed until, instead of being home for dinner the night before our season opener, I made it through the door with just enough time to change clothes and head out hunting.

The rain was constant and relentless, and by the time dawn came, I was soaked. By noon I'd had enough. For the first time in my life I left the woods without a deer to go home while it was still daylight on opening day. When I got there, I hung my incredibly heavy wool coat on a chair in front of the wood stove and went to bed. When my wife came home, she found a bright red ring on the carpet where the coat had drained, taking the red dye with it. That was a decoration in our living room until I replaced the carpet several years later. My point is not so much the way the dye will run, but that the old-style wool coat is just like a big sponge and holds a lot of water.

The Beagle coat, by contrast, uses specially treated wool that is very water repellent. In one version there is also an inner layer of breathable, waterproof barrier material to keep the hunter even dryer.

"What sold us on these Beagle coats," Shane told me, "was when Lanny tried one a few years ago. It was pouring rain all day and we were all soaked by the time the day ended. As we undressed in camp Lanny said, 'Feel my shirt.' Even though he had been out in the rain all day, the shirt was dry. That was enough for me. I used Lanny's spare Beagle coat the rest of the hunt and I ordered one of my own as soon as I got home."

Do you scout before you hunt?

The odds of shooting a big buck always go up when you scout out the country and locate as many bucks as possible. If you can also learn their travel habits, you have a better chance of shooting them. But the answer is something contrary to that truth.

"No," Lane would tell the audience member who asked. "We usually do our scouting as we hunt."

What they usually don't explain because of time constraints and all the other hands waving in the air is that some of the places the Benoits are hunting these days are a 30-hour drive to get to and it's not easy to just pop in for a weekend of pre-season scouting.

Besides, during the fall, big-country deer are in transition. Food sources are changing and when combined with the rut, the deer can move far and often. Where you found them when you were scouting in October may not be where they are in November when you are ready to hunt.

The Benoits often go into a place to hunt for several weeks at a time. As a rule, they are in no hurry to shoot a buck and they often spend the first several days learning the area and the deer movement within that area. By the time they are serious about shooting a buck, they have a good idea of where the best bucks are located.

However, the great thing about tracking bucks is that it doesn't always require a lot of scouting. You simply find a big buck track that is a likely candidate and you follow it until you kill the deer. It may be a buck you found several days ago and came back to hunt, or it may well be the first time you have seen that buck's tracks. You don't have to "pattern" him or learn his travel corridors, bedding area, feeding area, or anything else about him. You have seen his track; you know he is a big buck. You have followed it far enough to know he probably has a good rack; what more information do you need? On the grand scale, it doesn't matter where he is going as long as he is leaving tracks. You can follow him to his bedding area as well as you can to his feeding area. Finding a "primary" scrape or a "signpost" rub will tell you it's a buck in front of you and will delay him a bit so you can close the gap, but they are really not all that important to shooting this buck. You may need that information if you are going to ambush him from a stand, but in this case you only need his track on the ground to find him.

He may or may not come by your ambush site; that's up to him and the whimsy of fate. But it's a sure bet that the buck is standing at the end of the trail you are following. If he made these tracks, he is ahead of you on that track, plain and simple. If he decides to go follow a doe, or to take off into uncharted territory, you are out of luck if you are waiting along the "funnel" where you put your treestand. But if you are tracking, you simply follow him wherever he decides to go. Assuming you don't give up, one of three things will happen: you will lose the track, it will get dark or you will shoot this buck. You cannot make that last assumption when stand-hunting after scouting.

Tracking is a great way to hunt trophy bucks when you are in a new area, as you can often be effective right out of the gate. It's not unusual for one of the Benoits to be short of time due to work or family commitments, to arrive in the hunting area and to shoot a big buck in just a few days.

With the more "conventional" styles of hunting these days, you must spend a lot of time scouting out locations for stands. To do it right, you must spend a lot of time checking the area to learn deer-movement patterns and to figure out what the area holds for bucks. This, of course, disturbs the deer, as scouting is intrusive. It can, at least theoretically, cause them to move on to a place with less human activity. But even if they stay put, you are wasting a day or more scouting and alerting the deer to your presence. If you are a tracker, you are hunting as soon as the sun comes up the first day. Often you will kill the buck the first time you park your truck and go into the woods. By the time they are "disturbed" by your activity, you are digging out your dragging rope.

You don't need to scout to know the best ambush locations because you are a walking ambush. You will always have a trophy buck in front of you when you are tracking and you go where the buck goes, rather than waiting someplace you hope he might wander past.

Do you use scent?

This one is getting old, but here goes. The boys always answer with, "The only 'scents' we use is 'common sense'."

The question gets asked every seminar and they always answer the same way. The audience always laughs, so I guess it's not worn out yet.

The techniques that apply to making the use of deer scents successful in whitetail hunting do not really apply to tracking. Except perhaps cover scents.

The idea of a doe-in-heat scent is to attract a horny buck to a place where you can shoot him. To do that, you have to wait in ambush on a stand, someplace where the buck cannot smell you. It's impossible to use this method when tracking deer. If you put the doe-in-heat scent on yourself, anytime the buck can smell it, he can also smell you, which negates the usefulness of the scent. However, it does make some "sense" to use a cover scent. The deer can still smell you, as no cover scent will completely block the human scent from a deer's nose. But a good cover scent will sometimes buy you an extra second or two. However, the Benoits don't use any commercial scent.

The truth is they do use some scent, although not commercial scent. Shane will rub snow that is stained with deer urine on his clothing as well as evergreen branches. He calls it the "scent of the woods" and he believes that it may provide a slight edge in the same way that any cover scent will.

Lanny has a theory that the longer he is in camp and the "stinkier" he gets, the more bucks he sees. "I don't think they know what I am when I am getting ripe," he chuckles. "They don't expect a hunter to smell like that and sometimes they hang around to see if I am a man or a wookie."

If you are tracking a buck and you don't get him that day, do you go back the next day to where you left the trail?

As a rule, no. By morning that buck will have 12 or 14 more hours of traveling time on you, on top of what he already had when you left the track. If he is moving, it's very hard to make that up. If you have been doing your homework and know the area, you can probably make a

Lanny & Landon Benoit on the track in New Hampshire 2002. Bryce M. Towsley photo.

Tom Blais photo.

good guess about where he is headed. It's better to spend some time trying to find a fresher track he made. Drive the roads around the block of woods he was in to see if he has crossed anyplace. If he has, drive around the next block and so forth until you finally isolate him in a specific section of woods. Of course, in the North Country, that may only narrow it down to simply a huge piece of woods rather than the humongous section you had isolated before. But at least you have cut the distance to the buck and the possibilities of where he is lurking about.

If he hasn't left the block of woods that you were tracking him through the day before, then you may want to go back and pick up where you stopped. Chances are good he has found a hot doe or is tired from avoiding you all the day before and has bedded down someplace.

The reality is that you can't always cover every side of a piece of land and it's possible that the buck may exit someplace you can't get to, but you should always try to isolate his location as much as possible before starting tracking again.

Chances are that in the course of doing that, you will find another fresh buck track that you can follow. It may not have been made by the buck you were on yesterday, but if they are of at least equal quality, so what? He is here and available and how do you know he isn't a better buck than the one you were hunting? But if the buck you had been following was exceptionally large, you may want to stick with him, forsaking all others, at least for a while longer. In that case, try to figure out where he is and then plan accordingly.

The key is to hunt more with your brain than your feet. You cannot outwalk a whitetail buck in his prime, but unless you come from really poor genetic stock, you should be able to out-think him.

What about the wind?

This comes up at every seminar, and the Benoits have been giving the answer by rote for so long, I think they sometimes fail to explain it adequately.

The canned response is that "the wind in the mountains can blow in all four directions at any given time. We don't pay any attention to it."

I heard Larry say that 25 years ago at a seminar and I heard one of the brothers say it a week ago at another seminar. It's correct as far as it goes, but sometimes that is not far enough.

What they mean, of course, is the wind can constantly switch directions in the rough terrain and unpredictable weather patterns of the North Country in November. It might be at your back at one point, but 10 minutes and 200 yards later, it's in your face. Anybody who has tracked deer likely knows exactly what I am talking about here.

The relevant point that is often not made is that they are trackers, and as such, they must go where the track takes them. If the wind is wrong, what are they supposed to do, leave the track? That would hardly work, particularly when you consider how often the wind direction and the track direction can change. They must follow the track where it leads, regardless of which way the wind is blowing.

When the wind is wrong, very few deer will fail to notice the scent of a man and act accordingly. That means at times the wind will betray the hunter and cause the buck to run away, when with a different wind direction, he might have gotten a shot. That's just part of tracking bucks. The only thing you can do is to keep on the track and hope the next time you catch up with that buck, the wind is in your favor and not his.

With a prevailing wind, bucks on the prowl usually travel with their noses pointed into the wind or, more often, into a crosswind. That's because they are trying to find does in heat. Sex is more important to them at that moment than avoiding danger. The bucks locate does by smelling a hot doe's lusty scent, so by moving into the wind or into a crosswind they are covering the most ground possible. That's to a tracker's advantage because he will usually be behind the buck, where the deer can't smell him. When the buck stops to bed or to court a doe, that can change and all bets are off. The best you can do is hope that luck is with you. If not, there is always next time.

Shane Benoit rattling horns in Ontario in 2002. Bryce M. Towsley photos.

How do you know when you are getting close to a buck?

The best indication is when you see him standing in his tracks. Other than that, it is simply a matter of reading the sign. You can see the tracks are getting fresher. Compare them to your own tracks, and when they start to look the same, you are probably getting close. Or it might be the buck is starting to feed and will bed down soon. Also, look for the tracks made by one or more does that might be traveling with him. If the doe is puttering around, that will delay him and likely means they will be stopping or bedding down.

You should always be careful, though, to be looking for the buck at all times, as you can see them at anyplace and anytime, even when you think he is way ahead of you. If you are always looking, you won't be caught off guard or surprised when you catch up with him.

Do you guys hunt together?

Yes, they all hunt with each other at various times. Of course, too, they have their favorite pairings with personalities and hunting styles that complement each other.

Landon told me he has never shot a deer except with his dad. He and Lanny always hunt together when they are both in camp.

Lanny and Shane often hunt together as well, double-teaming or simply riding the trails looking for tracks.

Lane was more of a loner and was apt to be off by himself most of the time. He used to double-team with his buddy, Dave Coker, quite often.

In the past 4 years, any and all of the Benoit Brothers will usually have a cameraman with them to film for the videos. Double-teaming means that two hunters and a cameraman are starting to become an entourage. Too many people cause problems, so these days the Benoits usually hunt alone, except for the cameraman.

Do you use grunt calls?

They never used to, but lots of things have changed in recent years. They use them quite often now.

When you are very close to a buck and perhaps he even hears you, but still doesn't know what you are, blowing a grunt call can have a dramatic effect. The Benoits only hunt for mature, dominant bucks. These bucks are usually pumped full of testosterone and are ready for love or ready to rumble, and they don't much care which. Blowing a challenge on a grunt call when you are close will often cause the buck to charge back at what he thinks is a rival buck. If nothing else, it will often confuse the buck about just what is coming. If he thinks those footsteps are another deer, he will not run away, but rather will wait to make visual contact.

Also, blowing a grunt call at a buck that is moving but is not too spooked will often cause him to stop.

How about rattling?

Tom Blais has been filming the Benoits for four years and has had a positive influence on their hunting techniques. Tom is an avid and experienced whitetail hunter and a big advocate of rattling horns.

While they don't do it a lot, the Benoits do use rattling some, particularly Shane. They see it as a tool that can be utilized in some situations. For example, when tracking a buck that is isolated in a small patch of woods, he will sometimes simply circle around you and refuse to leave. Often that's because it's too thick and noisy, or because the wind is wrong. If for those or some other reason you can't go in and shoot him, sometimes rattling will bring him out. Even if he winds you and spooks, at least you have him out of that bad section of woods and where you may be able to track him better, so nothing is lost in trying.

Shane and I tried rattling in this type of situation several times while hunting in Canada during the 2002 season. The bucks simply were not responding well to rattling at that time and we didn't have much luck. Any experienced horn rattler has been through periods like that and knows that it's simply a matter of timing. For whatever reason, those few days were not the time to rattle. But Shane's faith in the technique, if not in my skills at executing it, was illustrated when we left one unsuccessful location. "Tom will be here in a few days," he said to me. "He actually knows what he is doing and we can rattle in some bucks then."

Thanks, pal.

SECTION THREE

MY "EXCELLENT BENOIT ADVENTURE"

Chapter Seven

Ontario 2002

This is a long narrative of a two-week trip I made in 2002 to hunt with the Benoits in Ontario, Canada. My primary focus was to shoot photos and gather information for this book. While those kinds of activities get in the way of serious hunting, I did buy a license with the intent of hunting and shooting a good buck myself. This is written from my perspective and its intent is both to entertain and to teach. Throughout it you will find tips, tactics, techniques, and tidbits about the Benoit's hunting style. But you will also find a lot of insight into the personalities of the Benoit Brothers and how they approach deer hunting. Included in all this are some of the changes they have made in equipment and hunting style.

Because I make most of my living writing about and photographing hunting, I have been lucky enough to have experienced whitetail hunting just about every way it is legally practiced and in most of the best places. I can truthfully say that hunting deer with the Benoits is always a unique adventure. They live a simple and almost primitive life while deer hunting. They bring a small amount of gear and almost all of it is for hunting. They have little time or use for frivolous things or even many of the things that most of us think of as "necessities." This minimalist approach works well for them, but after several days of riding in Shane's truck listening to the same Enya CD (the only one he had in the truck) over and over and over and over, I think he takes this "minimalist" thing way too far.

On this hunt the Benoits and several friends and groupies were packed into a single wall tent, "barracks style," with very little personal room other than that space occupied by their cots. Although the tent had an attached kitchen area that was well stocked, while I was there they never prepared a meal in the traditional fashion of most camps, where all or most of the hunters sat down to eat together. Rather, they mostly heated snacks or small personal meals as each of their schedules allowed or their needs demanded. Mostly, though, they eat on the go. If they are driving through town, they will stop for food at a restaurant or convenience store and usually get it to go. Each of them keeps a "grub box" in their vehicle that is well stocked with snacks, canned goods, and junk food. It takes a lot of energy to hunt hard all day long, and they are constantly eating something, but they have few clearly defined meals.

While they would share a drink and a few minutes of the day's stories each night, clearly camp was not a place for a lot of socializing. Rather it was a place to recharge their tired bodies and in which to endure the hours of mandated abandonment of deer hunting that is forced on them by the lack of daylight. They reminded me of caged animals after dark, submissive to the inevitable, but straining for the freedom that would come with the dawn.

The Benoits are incredibly focused and will let nothing short of a nuclear holocaust distract them from deer hunting. They are in camp only to sleep and very occasionally to eat. If it's daylight, they are out hunting. They never seem to get bored or "burned-out" and it's an amazing thing for me to witness how they maintain the same drive and enthusiasm for deer hunting on the last day that they started with on the first day. If I were forced to identify one single secret to their success, that would be it. They truly expect every single time they head out to hunt they will shoot a trophy buck that day and they keep going, keep focused, and keep hunting, no matter what.

OCTOBER 26, 2002

It is closing in on midnight and I am trying to eat a badly deteriorating sub sandwich that is spewing its contents all over the front of my shirt. At the same

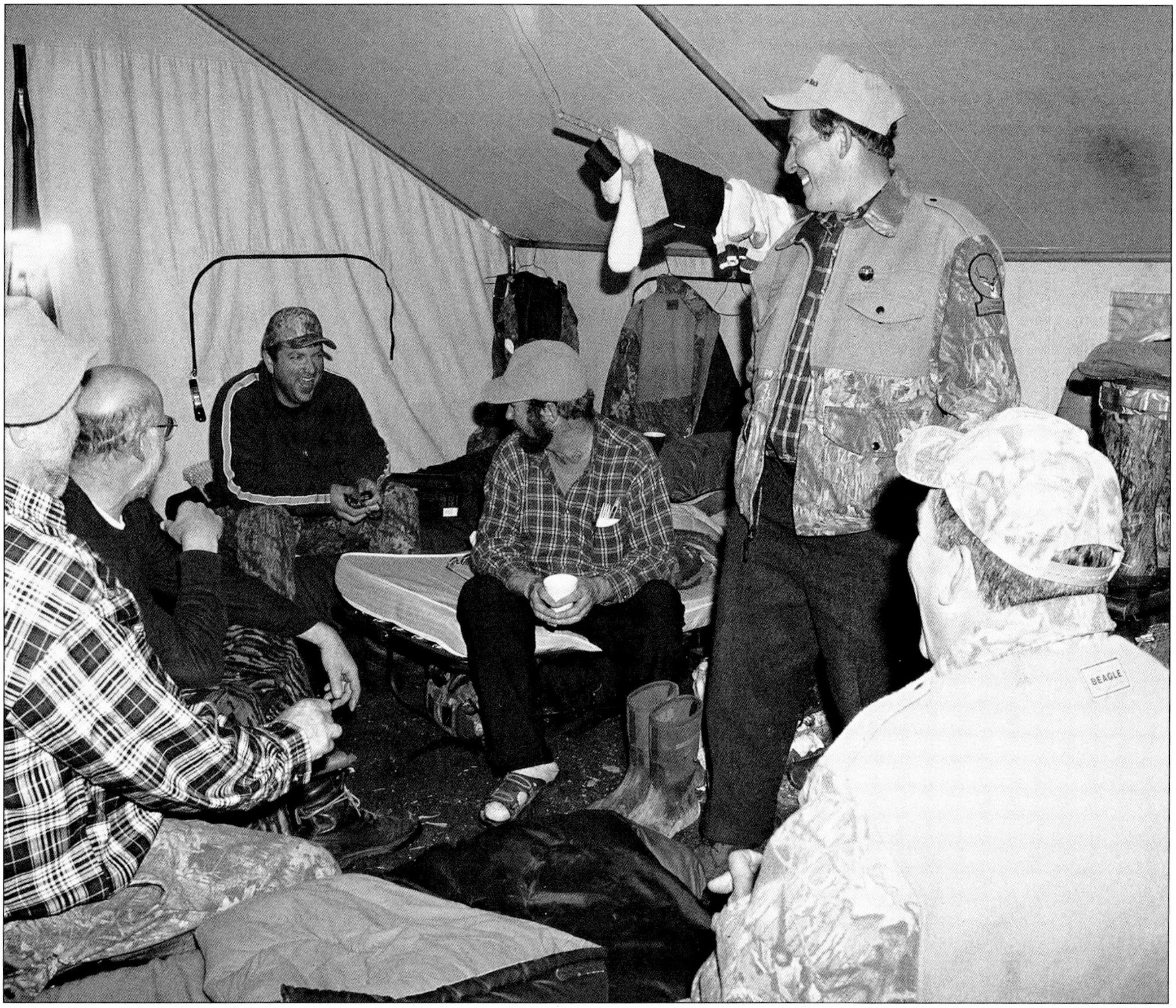

Inside the tent camp in Ontario 2002. Bryce M. Towsley photo.

time, I am driving my slipping and sliding truck while towing a misbehaving trailer down a desolate road that is snow covered and slippery. For the last hour I have been pretty much lost and just as the rapidly falling snow conspired with the whipping wind to cut visibility to about zero, my cell phone rang.

"Where the heck are you?" Shane Benoit asks.

"Somewhere in Canada," is all I could honestly reply.

The Benoits had started out a little ahead of me and were taking a different route initially. The plan was for our paths to converge several hours into the trip. They would stop for the night before I did, and we had planned to meet at the hotel where they ended up, but it turns out that at midnight Shane is about 300 miles from me. This trip is just getting started, but clearly things are not working out quite as well as I had planned. They had made it out just ahead of the storm that is impeding my progress and as a result had experienced a much more productive day.

I had gotten a later start this morning than I had hoped and quickly ran head on into a snowstorm just a few miles from my house. It was slow going, much of it with my truck in four-wheel-drive. Towing my trailer on slippery roads in high winds proved to be a challenge. By the time Shane calls, I have about 18 hours of windshield time behind me and I am exhausted. But I have no clue where the next hotel is located. It might even be the one they are in, for all I know.

When I finally find an open hotel a few hours later, I don't realize until it is too late that they are hosting a high school hockey team in a partying mood. I would have done as well to keep driving. I would have been that much closer to camp and I almost certainly would have gotten more sleep.

OCTOBER 28, 2002

It is mid-morning on the third day when I finally get close to where we will be hunting. I am following a confusing and vague set of directions to the camp when I notice a snow-covered truck with Vermont plates flashing its lights behind me. Shane has been out "tracking" me down. He had passed my truck on the main road while I was too focused on reading the snow-covered road signs to notice, but he had turned around to follow and chase me down this ice-covered dirt road.

We get to the campsite and quickly set up my tent. I am a bit of an insomniac and tend to ramble around much of the night. I like being self-sufficient, so I have brought my own camp with me. In looking at the way the main tent is filled with cots in close quarters—army-barracks style—I know I have made the right decision. I bring a lot of gear, and there is no place for that in the Spartan-style and crowded tent of the Benoit deer camp.

Shane and I wade through the snow behind their tent and start to put up my Cabela's Deluxe Alaknak II outfitter's tent. This tent is designed to go up fast and easy and as soon as I tighten the last guy rope, Shane slams the door on my trailer and locks it.

"This is a killing day. Let's get your license and get to hunting," he says with barely veiled impatience. "You can set up the rest of your camp tonight. I want to get to hunting."

So we go to town for my license. The first place we stop doesn't have them and the lady there insists we can't buy one unless we are hunting with an outfitter. We explain that we can hunt on our own and try to find out who has

Lanny Benoit. Bryce M. Towsley photo.

non-resident licenses, but she is so sure we can't buy one that she won't tell us. Shane is starting to vibrate with impatience to get into the woods, so rather than argue, we simply leave and drive to the next store.

Inside is a tall blonde girl who looks like every fantasy drawing of a Viking Warrior Princess ever pined over by a lusting adolescent. When she comes closer I can see her face is covered with blood, and I start to wonder just how much of it all really is fantasy and how much is real. I am checking her for a sword and wondering how she feels about middle-aged American men, when I notice that she has been working butchering and packaging meat. She smiles and says of course they have non-resident hunting licenses and suddenly she is simply a tall, blonde girl who works at the store and really isn't very threatening at all.

Our "hunt" isn't 10 minutes old when Shane spots a deer standing in the thick brush at the top of a steep ridge. We are only a few miles from camp and really not even "officially" hunting yet. Only the deer's head is

Shane Benoit reflected in truck mirror. Bryce M. Towsley photo.

showing and even that is well hidden by the brush and distance. I am amazed Shane spotted this deer, but I have come to realize he has an outstanding ability to see deer in the woods. It is impossible to tell what the deer is, and at first glance, we think it is a doe. But the neck is very large, which indicates a rutting buck. I grab my 10x40 binoculars and can see he is a 10-point with antlers colored to match the surrounding brush and trees, so that they are blending in and disappearing when viewed by the naked eye. Even after we know he has them, his antlers are hard to see without binos, although he is only 100 yards from us. I can see the antlers are covered with strips of reddish-colored bark hanging in strings, and at first glance, they look like velvet peeling. But this buck is long past all that. His neck is rut-swollen and his hard antlers are polished and stained from hours of rubbing trees. He is a very nice buck, one I would shoot in a heartbeat on most hunts. But I just drove 1,500 miles through the snow to hunt with the Benoits; somehow shooting a buck beside a logging road 10 minutes into it just doesn't seem right. I urge Shane to drive off before I weaken.

I secretly hope I won't regret this decision.

We ride the snow-covered roads as more snow falls to fill in the already blanketed landscape. We are eating up lots of miles as Shane shows me several of the places he found bucks last year. At each place we get out and walk the woods to see if they have returned. Many have, as indicated by the large tracks that litter the ground. We are also finding lots of new bucks in new places as well. This hunt is looking promising, and as we continue to look for tracks and study the land, we start to build a "database" of the bucks lurking about and begin to learn their habits.

The area has been burned off twice, the last time about 20 years ago, and it has been slow to grow back. The two very hot fires apparently killed everything and it took a while for the vegetation to begin the regeneration process. Right now it's in the mid-stages of regenerative growth, and as in most places with good soil, the larger trees are the size of my forearm and the bottoms are choked with the extremely thick brush of the relatively new growth cycle.

The land is a series of steep ridges oriented north and south to display the architectural design of the massive glaciers that once covered them. The land is interspersed with hundreds of lakes and thousands of creeks and streams to feed them. Most of the ridge tops show bedrock and are more open, with fewer trees and brush able to grow among the rocks. The valleys between the ridges are choked and tangled with thick brush, small trees, and blowdowns from the fire-killed trees. In places where the fires spared the trees, the spruce bud worm did not and those trees have also toppled to add to the confusion on the ground. As the afternoon progresses we see tracks from deer, bear, wolf, beaver, rabbits, and grouse, and I think that I like this place.

A couple of hours before dark, we head to a powerline where Shane had shot a good buck the year before. We walk in for half a mile and set up folding chairs behind

Lane with his 2001 buck. Lane Benoit photo.

a big rock that is perched on top of a small but high hill. We are overlooking a deep gully that crosses the powerline and is instantly recognizable to a deer hunter as the kind of place deer love to travel.

The Benoits are deer trackers, pure and simple. When hunting with them in the past, I was often struck by how they are constantly in motion. They all exude an energy during deer season that is barely contained and is always seeping out the cracks to drive them on with a perpetual motion. It's a raw and unharnessed force that's constantly propelling them to go further and faster. I don't know for sure what it is, and I can't define it or even describe it adequately, but I am certain that it's never still. So I am still dealing with the shock of sitting on a stand with a Benoit when the first buck appears. He comes from a direction we don't expect and the little 4-point buck is halfway across the powerline before I notice him. He continues on his path until he's just 50 yards from us when he hits the trail where we walked in and smells our tracks. This little buck is no fool; he simply looks along the track until he sees us sitting on top of the hill. The rock we are depending on for cover is of no use from that angle and he quickly spots us silhouetted against the gray sky. Not sure what we are, he runs only a short way into the woods and stands in the trees staring at us for several more minutes.

A mix of rain and wet snow is falling as dark begins to put out its feelers. I am looking through Shane's scope to see how it gathers light. When I swing the scope to the dark trees across the power line to look into the shadows they are creating, I can see a doe standing on the edge of the trees, but she is alone. Then it's dark and we must leave. As we trudge back to the truck through the gathering cold, I consider that it's been a great "first" day.

OCTOBER 29, 2002

Shane and I hunt together. This is the first full day of hunting, and as usual, the Benoit game plan is to drive the passable roads and walk those a truck can't get down. We are not so much hunting as we are building a database of information. The Benoits like to get a feel for the bucks in the area—where they are living and traveling, what they are doing and where their "favorite" places are. If a track looks promising they will follow it, but mostly they are just scoping out the area and learning all they can about the whitetail activity. While I only have a few days, they are here for a month, and plenty of time remains for them to shoot a buck. To a man, they are in no hurry to end it this soon. Even though they are driven to hunt, they seem almost casual about actually shooting a buck.

I am reminded of the bear hunters I used to run with. They called it bear *hunting*, but shooting a bear was not a big part of the equation. These were hound men and their joy was in running the dogs. On occasion they would allow somebody to shoot because, after all, it was bear *hunting* and hunting, to remain valid, requires that game be taken. But clearly it was nothing more than justification for what they truly loved to do, and that was to chase black bears with their hound dogs. The Benoits are from the same mold—it's not so much about shooting a buck as it is about hunting whitetails. They will procrastinate, stall, and find every reason in the world not to pull the trigger. It's a subconscious motivation and one they probably are not even aware of on most levels. I don't think it's something they think about, and if asked, I am sure they would deny it; but it is strongly evident to me, and I see it in all three of the Benoit brothers. To shoot a buck is the ultimate goal in the most gaunt and shallow of explanations about what they do, but that's not what they love most or what motivates and drives them. That is simply the love of hunting whitetails and the joy they find in tracking big bucks. Pulling the trigger puts an end to all of that and in some light will appear as an almost undesirable act. They will eventually shoot a buck on this hunt, of that point each of them is extremely confident, but it will be only when they are ready and when the timing is right. They have the skills, ability, and confidence to wait until the last week or even the final few days of the season.

Time and again I have seen this pattern, where they shoot little or nothing for weeks and then in the final days of the season strain the game pole to the breaking point. When they do pull the trigger, they are, I am sure, filled with the same range of emotions any true hunter feels, but they also must experience a sense of loss in

Wolf tracks. Bryce M. Towsley photo.

knowing what they love most in life is finished and gone for another year.

The ground is covered with a light dusting of fresh snow and there was clearly a lot of deer activity during the night. We look at lots of tracks and with each one Shane puts another piece on the table that is supporting this mental jigsaw puzzle representing the buck activity here.

We stop to look at one big track, and Shane and Dave Coker, who is following along behind us, discuss the deer. The buck has big feet, as indicated by the huge tracks, but they think he is young because he is not flattening his feet out on the hard surface of the road. This would indicate that his weight doesn't match his feet and frame. His length of step and foot size are both large, which indicates that, while this is likely a large-framed buck, he has not filled out in weight yet, so he is probably a young deer. Sort of like a teenager who has sprung up to the height and framework of an adult, but not the weight that will come with maturity. We think it may be the 10-point that Shane and I saw yesterday, as this is close to the same location, but this deer looks bigger. In the end they decide not to follow the buck, although I can't help but secretly wonder how much trouble he would be in if this were the last rather than first week of the hunt.

We are seeing a lot of wolf tracks in the road this morning and I wonder if they are as selective in their hunting as we are. I suspect not, and I wonder how hard it is for a deer to grow old here.

Shane and I go far down the narrow road to a large lake. Shane had mentioned yesterday he had wanted to check out the thick and remote country along the edge of this big lake. We quickly cut a big buck track entering that thick and inaccessible section of land. We make a huge circle on the trails and roads that border this section and an hour later we know that the buck has not exited. We have three sides of the block covered. Two we looked at, while the lake forms a border of the third. It's possible that he simply continued on a straight course and is deep in the woods on the bearing we can't reach. But this was not a buck that was in a traveling mood, and Shane's guess is that he has bedded down on the wind-protected side of one of the steep ridges.

We walk a side road that runs perpendicular to the "main" road, cutting deep into the woods to split the land down the middle. We find that the buck has not crossed and deduce that if he is still in these woods, we have just narrowed the possibilities by about half. Our guess is the buck is probably still in the woods along the lake, unless he has traveled out the one end we cannot check, but we have now made those woods smaller. We also find two more buck tracks entering this section of woods. Shane points out the wisdom of checking the area as completely as possible to get a handle on what is going on. Not only have we confirmed as much as possible that the first buck is likely still in this piece of woods, but we have also discovered two others that are in there as well. This would indicate something they like. Perhaps a hot doe, but it's still early in the rut and we are not seeing many indications of breeding does. Shane thinks it's probably just as he suspected when he found this place last year, that this is simply an area that bucks like, a place where they feel comfortable. It's a natural travel corridor, as the 5-mile-long lake forms a barrier that couples with another lake about a mile away to shape a classic, although wide, "funnel" between the two. Any deer that's wandering must come through here, but also this long series of ridges forms a natural travel route between the two lakes.

One of the bedrock ridges in Ontario. Benoit Brothers photo.

We finally locate the big buck's track on yet another grown-over road leading to an isolated camp on the lake. We follow it into woods that are incredibly thick. The only open areas are the ridgetops where the bedrock, exposed by the relentless winds, allows little vegetation to take hold. While these higher areas are "open," comparatively speaking, even they are thick with small trees and brush. There is a lot of buck sign—rubs, scrapes, and tracks—and they seem to favor running the parallel ridgetops. Perhaps because it's easier to move in the thinner vegetation, and they know that the safety of cover is only a jump away. I doubt they are aware that humans are after their hides this early in the game, but the wolves no doubt are always on their minds. The bucks seem to move in one of two general directions: east or west through the thick brush between the ridges, or north and south along the tops of the ridges.

We decide to move up one of the ridges and Shane says he wants to stop to try to rattle the buck out. Again, I am in shock. I look at Shane's rifle and see a scope rather than a peep sight and the trademark green-and-black-checked jacket is gone, replaced by a high-tech wool coat in a camo pattern. He has binoculars, a grunt call, and he wants to stop to rattle antlers. I look around for pods, sure that there has been an invasion of Benoit Body Snatchers. I decide if he pulls a treestand out of his truck later, I should probably shoot this alien invader inhabiting Shane Benoit's body.

As we approach the ridgetop, a buck spooks. He was standing about halfway up and off to the side where he was hidden by the thick trees and brush. He watched our approach, but didn't spook until we passed and the steady quartering wind allowed our scent to reach him. I hear him leave as his hoofs hit the ground, but do not see him. Shane is a few yards ahead of me and has a different view. I see his rifle snap to his shoulder as he watches the buck charge off. Then we both see him topping the next ridge and within seconds he is over it and gone.

We are both pretty sure it's a different buck than the one we are tracking. A quick check of the tracks on the ground confirms that, so we try rattling anyway, giving it half an hour with no success. We continue on the track of the bigger buck, and as we do we are passing a lot of buck sign, both from him and from many other bucks. Surprisingly, there are few tracks from does or fawns. Almost all of the tracks here are from bucks. Clearly this is a place where bucks feel comfortable. It's probably the whitetail equivalent of a hoary old camp that is so infiltrated and infested with testosterone that only men are comfortable inside its walls.

The snow is sparse along the windblown tops and there are lots of tracks from many different bucks. It's very hard tracking, and we have our heads down looking at the tracks too much, which is probably why we didn't see that first buck in time. It's hard to watch for deer and follow the tracks at the same time. For one man alone, it's all but impossible. We are "double-teaming," where Shane is tracking while I keep my eyes sweeping for the buck, but it's still probably a hopeless cause. The snow is frozen hard and is crunchy. Walking is very noisy and clearly we need more snow to allow easier tracking and to make our footsteps less vocal.

We stop at noon on a windswept and barren section of bedrock. We eat cold SpaghettiOs and Beefaroni from small "personal size" cans we had pilfered hours earlier from the "grub box" that perpetually resides in the back of Shane's truck. I start to scoop the cold and congealed glop out with my hunting knife, but I am so cold I can't trust my hands and am afraid I'll slice off my tongue, so I use my fingers. This is a source of hilarity to Shane until he finally hands me a plastic spoon. After that I emulate him and carry one in my shirt pocket on each day of the hunt.

Sometime after lunch we find some odd-looking buck sign where a big-bodied deer has made a single, deep gouge in a pine tree. We also find a similar mark on a dead tree, but here there are two gouges. There is hair in two locations on a small tree next to the gouged tree. The white hair on one tree indicates he was pushing the tree around with his butt while he made twin passes at the larger, dead tree with his antlers. He is clearly a big buck, but he seems a bit confused about exactly how this tree-rubbing thing works.

Shane Benoit eating lunch in Ontario. Bryce M. Towsley photo.

We track this buck through a bottom absolutely choked with small birch trees and tipped over, burned-out tree carcasses. There are so many blowdowns from the fire-damaged trees that, without following the deer path that weaves through, human passage would be almost impossible. The genius of navigation these deer possess is strongly evident as we twist and turn through this seemingly impassable section of woods. Clearly a multitude of bucks travel through here often, and this would be a great location for an ambush. Except there are no big trees for a treestand and it's far too thick to use a ground blind. As I think about this, I realize perhaps one reason they travel through here so much is they feel safe. My guess is not only is it "hunter proof," but they can also easily escape from marauding wolves in this thick cover. Obviously, they know this at some level and travel freely through here.

As the trail approaches the ridge, it begins to split and disperse like a river approaching its delta. By the time they climb the ridge, the one trail has become many, but for a stand hunter the ridgetop would be the only choice. There still are no big trees for a treestand, but a ground blind might work here. We find a spot that overlooks the exit at the bottom where the trails begin to split and mark the location with a GPS so that we might return to take a stand later in the week. We talk about doing exactly that, but we both know we probably never will.

We follow the buck's tracks up the ridge and on to the top where he turns south. The snow is thin here where the wind and sun have worked and worried it. There are many different buck tracks and it is getting impossible to stay with one deer. We finally decide to declare the buck the winner of this round and to head back to the truck.

It's the first full day of deer hunting the Benoit way and neither of us is as "woods" conditioned as we need to be. Shane has been carrying his heavy video camera and has somehow wrenched his back, so the weight is aggravating the injury and I take the camera from him. I have a torn cartilage in my right knee on which I had been stalling surgery until after hunting season. Of course, I catch my foot on a root and twist the knee until it feels like a hot knife shooting through the joint, and I choke back a pain-induced scream. Shane soon follows my lead as we both collapse on the ground. The grimaces of pain, though, soon turn to laughter.

"This 'getting old' crap ain't all it's cracked up to be," I wail. Shane is the "baby" of the Benoit family, but like me, he is staring hard at fifty years of age. We sit there on that ridge for a while, neither willing to admit we need the break. To pass the time we talk about getting old and all the things we "use-ta-could do" but can't or don't want to do anymore. This leads to a discussion about how getting older has affected the Benoits' hunting styles. Shane points out he hunts smarter now, more with his head and less with his feet, and that this change has actually resulted in more and better bucks.

"I realize now that thinking is better than bulling and jamming," Shane says. "I just wish I had realized that years ago."

Later, as we are driving back to camp, we round a corner to see a very large buck standing in the logging road. He appears very tall and long-legged, almost like a moose. His rack is tall and wide and Shane thinks he sees 9 points. I bail out of the truck, load my rifle and rush up the hill, but he has picked well where to stop. The buck is watching and listening to my approach. I hear him crashing through the brush as he runs away, seconds before I crest the steep hill.

Back at the truck, Shane says he thinks this buck is in a traveling mood and getting a shot at him will probably require a lot of time and effort. He admits he is not up to it because of his back, but my knee feels better and I am fired up. I take the trail while Shane waits at the truck. The buck heads through some evergreen trees where there is almost no snow cover. I am forced to watch the ground too much in order to follow the track. It's slow tracking, and unless I can move faster, I will have almost no chance of seeing the buck. I follow up the hill into better snow, but the brush is very thick. The buck is not running, but is walking with long, purposeful strides that are eating ground at a good rate, and I am starting to realize that Shane was right. This is a buck that's going to be hard to catch. I have followed the track for some time now and his pace has not wavered. I know that to catch him will take a lot of time and effort, but I hate to admit it just yet. Finally, I have little more than an hour until dark, so I leave the track and try to cut on a straight line back to the road.

Some odd buck sign that Shane and the author found while hunting Ontario in 2002. Note the gouges on the trees. This buck was confused about this "tree-rubbing" thing.

Benoit Brothers photo.

Shane Benoit on the track in Ontario 2002. Note how thick the brush is.

Bryce M. Towsley photo.

Finding the road is taking a long time and I have walked a very long way. When tracking a buck it's easy to lose perspective on time and distance, and I don't recall having come this far. I am sure I am headed in the right direction, but I start to second-guess myself. I have no compass, GPS, or fire-starting tools. The GPS and fire starter I had forgotten this morning when leaving camp. The compass was in my heavy coat back in Shane's truck. I was concentrating so hard on the difficult track that I didn't watch the land and now nothing looks quite right. While I try not to think about how lightly dressed I am, I force myself to trust my instincts and continue in the direction I am still pretty sure is correct. Finally I hit the road, but the track had run quartering from it and it's a long way back to the truck. The approaching night is muting the colors when I finally open the door and tumble into the warmth of the heater.

I realize I have dodged a bullet, even if it was a small one. This is how hunters die—not on elaborate expeditions deep into the wilderness, but on "short" hunts that were only supposed to last a few minutes. I think of the other times in my long hunting career when I have gotten into trouble, and many are consistent with that thought. I remember the time I beached the boat to climb a hill and look at a caribou, but wound up hours later standing in the rain and stranded on the edge of a wilderness lake. I think of the time we left the Range Rover to look at a herd of Cape buffalo and found ourselves hours later stumbling lost and waterless through the 115-degree heat. Another time, a quick fall turkey hunt ended with me "camping" for the night under a spruce tree, wet, snow-covered, and close to hypothermia. The common theme was that I had only planned to be gone for a few minutes and left unprepared. In reading hundreds of accounts of other hunters in trouble, that same theme often emerges, and I remind myself again how important it is to always be prepared.

I know to always have a knife, two ways to make a fire, and a compass with me every time I step into the woods, but like anybody else, I sometimes get lazy. Due to sloppy habits and muddled thinking I broke those rules this day. Nothing happened this time, but that's not the point. It could have. It almost did.

I say nothing about this to Shane, but instead concentrate on telling him about the buck. But once in the truck, I quietly put the compass in my shirt pocket where it belongs. That night at camp I put the GPS on my belt and a butane lighter and a magnesium fire starter in my pants pockets.

It's been a great day and we all gather in my tent to toast with a sip of Kentucky's finest. Dave Coker has a great story about three different bucks in front of him all at the same time. They are all trophy-size deer that would make most hunters happy, but it's early in the season and

Above: Knife, matches, and magnesium fire starter. Always bring a knife and two ways to start a fire when you enter the woods. Bryce M. Towsley photo.

Left: Silva compass and Garmin Etrex GPS. GPS has changed big woods navigation and has all but eliminated the fear of getting lost. Bryce M. Towsley photo.

he elected to pass on them. There was a new cameraman with him who should have had some outstanding footage of these bucks posturing and sparring. New and trying to break into the business, this could have been footage that opened doors. He "filmed it all" but never turned on the camera.

Two hours past the arrival of black dark, one of our party, Jed Ruhl, has not yet returned to camp, and I am thinking of my afternoon. Dave Coker and cameraman Dave Jacques go to look for him. They find him a mile from camp, soaked with sweat, exhausted and happy. He shot a 10-point buck and has been dragging it since 1 p.m. Jed is not a big man and I think the buck outweighed him by 80 pounds or more. It's a testament to his toughness that he dragged the buck as long as he did. He says this is the same buck he shot at the day before. He went back today and tracked it for miles, and when he realized he was close, he blew on his grunt call. The buck charged down his back trail and right into his destiny.

OCTOBER 30, 2002

Shane's back is still bothering him, so we take my Dodge truck because it's much larger and more comfortable than his compact Toyota (I also have a much better, not to mention larger, CD selection). We ride for miles looking for tracks, but in contrast to the day before, there is little fresh sign. The reason escapes us, but it's evident the deer are not moving. It's turned very cold and perhaps that's part of it, but these Canadian bucks are used to cold weather. We see one doe cross a remote logging road and get ready in case a buck is following, but nothing shows and finally we are so cold that it's doubtful we could hold a rifle still enough to hit a buck if he did show. We do see a red fox, which we watch for a long time. He stops at the top of a ledge and sits down, where he stares at us unafraid until I get out of the truck to shoot a photo.

We travel new roads into new country and into a huge, fresh clear-cut that runs for miles. We need firewood and stop to fill my truck from the scraps piled along the road. I had expected to see deer sign, as bucks like to walk in the roads along these remote and deserted clearcuts, but there are almost no tracks here.

This faint trail we are following comes to a remote railroad crossing and we have to wait for a very long train to pass. I regret that we didn't count the cars, but it had to be well into the hundreds. When they are finally clear, we can cross, and we take a shadow of a road that follows a huge power line. In a display of poor sportsmanship, or just plain stupidity, another hunter has parked his truck in the center of the road. I pull my rig into four-wheel-drive and go around it. I stop near the top of the hill, perhaps 500 yards past the truck to photograph a wolf track and

Jeremiah "Jed" Ruhl with a nice buck he took in Ontario 2002. Bryce M. Towsley photo.

am startled by two loud and very close rifle shots. I turn to see the other hunter exiting the woods and running for his truck. Apparently he was upset we were driving down this public trail and interrupting his "hunting." He showed his dissatisfaction by shooting, I suppose to scare or intimidate us. I am saddened to think this level of "sportsman" is still among us, but we get back in my truck and continue on so we won't bother him further. We stop often to check out tracks, some we follow for a bit, but none is fresh enough to excite us. We stop in several places and walk ahead to rattle antlers at likely deer crossings. But the deer activity is slow today, and we don't see another whitetail for quite some time.

Hours later we enter yet another clear-cut where Shane located a big buck last year. He spots a doe 300 yards away (I verified it with a rangefinder) with only her head visible. This is the first deer we have seen in hours. The remarkable thing is how Shane was able to see it, and I marvel again at his outstanding deer-spotting ability. We watch the doe with binoculars for a while, but it's alone, so we leave it and head for the powerline stand where we had hunted the first night. In the trail to our stand are tracks made by a very big buck. He had crossed through the gully our stand overlooks, and we think we made a mistake not coming here last night.

It's extremely cold and windy. Waiting on this hilltop is brutal work, and the lack of deer activity is doing nothing to make it easier to endure. I finally see a lone doe just before dark. She is 400 yards away, near where Shane shot his buck last year. We watch until dark, but clearly she is a social outcast with no companions to help her through the cold night ahead.

Back at camp we learn that Lane's day was more active, as he had shot a large and beautiful wolf. The 120-pound male was in peak condition with fur as prime as I have ever seen. Lane had seen ravens working an area near a frozen beaver dam, and had quietly crept in to see what they were fussing about. He caught the wolf feeding on a beaver carcass, and took him cleanly with a single 30-06 bullet. I have hunted in wolf country many times in a bunch of different locations. I have held a dozen or more tags, and while I have seen several, I have never had an opportunity to shoot one of these magnificent trophies. I am happy for my friend's success, but at the same time I am insanely jealous.

Tonight we sit in the tent around the big wood stove and discuss the way the Benoit Brothers have changed their whitetail hunting tactics. One point they discuss is the warming winters that have been a trend in recent years and the increasing lack of snow during hunting season. (Although, as I write this in February 2003, the Northeast is experiencing one of the snowiest and coldest winters in decades.) While we have no lack of snow at the moment, during the 2001 hunting season in Canada, they hunted all but a few days on bare ground. In recent years Maine, Vermont, New Hampshire, and even Canada show bare ground through much of the deer season and leaves are the forest's carpet as often as snow during the deer-hunting season. This has

Lane Benoit with wolf in Ontario 2002.

Bryce M. Towsley photo.

forced the Benoits to adapt and change tactics. They can track on bare ground under certain conditions, but only for a short distance and in reality it's not very effective unless the buck is very close to start with. Bare-ground hunting is a tough situation and tracking is not always viable, but the Benoits are deer hunters and predators, so not hunting is never an option. They have been able to adapt their whitetail knowledge with new hunting techniques to continue to be successful despite the lack of snow. In the past couple of years, all of the Benoit Brothers have taken big bucks while sitting on a stand. It might appear as a sacrilege to a tracking purist, but they did what they had to do. Even if tracking is not possible, not hunting is never an option.

For the past 4 years Tom Blais and Great Northern Productions have also been filming their hunts. While the Benoits have made a few changes to their hunting style when there is snow on the ground to accommodate the camera, they have had to make more drastic changes to their bare-ground tactics. The amazing thing, though, is they are probably taking more deer on bare ground as a result of all these changes than ever before.

This is proof that a great hunter is never one-dimensional. If you are bound by a single hunting technique and have neither the skill nor the insight to adapt to conditions and to use other techniques, then you will never achieve a high level of success. A great hunter may have

Bryce M. Towsley in the Benoit tent camp.

Bryce M. Towsley photo.

Inside the tent camp in Ontario 2002. Bryce M. Towsley photo.

his preferred style of hunting and may be best at that, but he will also adapt to the situation when that technique can't be used and switch to another tactic. While the Benoits are trackers, they are also great hunters and they recognize they must change and adapt. They must adapt to the fact they are getting older, they must adapt to the fact the climate is changing, and they must adapt to the self-imposed changes brought on by the difficulty of filming their hunts.

We also talk about the changes they have made in equipment such as optics, boots, clothing, and guns. Shane tells how he once used 220-grain 30-06 round nose ammo and chuckles at the contrast with the sleek, plastic-tipped 130-grain Hornady Light Magnum 270 Winchester ammo he shoots today. Shane quietly says that the whitetail survives because it is so adaptable, and if the whitetail hunter is to continue to survive and be successful, he had better follow that lead by learning to change and adapt too.

Late that night I am deep in my sleeping bag and sleeping soundly when I am startled awake by a loud wolf howl just outside my tent. I lie in my sleeping bag and listen, wondering if I really heard it or simply dreamed that I did. But then I can hear them walking outside the tent. There are several of them, and they are close. I can hear them bumping and digging at my coolers outside the tent door, trying to get at the food inside. I curse the foolish Canadian laws that have my rifle cased and locked inside my truck as I slip on my boots and grab a flashlight. As soon as I move the zipper on the tent, I hear them rushing off into the woods and the beam finds nothing but tracks and a tipped-over cooler. The light of morning shows even more clearly the evidence of their visit, as their tracks are large and prominent in the fresh snow all around my tent.

Many so called "experts" state unequivocally that wolves will always avoid contact with humans if given a choice. Like so many other "truths" spoken by today's brand of wildlife "experts," this is clearly anything but the truth. I don't recall inviting these canines to raid my food supply and certainly they had a choice to stay in the woods and away from our camp.

I lie on my cot long into the night thinking about how wildlife management is shifting from true science to emotional thinking and to following the popular myths that are promoted as fact. This Disneyesque-style of wildlife

The "gang" hunting in New Hampshire. Bryce M. Towsley photo.

Wolf tracks. Bryce M. Towsley photo.

management, one where voter referendum and the tyranny of the masses is substituted for proven science and trained professionals, can only lead to bad things for wildlife and for hunters. It's hours before I am able to let that go and drift back to sleep. It seems that as soon as I do, the alarm clock is assaulting my ears and it's time to go deer hunting again.

I am thankful that at least for now we still have that option.

OCTOBER 31, 2002

It's 14 degrees Fahrenheit at dawn, the fire went out hours ago and my tent is cold. I feel an intense hatred growing for the alarm clock and I lie in bed letting it ring for a long time before I poke an arm out into the cold air to shut it off. It takes a superhuman effort to leave the warm comfort of my huge sleeping bag and step into that refrigerated mass of arctic atmosphere. I dress as quickly as possible with fingers too cold to work the buttons and then stuff my cold feet into boots that are stiff and icy.

It is very cold this morning and everything is frozen. The food in the coolers is all frozen. All my water has turned to ice, even that kept inside the tent. Brushing my teeth is impossible and will have to wait for another time. This relentless cold is wearing me down, and it's hard to believe I will ever be warm again. What seems like hours later, the wood stove is finally warming the inside of the

Box of Hornady Light Magnum SST 270 130-grain ammo in the pocket of a Beagle jacket. Bryce M. Towsley photo.

tent just a little. But in this cold, that's enough; except it's wasted as I leave it behind to follow Shane to the frost-covered truck where we "mount up" for another day.

I discover that all the soda cans in the back of my truck have frozen and exploded. There is frozen soda all over everything. It's not a mess right now, but it's got to warm up sooner or later, although at times I question that fact. Intellectually I know it will, but it doesn't seem like it right now.

We wait for daylight along the road near a place the bucks often travel. A familiar truck with Vermont plates passes us in the dark. We have been seeing it all week and Shane comments on the difficulty in finding a place to be left alone to hunt.

"I know those guys," he says. "They came into our area last year, so we moved out and found this place. Now they have followed us here. The area we left to them last year was just as good as here, in fact I think it has more big bucks, but they have to follow us. They think we know something they don't, that we have some secret place that's full of big bucks, but we don't. We are just looking for some country where we can hunt without being bothered. This was a problem in Maine and is a big part of why we stopped hunting in the Jackman area. Every place we go, other hunters follow. I suppose we should be flattered, but it spoils our hunting experience. We don't like to hunt where the crowds are gathered, but rather the opposite. We will hunt in marginal country just to avoid them. But, they keep finding us and crowding us out again."

Things are slow all morning and at midday we stop by a remote lake to eat lunch. As we are sitting in the truck eating frozen sandwiches, we are watching the far shore in hopes that we might see a buck. I wonder if we could even consider shooting that far when Shane, who must have been thinking the same thing, asks how far I think it is to a big rock perched on the edge of the lake. We both make our guesses before I step out of the truck with my rangefinder to find we are both wrong. It's 405 yards from us, which to an honest rifleman is a very long way.

We decide to try a little long-range shooting, and Shane hits the big rock with his scoped gun three out of five shots, which is good shooting. With his peep-sighted gun he manages to hit it only one time out of five tries. But the front bead is larger than the rock at that distance and it covers it up completely. Hold over is a guessing game because he can't see the target. Clearly it's too far for shooting with iron sights.

I am watching through a spotting scope mounted on the truck window and I can see the bullets arch into the rock. With high-velocity bullets such as those from his 270 Winchester, I have only witnessed this at extremely long range when the velocity has started to drop. Today they gleam like miniature fighter jets as they track through the cold, clear Canadian air. They appear to cleave it like ice, as they leave a brief contrail that is visible behind them for just a fraction of a second.

All week I have been watching the master at his game in tracking bucks, but now he wants to romp in my playground. I make a good portion of my living writing about guns, and as a result I shoot a lot. I also shoot a lot because I love to shoot. One of my big thrills is long-range rifle shooting. I was privately getting a little cocky about showing off, but it's so cold I am worried about trigger control when I can't feel my fingers.

I have three rifles with me and I shoot each of them several times at a patch of snow on the rock. I hit the snow or very close to it every time. The last three shots are with the three different rifles, and they form a group that is less than 6 inches at its widest point. I have shot enough publicly to know this is a great time to quit, so I case the rifles and jump back in the truck. Shane doesn't say anything, but I figure it's because he is in such awe as to be rendered speechless.

We spend the afternoon scouting for tracks, and we walk the trails, stopping often to rattle; the bucks simply are not interested. Shane has been telling me about a peninsula on a lake where a big buck was hanging out last year. It was clearly a "favorite place" for this buck and he was able to find him at home several times last season. With a rather narrow peninsula, it would appear to the uninitiated this buck was headed for immortality by posing for photos with a Benoit holding his head up. But, as anybody who has ever hunted whitetails knows, things are not always what they would seem. The buck escaped without a scratch several times last season. Not just from Shane, but from all the Benoits. They combined their talents to do battle with this buck, but the cagey old general won every skirmish. The only serious mistake he made was when he ran out to cross the road in front of Craig Jaques. Had Craig been ready, he would have had an easy shot, but his truck was having alternator problems. When the buck appeared, he had a Craftsman wrench in his hand rather than a Remington rifle. The buck sauntered off with an arrogant swagger and was gone long before Craig could arm himself. Time and again, both the buck and the Benoits returned to this spit of land and time and again the buck escaped.

Shane Benoit sits at a bench and glasses across a lake to look for a buck that lives on a peninsula.

Bryce M. Towsley photo.

Shane and I walk the peninsula to see if, like us, the buck had returned this year. While we find lots of deer sign, including some recent rutting activity, Shane is unable to locate his distinctive tracks. After an hour of searching, he concludes the buck has not returned. Maybe he finally took the hint that his luck was stretching thin and moved to a less Benoit-infested section of woods. Or perhaps on some cold and lonely winter night, the wolves finally did what the Benoits could not and this worthy adversary greeted his fate.

It's too late to follow a track, so in the last hours of the day Shane wants to sit on a big ledge overlooking a crossing that was seeing a lot of use last year. There are old tracks from big bucks in this aging snow, but there are few fresh tracks. But as Shane points out, big bucks in big woods generally travel in a big circuitous travel route (or as the Benoits call it, "his swing") that takes about 3 days to complete. Shane is convinced a buck will cross here again soon in spite of the lack of fresh tracks. This was a well-used crossing last year, but a wild card has appeared in the form of a new beaver dam that has altered the deer movement leading up to this place.

I walk up the logging road about half a mile and sit at another crossing, but I don't like it, so I move. I find another location I like much better overlooking the same crossing. I hunker down in the icy rocks and pull back into my wool coat. It's very cold and windy. It's not just the cold now, but that it's been with us for so long without pause. For days now it has been uncommonly frigid, even for Canada. With the tent camps, it's hard to ever really be warm and it wears on you psychologically, as well as physically. Waiting on stand allows a lot of time to think, and as I consider this relentless cold, I believe it would cause a lot of casual or less-dedicated deer hunters to call it quits. One of many keys to the Benoit success is they are even more relentless than the weather. They keep working and keep hunting no matter what. They don't go back to camp because they are cold and they don't quit the hunt because they have been cold for too many days. They instead keep working as hard as they can and they keep focused on the goal. That closely focused persistence is a big factor in their success.

Just before dark a doe comes out and crosses 150 yards in front of me. She keeps looking back over her shoulder, so I brace my 35 Whelen on my knees and slip off the safety. She turns back and disappears into the woods that birthed her. A few minutes later she reappears, not with a buck, but with two fawns. I slip the safety back on and relax my grip on the rifle. They all run up this icy logging road straight at me. The fawns are slipping on the ice and having trouble with traction. This is their first winter and may well be the first time they have encountered slick ice. Mama,

Bryce M. Towsley with a large whitetail buck taken in Arkansas 1999. Without binoculars, he wouldn't have gotten this buck. Kevin Howard photo.

on the other hand, has no trouble at all with the footing, a result I suspect of several years of practice. They come very close to me, only a few yards away, and begin to feed in the high yellow grass along this opening on the edge of the road. In this fading, flat, gray light I realize if I take my eyes off them and look away, they are almost impossible to see again until they move. It makes me wonder how many deer go unnoticed by even the best hunters. I suspect it would drive us crazy to know the truth.

The deer feed for some time before the doe goes back into the road and starts up it, looking intensely at something behind me. I wonder if a buck has finally made an appearance. I could use the rocks I am hiding in to cover me as I stand and turn to look, but I can't move as the two smaller deer have me pinned down. The doe is moving up past my position only a few feet from me. From her body language, I think perhaps it's a buck behind me, but I can't do anything but watch. Finally, she walks into my scent stream, and like a puff of smoke on a windy day, they are all gone. I am cold and it's getting too dark, so I start the long walk back to the truck.

Shane is there with the heater going and I am thankful. He tells me how he came close. He could actually hear a buck rubbing a tree near the beaver pond, and even see the top of the tree moving, but because it was back in the shadows, he could never see the deer beyond a few flickering movements.

In my never-ending quest to bring the Benoit's choice of equipment into the new millennium, I explain how good binoculars would have helped him in this situation. With a pair of high-quality 10x40 binoculars, he would have been able to look into those shadows and perhaps see the buck. Of course, shooting him with a peep sight would have been impossible, but Shane's rifle that day wore a scope.

During the long drive back to camp I tell him about my best week of deer hunting. A few years back I shot a big, long-tined, 9-point whitetail along the Belle Fourche River in northeast Wyoming. Then exactly one week later, I shot a huge 10-point while hunting in central Arkansas, my best buck ever. My point was that I located both bucks under difficult conditions by using high-quality binoculars. Without the binoculars and my willingness to use them, I would not have taken either buck.

There are new and changing tactics being employed by the Benoits—tactics that are an addendum to tracking, not a replacement. These have been a catalyst in some of the changes in their equipment and Shane says that after the frustrating half hour he spent tonight, he can see the truth in my argument.

Realizing I had won my point, I did a rare thing and shut up.

NOVEMBER 1, 2002

A new month. Winter is closer and the air feels it today. It's cold and thick and seems to have a substance you can see. In the flat gray light, it's as if you are looking through a diffuser designed to scatter and weaken even more the feeble November North-Country sunlight.

Shane Benoit using Swarovski 10X42 binoculars to look for a buck he knew lived across a lake.

Bryce M. Towsley photo.

The humidity is high, making it seem colder, and it feels like it will snow soon.

Shane and I walk to a high ridge overlooking a big lake and set up to rattle. It's cold, and given the response so far, neither of us has much faith in rattling today, so we give it up too soon.

After abandoning our setup, we only walked a short distance before we found a fresh track running away from us. Could this have been from a buck responding to our rattling? There is no way to know, but the lesson is clear that we should have stayed for the pre-agreed length of time rather than abandoning the stand too early.

We take the track and follow it for several miles. But when the buck moves up high to run the top of one of the barren ridges, it becomes hard to follow. There are lots of other deer tracks and the snow has been blown thin on this exposed rocky ground. The main vegetation here is a carpet of thick and low-growing blueberry bushes. The effect is like a covering of cheaply made deep-pile carpet. This makes tracking even more difficult as the bushes spring back from the weight of the buck's foot and fill the track with the loose, powdery snow. Identifying the track as "our buck" is all but impossible. Because there are so many other deer tracks, at times it's hard to even tell which direction "our" track is headed. But Shane stays with it in his patient and methodical way, and he sorts it out until the buck heads back down into the woods. At least we think it's the same buck, but we can't be sure. What we do know is it is the track of a good buck, and it's headed into an area where the snow is better for tracking. If it's "our buck," we have lost a lot of valuable time. If it's a different buck, it probably doesn't matter.

A few hundred yards into the thick cover we find a large, fresh bed with a couple of scrapes and a fresh rub all clustered together. That tells us it's probably a different buck. The sign looks fresh and Shane looks at the location of the stains in the bed, smells them and says it's a buck. I take the opportunity to sarcastically point out that, with tracks leading from the bed to the scrape and then to the rub, I had pretty well figured that out all on my own. Shane calls me a bad name as he gets down on his knees and smells the scrape. "Even though he is scraping, he is not 'rutty' yet," he says. This time I take his word for it.

The buck took the time to work the scrape and rub a tree before walking off, and clearly we hadn't spooked him, so he is at least some distance ahead of us. The bits of bark that fell from rubbing the tree are high on the soft snow and have not melted down into it at all, which tells us he is not too far ahead, though. We take a minute to talk a little about the sign this buck is leaving.

"A mistake most hunters make is they try to smell in the center of the scrape to see if the buck has freshened it recently," Shane says. "But the buck is usually standing so that he is urinating in the edge of the scrape instead of the middle. The hunter should be smelling along the outside of the scrape rather than in the center."

The track leads us through some thick and sheltered areas where there is a lot of fresh deer sign. The trail is worn very deep into the ground, and at one point where it drops down a steep bank, it cuts deep enough into the earth that the top of the ground is level with my knees as I walk along the trail. I am reminded of reading the book *A Hunter's Wanderings in Africa* by the great African explorer, Fredrick Courteney Selous. In this book there is a passage in which he describes a similar place, a trail made by hippos and worn more than 4 inches deep into very hard and solid rock. He noted that to do this, the time they have been using the trail "seems almost beyond calculation."

In this case, figuring the time is much easier. Clearly a lot of deer have been using the trail often and for a long time, but given the changes in vegetation from fires, we know it's more likely been 5 years rather than 500. To erode the trail this deep in that short of time has taken a lot of deer activity. Obviously, this is a place they like, and the trail soon intersects several others. These trails run out like spokes on a wagon wheel, with a thick patch of brush about 5 acres in size as the hub. The ground here is littered with fresh scrapes, and everywhere you look trees are weeping from fresh scars caused by antlers rubbing the bark off of them. If nothing else, following this buck has shown us a great location for a stand. There are a few surviving big trees here that were protected from the fires by surrounding wetlands. We are able to isolate several good treestand locations and I mark the spot on my GPS. I have a portable stand back at camp, locked in my trailer, but I know we won't be back. If I were simply here to kill a buck, I would be in one of these trees when dawn peeked into the dark tomorrow morning. My goal this trip, however, is to write a book on the Benoit style of hunting and shooting a buck is secondary. The "new generation" of Benoits may have "evolved" a lot in hunting techniques and equipment, but I don't think Shane is quite ready for an all-day sit in a treestand just yet.

There are lots of bucks of about the same size in here and it's hard to stay with the same track. The snow is light and it finally becomes clear that sorting out this buck's tracks from the hundreds left by his clones is not humanly possible. This illustrates all too well why it's important to try to find the track of an exceptionally large buck. We have many hours and several miles invested in this buck. While he is well over 200 pounds, so are half a dozen other bucks using the area. With the track of a bigger buck, we would be able to see at a glance we were on the right trail; but with this buck, we have to fight for every footprint because he simply is not exceptional enough to distinguish himself from the pack. Shane mutters that he is forced to have his head down looking at the track too much and that it's taking too long. The buck is traveling today, and every minute we spend sorting out his track, he is opening the gap between us. We have both known for a long time this is not a good cause to champion, but we stubbornly keep going. Reality, though, dictates we accept the inevitable sooner or later and at some point

Shane Benoit smells a scrape to see how "fresh" it is.

Bryce M. Towsley photo.

Note that this bark has melted slightly into the snow, which indicates it has laid on the snow through some daylight hours, but not many. Bryce M. Towsley photo.

we admit defeat yet again.

I have lost track of how many bucks we have followed, only to be forced to quit by snow conditions, dark, or the fact that most of the bucks are of similar size, making it hard to stay with one track; but it's a mounting tally. I am comforted by knowing that while the bucks win most of the battles, the Benoits always win the war.

Early afternoon finds us back in the truck searching for a big track. Shane likes to drive because he says that's when he sees all the deer. But this time, I spot the buck first. We round a corner and standing in the road is a huge buck. Shane is looking to the side rather than at the road ahead, and he sees the buck a split second after I do. As we skid to a stop, the buck slowly walks into the woods. I jump out of the truck, load my gun and take the track. When he hits a well-used trail, I stop looking at the track and move fast. I am eating ground at a rapid pace, but a glance down tells me his track is no longer on this trail. I turn around to backtrack and see Shane trotting along on my track, so we set up to double-team the buck.

The buck only runs for a short distance, and he is walking almost as soon as he is out of sight of the road. Clearly he wants to cross and his track is making a circle back toward the road. About half an hour into it, we know we are getting close, as we can hear another hunter's truck passing by. Suddenly the buck is right in front of us and instantly Shane has his gun pointed at his ribs. It's an easy shot and this buck doesn't realize he is dead already. But we are trying to fill my tag. Shane wants to wait for his cameraman, Tom Blais, to arrive so he can shoot a buck on film. He also has more than two weeks left to hunt, while I need to head for home in a couple of days. I, too, can see the buck clearly, but only one antler and his right ear. Shane is hissing for me to shoot, but I have nothing to shoot at. I sidestep to get a view of something important to point my gun at, and that movement is all the buck can take. He jumps what looks to be 20 feet from a standing start, and I know my shot is behind him even before the firing pin drops to the primer. Faster than you can think about it, he is gone.

We, of course, follow to make certain, but there are no red stains on the snow. We stay on the track and perhaps half a mile farther, and as might be expected, he is still running. So we move fast, almost trotting on the track, trying to keep the gap between us as small as possible. We won't gain any ground until he slows to a walk, but he will sooner or later. The idea is to be as close as possible then so we have the least amount of ground to make up to catch him again. But this buck has another surprise for us.

We move fast over the top of a ridge, and in the thick brush along the bottom, we see the buck running away. He descended the ridge in a full-out run, but at the trail along the bottom he stopped to work a scrape. Certainly, it was odd behavior for a buck and it's probably an indicator the rut was finally starting to affect his thought process. It is thick here, and I doubt we would have gotten a good shot had we been sneaking rather than moving fast, but it's still discouraging.

It's late in the day and this buck is going to take a long time to catch again. Shane points all this out implying that our chances of catching him before it's too dark are somewhere between slim and none and slim has left for the day. I insist we keep trying, and he agrees. But we only follow a little farther before I realize he is right and call it quits.

"What killed us on that buck was that other truck," Shane explains. "If it hadn't come along when it did, the buck would not have stopped to listen to it. We would have come behind him as he was walking away and we would have had a shot. When you catch a buck that's walking away from you, he can't see behind him and the sound of his own footsteps will usually cover any slight noise you are making. I have shot a lot of bucks that way, and it's the best possible scenario for a tracker. But he stopped to listen to that truck and he heard us behind him. That's when he turned to look at us and he was on high alert. When you moved for the shot, it was all over. The speed with which he got out of there tells us that he was wound pretty tight."

That night we drive to the gas station/store with the "Viking girl" and rent their public shower. The hot water feels good, and for what seems like the first time in days, my feet are warm. The soothing effects of the hot water help to drive out the demons of frustration, and by the time I am dressed, I am ready for the pizza Shane has sitting on the little table.

About the time we have it reduced to a few red stains on our clean shirts, Lane comes rushing through the door. After ordering his own pizza, he sits down and tells us how he had tracked the same buck from daylight to 3 p.m. "I wore out that new cameraman," he chuckles. Too tired to talk, the cameraman painfully nods in agreement. Lane goes on to tell us how they saw another pretty good buck while they were tracking the first one, which happens quite often. The second buck saw the first one pass and when he heard the hunters approaching, he assumed it was another buck and hung around for a look—probably so he could assess his status in the pecking order and to see if it was a friend or foe. With a Benoit showing up, a buck usually realizes too late that it's the latter and finds out exactly where he stands in the pecking order.

"He was good," Lane says, "but it happened too fast to film it, so I let him go . . . this time."

Shane Benoit in truck.

Bryce M. Towsley photo.

NOVEMBER 2, 2002

There is a large lake at the end of the road where we are camped that has several camps sparsely scattered around its long shoreline. Most of the camps and houses are only accessible from the water, so there is a landing at the end of the road to accommodate all the boats. Most of the traffic is summer use, and the place had the deserted, desolate and lonely look that's unique only to a collection of boats in winter. Shane and I stop there shortly after daylight and glass a large island about a mile away. There appears to be a small strip of land connected to the island from an area we know the deer like to use.

I am setting up my spotting scope to check it out, when I see a deer running along the bank on the near edge of the island. By the time I get the spotting scope focused, that deer is in the woods. But there is still one standing on the shore and I can see that it's a very big-bodied deer. Although I can't see his head because it's hidden by some brush and the distance, the body size indicates the animal has to be a big buck. Finally, he moves his head a bit and through the 40x Leupold, I can see he is indeed a huge buck. We watch until he melts into the brush, with his nose planted in the tracks of the first deer. I am sure the first deer we saw running was a doe about to come into heat and that this buck is on her trail. He will be preoccupied with her for a while, and after a short discussion, we decide to go to the island and try to get him.

Shane and I have a heated discussion about the route before we set out. The "shortcut" that won out turns out to be a mistake. The first half mile is not too bad walking and we actually run into a nice buck heading up the trail we are walking down. In another location, even a few yards either way on the trail, we might have gotten him, but luck was on his side. His head popped up over the top of a sharp ridge just as we came up the other side. We made eye contact, and by simply ducking his head, he was out of sight. By the time we ran to the top, he was long gone, back into the thick brush where visibility was measured in feet.

Right after that, things take a turn for the worse, and as a result, it is more than two hours before we even see the island—not that it is all that far, but because it is so thick. At one point we are crashing through impenetrable brush so thick and so full of blowdowns from trees killed by the spruce bud worm and the fires it is almost impossible to get through.

The new-growth trees are packed together so thick, my friend, Gary Sefton, would say, "A dog has to back up just to bark." Because of all the deadfalls and this thick brush to catch them before they hit the ground, the logs shoot off at all kinds of crazy angles, and we are stepping over as many as we are crawling under. It's impossible to walk quietly because the dead, dry trees and branches are brittle and frozen and they break easily. When they do, it's with the volume of a firecracker.

We are cut, scratched, poked, shin-scraped, and ankle-twisted before we are halfway through. Anybody who has been whipped by a twig on his nose or ear on a cold day knows how aggravating this can be, and it is happening every few minutes to us. When we are not being whipped by the new-growth branches, the old, dead limbs are stabbing us like rapiers. It all causes the adrenaline and frustration to well up as anger, which manifests itself to the point where your vision turns red and murder fills your heart, but there is nothing to fight. This, of course, makes you even more frustrated and much angrier. Punching and kicking is useless, cursing doesn't help and rage only makes things worse. You can't bully your way through and begging brings no results. It's a bad place to be under any conditions, but when you are under the illusion that you are stalking a buck, it brings new meaning to the word "ridiculous."

It appears a strong wind came through here and toppled a lot of trees sometime in the past few months, and the thick areas are so bad even the deer are no longer using them. There are lots of clearly defined old deer trails, but they are all abandoned and unused. This section of woods seems to be endless, and it's a frustrating hike because now that we are in here, it's uncertain what the best way to get out is. I am reminded of the joke about the swimmer who was three-quarters of the way across the lake, but realizing he couldn't make it all the way, turned back. Once committed, we don't know if it is best to keep going in hopes the end is close or to turn back through where we already came, exit, and try to circle around. With the ever-present Benoit optimism, Shane keeps us

This "island" is connected to the mainland by a small sandbar. We spotted a big buck with a doe on this island. Bryce M. Towsley photo.

Shane Benoit looks at a buck through a Leupold spotting scope. Bryce M. Towsley photo.

going forward with the thought the end has to be close.

This mess continues right to the shoreline, but finally we hit the lake. The problem is we had gotten off track in navigating that hellhole and are half a mile too far down the lake from the island. So we travel parallel to the lake through more of the same until we finally reach the narrow sandbar that connects the lake with the mainland.

The sandbar is perhaps 25 yards across at its widest point and is grooved deeply with a heavily used deer trail. Along the trail are two very fresh tracks, a doe and an extremely large buck, both heading out to the mainland. We'll never know if they heard us coming and realized how vulnerable they were, or if it simply took us so long to get there that they wandered off, but it really didn't matter. Our buck, and apparently our luck, was gone.

We set up out of the wind on the mainland shore and eat a snack while we watch the island. We can plainly see the spot where the deer had been when we saw them from the boat launch. Shane says we will stay for a couple of hours, which I doubt, having sat on stand with him before. We rattle, of course with no results. After 45 minutes Shane is wiggling his feet and I can tell he is getting cold. He wants to move, and to be honest, so do I.

We cross the sandbar and Shane sets off to circle the island to see if he can find another buck. I climb up on a fallen log on the edge of the sandbar so I can overlook the choke point the deer must come through if they plan to exit the island without swimming. If it comes, the shot will be very close and will probably happen very fast, so I stay alert, with my gun ready. I listen for advance warning of a deer's approach, but years of shooting and injuries have made my ears unreliable. It doesn't matter; the deer are gone. But they left their calling cards, as Shane found a very large bed, clearly made by an exceptionally large buck. No doubt, it was the same buck we saw from the shore and the same buck that left the departing tracks on the sandbar.

We take a different route out, staying to the higher ground. We find it's the same way the deer went when they left. It's the way I wanted to go to begin with, but it's still a long walk back to the truck. This sandbar would be a great place for a tree stand, but the only way to effectively hunt it would be to approach by boat or canoe. There is simply no overland route that can get you there fast enough to make hunting effective. I suspect that trying to get in or out in the dark would be suicide, and waiting for daylight to walk in would have your arrival too late to catch most of the deer movement. Then you would have to leave well before prime time in order to safely make it back to the truck. With a

Shane Benoit sitting on a ledge on top of a ridge in Ontario. Bryce M. Towsley photo.

boat, however, you could sneak in quietly to the shore just down from the sandbar and have a trail pre-cleared for your approach. With a stand on the east shore and a prevailing west wind, it could work. If we hunt here next year, I will bring my canoe.

It's late before we get back to the truck and eat a long delayed lunch. We then drive to a big clearcut and collect more firewood. We cover some remote roads looking for a track we can hunt tomorrow, but the deer are not moving and the snow is disappearing. Even though it's cold, the sun and wind are thinning it in most places and picking up new tracks is getting harder and harder. We need some snow, we need a break, and with only a few days left, I need a miracle.

NOVEMBER 3, 2002

I have to be home soon to help conduct a youth deer hunt, so with only a few days left, I need to spend some time with Lane and Lanny. I want photos of them and more information for this book. Shane and I hoped we could shoot a buck together, but time has simply run out on us.

I have passed on lots of good bucks, bucks that I would have been very happy to shoot, but I have laid down some rigid personal guidelines on just how I want to take a buck on this hunt. If simply killing a buck was the goal, I am secure in the knowledge we could have easily done it many times over, but I want a buck that is purely and truly taken while tracking him with a Benoit. Shane and I came close several times, and if we had been seriously hunting, it would have ended much sooner. But every time we should have been serious about deer hunting, I had a camera in my hands instead of a rifle. Often I would call a halt to the hunt while we photographed something that caught my eye, and the buck was using all that time to put more distance between us. It's all but impossible to shoot photos and hunt seriously at the same time, but the book had to come first. It seems like that's always the case when Shane and I are hunting together, and I promise myself that next year if I hunt with the Benoits, I will leave the cameras in camp.

Lane and I drive for miles to some different country to hunt. I still have my rifle with me, but the next few days will be spent on learning more about the techniques that Lane and Lanny use and in shooting photos of them. I accept that the chances of my actually shooting a buck are pretty slim.

We drive a long way, to a spot where Lane has hunted in years past and where he actually took his buck in 2001. This area has escaped the fires and looks a lot more like the Maine woods. It is predominately evergreen trees: spruce, pine, and fir with some hardwoods mixed throughout. The trees here are older and larger and the woods more open. There is less brush than in the burned areas and far less ground trash to deal with. Unquestionably, these are better woods for tracking, but the unanswered question is, do they hold the deer the other area did?

This new place has a lot more hunters on the roads and lots of the trucks have green Vermont license plates. As we turn off the main road, one hunter standing by a Vermont truck flags us down. He sees my Vermont plate and asks where we are from. I can tell by his eyes that he recognizes Lane as a Benoit, but he is reluctant to come out and ask him his name. Inquiring about our home is a polite way to backdoor the question. But Lane is very protective about where he is hunting, and he gives the poor guy evasive answers until finally he wishes us good luck and walks back to his truck. Clearly, Lane wears his fame reluctantly.

Not too far down this remote road we see a small-racked buck cross in front of us and run up the bank. "That buck has no idea how lucky he is that he was born with a runt of a rack," Lane laughs. "If he had a rack to match his body, he would be in a lot of trouble right now. It's a good thing we saw him, because I think he was big-bodied enough that we would have taken his track if we hadn't seen that little set of horns."

We park and walk a mile or so into where Lane shot his buck last year. There is almost no deer sign, yet when Lane hunted here last year, the place was full of bucks. It goes to show how it can all change and for no apparent reason that we can see. But if you don't watch the sign and get out when the deer are not there, you can burn up a lot of valuable time hunting in a location that "used to be good."

We only spend about an hour looking around before we hike back to the truck and drive on to another place Lane knows about 4 or 5 miles down the road. This time we hit paydirt.

There isn't much deer sign along the road or even along the foot trail that penetrates deep into the woods. But when the trail ends, so do most of the boot tracks. Some of the hunters ventured for a distance past the end of the trail, but before long, they obviously got nervous about the big woods and turned back to the safety of the trail.

It isn't very far past the last bootprint before we start seeing lots of deer sign. The deer clearly avoided the road and the trail where hunters were common, but as soon as we got into the deep woods where the other hunters dared not enter, we found deer and lots of them. We walk right up to a bedded fawn that stands up when he sees us about 10 feet from him. We stand staring at each other for a few seconds before he realizes he has messed up and disappears into the brush. Off, no doubt, to tell his daddy and his uncles there is a Benoit coming and things are looking grim.

We track several bucks this day, never staying with any particular one for more than an hour or two. Lane cautions me about getting hung up on one single buck. "If you come across a track that is bigger or fresher or just 'feels' better to you, take it," he says. "One big buck is probably as good as the other, and the new one doesn't know you are after him yet, which gives you an advantage. If the buck you have been tracking has been jumped a time or two, he is going to be a lot harder to kill than a buck that is unaware you are hunting him. So if you have plenty of big bucks in the area, don't worry about staying on the same deer all day. Go where your instincts take you."

We are close to bucks much of the time and actually see one buck a couple of times, but never long enough for a shot. We can no doubt shoot a buck but for the fact we keep stopping to take photos and to discuss what the sign is saying.

While I have hunted a lot over the years with Larry, Shane, and Lanny, this is my first time on a track with Lane, who is a loner and was never much interested in having a writer tag along. He is a big, burly guy with an aggressive air about him and he surprises me with not only how fast he can move through the woods, but how quietly he does it. He seems not so much to walk through the timber, but flow through it. He looks almost like he is liquid as he slips and turns to avoid the branches and brush. His movements are fluid and smooth and appear much slower and more relaxed than they really are. Clearly he is a guy who has spent many hours learning the ways of the woods, and he has developed the skills needed to successfully track bucks in this aggressive style.

Even though he is moving fast, Lane rarely looks directly at the track. Instead, he is always watching ahead, always moving his eyes. He not only looks for the buck, but he is following the track out far ahead of him and planning his route. He sees the track, not at his feet, but 50 or 100 yards ahead. This keeps his eyes up where they belong to spot deer and it allows him to move very fast along the track. At times I have trouble keeping up while still staying quiet. If I had to watch the track too, I couldn't do it nearly as fast as Lane is moving. We talk about this later, and he explains how he thinks that speed, combined with smooth motion and quiet passage, is important to catching and shooting big bucks.

One good buck is staying just ahead of us and we are very close for an hour or more. At one point he stops to watch for us, but he picks his hideout well. When we finally see him and make eye contact, he bolts before we can even think about shooting. As he dashes away, 50 yards down the trail, he runs right through the center of a bedded pack of wolves, which all jump up and chase him, preempting our efforts.

Talk about a bad day for a whitetail buck! First, he has a Benoit on his trail, and as if that's not bad enough, he then stumbles through a pack of wolves. You know this buck has to be looking up at the sky and wailing, "Why me?"

We figure the wolves have control of this one, so we turn east to head cross-country. Soon enough there is a giant beaver dam in our way. It's frozen, but with flowing water underneath, you can never tell how safe the ice may be in these situations. There are wolf tracks in the light dusting of snow that covers the ice, but Lane and I both weigh twice as much as most of them. And while they have four feet to distribute their weight, we only have two.

I have a few pounds on Lane, so I gallantly let him go first. He crosses the cracking and moaning ice with short, quick steps. I follow and the ice cracks loudly under my feet. I was a beaver trapper for a long time and I have negotiated some very thin ice over the years. You learn to develop a way to make your footsteps light when a frigid dunking is the price for not mastering the technique. It's been many years, but it came back to me fast. The trick is to not panic, but to keep moving, smooth and steady and never put your full weight on any one foot. I have water flooding the ice and pooling around my boots, but I make it to the other shore still warm and dry.

The bank is steep on the far shore and it's a tough climb to a high rocky ridge that overlooks a vast "beaver meadow." A beaver meadow is an opening left by an old beaver dam that breached. With its comparatively wide vista, this overlook appears to the uneducated eye like a great place to sit and watch for deer, but as we talk about it, we both mention how rarely we see bucks out in these openings. The body heat we had generated by the climb up here is soon dissipated by the cold wind. This ridge is too steep to climb down the other side, so we head north along the spine and soon find the tracks of a deer traveling ahead of us. They lead out to an overlook and disappear. I walk to the edge to see where the deer had jumped or fallen off the ledge. It's about 10 feet to the rocky ground below, but the deer appeared to land on his feet and, judging from the tracks, walked away unhurt. I almost think he simply got sick of looking for a way off this ridge and jumped. Good for him, because I am ready to get down too. I just don't think I would fare as well by jumping.

Lane Benoit looks at a track in Ontario 2002. Note cartridge in track. Bryce M. Towsley photo.

The long ridge finally ends where a brook passes through and the steep slope has been eroded enough by eons of passing water to allow a complicated and slippery climb down to the valley floor.

Across the beaver meadow, we run into a bottomland choked with willow and alders. It's full of buck sign, with a lot of scrapes and rubs that are very fresh. We pick up a good buck track and follow it for a short distance before we jump a doe out of her bed and she goes crashing off through the brush. We can hear another deer get up and follow her. It is, of course, our buck. Had we not spooked that unseen doe from her bed, we may well have shot him as he lay sleeping. But as they always seem to do, this buck had planned well. It happens too often to be coincidence that the buck will bed behind the doe so that anything following their trail will encounter her first. Chivalry may well be dead among whitetails, but this blatant exploitation of their girlfriends has kept countless bucks alive. Protected, I suspect, both from bullets and from wolves.

Near the beds we find where the buck put his nose down to smell where the doe had urinated. This gives us a clue as to why he is sticking so close to her, as she is probably very close to coming into heat. His antlers imprinted clearly in the snow when he did this and we can see that with brow tines he is likely a wide 10-point. Six neat holes in the snow clearly defined the tines on each side. The main beams didn't show, nor did the brow tines, but with "three up" on each side, it is most likely carrying 10 points.

This large alder swamp is full of scrapes and rubs and clearly several bucks are using it as a bedding and

Above:

Lane Benoit in Ontario 2002.

Bryce M. Towsley photo.

Wolf bed. Bryce M. Towsley photo.

staging area. I am photographing some rubs when Lane looks up to see a buck watching us. The buck runs off as soon as he makes eye contact, so Lane takes the track, but jumps the buck in a very short distance. Lane had assumed the buck would run off, so he was moving fast on the trail, but in reality all the buck did was melt back into the brush when he realized we had seen him. He was standing just out of sight and listening for us when Lane bumped him.

Lane points out this is his and several other bucks' "favorite" place. At one end of this basin is a high, steep bank overlooking a small opening in the thick woods. With lots of trails and intersections converging in the opening, it would be a good place to take a stand, and Lane vows to be back here in the morning.

It is a long hike back to the truck and the grub box. By now it's too late in the day to take another track, so we decide to check out some of the places that held bucks in past years. The first location is where Lane started the track of a good buck he eventually killed a couple of years back.

"It's another one of those 'favorite places' that bucks just seem to like," he tells me. "There is always at least one good buck hanging around."

We find he is right, but in spite of seeing a lot of rubs and plenty of big tracks, Lane is disappointed.

"Usually there is a lot more buck sign here than this," he tells me. "Most of this is a few days old too. I think that a doe or two must have come into heat and drawn them out of here. This is kind of a 'bachelor pad' where they hang out until the does start coming into estrus. Then they abandon it for a week or two while they are distracted with the business of procreating. They will be back later in the month, but by then the hunting season will be closed and we will be gone. For now, it only tells me that we need to look someplace else for bucks."

We burn the rest of the afternoon checking places where he had found bucks in the past. "It's important to remember the best buck places," Lane explains, "not only because they come back year after year to them, but also because when the bucks are not there, it gives you a clue as to what is happening and where they might be. Now, we are not seeing a lot of fresh buck sign in many of these places we checked. They were here a few days ago, but nothing is fresher than that. Something changed pretty fast to make them move out, and this time of year, that means the first of the does are probably coming into heat.

Lane Benoit glasses from a high ridge overlooking a beaver meadow.

Bryce M. Towsley photo.

Deer bed in snow. Bryce M. Towsley photo.

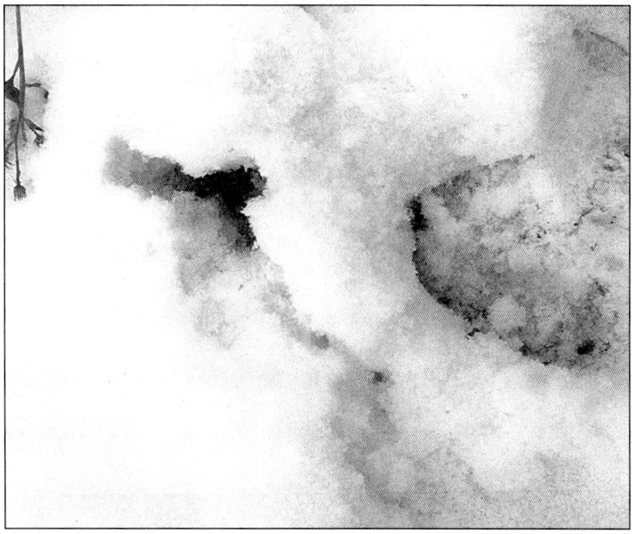

A doe urinated here, but the track is from a buck. He stopped and smelled this urine, then he followed the doe. Bryce M. Towsley photo.

So we go and look for the big bucks in the places where we usually find the does.

"It is so important to cover a lot of ground and to remember what you find. It's all part of the puzzle and, like any puzzle, it forms a clear picture when you put all the pieces together."

We drive some other logging roads until dark, but there is very little deer sign and few big tracks crossing. As often happens, as soon as the does start coming into heat, the bucks stop rambling around and stick with the girls. The number of big-buck tracks crossing the roads decreases dramatically. That's another clue the does are hot and the bucks will be with them.

Lane points out the importance of finding the deer first and then hunting them. He laughs, "Today we found out where to look for the bucks, tomorrow they are going to realize they are in trouble!"

NOVEMBER 4, 2002

This is to be my last day here, and Shane and Lanny have it worked out for me to go with Lanny in the morning. Somehow the signals get crossed, and when I get to their tent in the morning, Lanny has already left.

I have some photos that I need to shoot, so I spend a few hours working on that. While photographing tracks, I walk up on a pretty good buck that I can easily shoot. He really isn't all that big, and I just don't feel right shooting him, even on this the last day, so I watch him walk off.

I am heading back to camp to meet with Shane and driving a little too fast on the icy road. As I top a hill, about halfway down the other side is a two-wheel-drive truck sideways in the road, blocking both lanes. The driver is standing in front of it waving his arms. The banks are too steep to drive off the road and my only option if I can't stop is to hit his truck. Standing in front of it is a really stupid thing to do, as it is about to lead to turning him into the filling in a truck sandwich. But then, getting stuck across both lanes trying to turn around on a blind hill is a stupid thing too. I manage to stop just a few feet short of hitting his truck, and it takes a long time to calm down and to trust my legs enough to get out of my truck.

"Gee, I never thought of that," he says when I explain how close he came to dying. As we work to free his truck, I realize this guy has no business being out in the wilderness at all. We get his truck turned around and I suggest he go back to town. He doesn't argue, so maybe he isn't as dumb as I think.

I decline to go with Shane to look for Lanny. Instead, I finish some of the photos I need to take around the camp and decide to break camp to get a few hours head start on the long drive home.

THE TRIP HOME

The trip home was a disaster and it turned out I needed

every extra hour that head start bought. I drove much of the 1,500 miles in falling snow on slippery roads, and at times I had to stay in four-wheel drive for hundreds of miles at a time. One late-night stretch between gas stations was so far that if I had not carried two 6-gallon cans in the trailer, I would have been stranded.

I was fortunate at that point that I could get the gas out of the trailer to fill the truck. Before leaving camp, I changed into street clothes and threw my wool pants into my trailer then locked the door. It was only when I was "reminded" that my trailer lights were out that I realized the key to the padlock was inside the pocket of the wool pants.

Late that night I found myself in a Wal-Mart parking lot trying to beat the lock off the door with a hatchet. I expected any minute to be arrested for breaking and entering of a trailer.

The snow, cold, and road salt had taken their toll on the wiring on my old trailer and I had to stop several times to make repairs. Each time I would fix a wire or a light, another would break soon after. Finding an open store to buy parts was difficult in this long trip through rural Canada and I wasted several hours looking for tools and materials.

Ontario is one of the last places in Canada where non-residents can hunt whitetails without paying an outfitter. But hunting there poses a constant risk of running into trouble with the law. The gun laws are so complicated and ill defined in the material available that it's all but certain a hunter will be in violation. The camping laws blatantly discriminate against hunters, as much of the area we hunted allows public camping except during deer season. Further, and I suspect because of the Benoit's fame, we experienced almost constant attention from the conservation officers. They stopped people from our party several times, harassing them and making threats. They harassed the private landowner where we were camped and pointedly questioned him about the "Americans." They even sent an officer into camp to question and intimidate the daughter of one of our party while the young girl was in camp alone.

While on my trip home, a police car came roaring past my truck like a SWAT team attack and crowded me off the road. All the lights were working and I wasn't speeding. My offense? I had a radar detector. I explained that I didn't know it was illegal in Ontario, and I would be very happy to lock it in my cargo trailer. Instead, the officer called me a liar and took the $100 device. Then he fined me an additional $175. Now, I am the first to admit that ignorance of the law is no excuse. However, I did think the response, the attitude, and the penalty were all extremely harsh. I can't help but wonder if things would have been different if my truck had Canadian license plates instead of Vermont.

I have been traveling to Canada for nearly four decades. In the past 20 years I usually made several trips per year, primarily these days to hunt or fish. I live just a few hours from the border and in my lifetime I have made many trips into Canada with few problems. But things have changed recently. We used to be friends, the US and Canada, but now I am seeing anti-American attitudes more and more when I am in the North, even from hunting guides. I had a bear guide this past spring who went off on a tirade about "Americans." He only shut up when I asked him what we ever did to him except hand him money, and he couldn't answer.

It's not just Canada, either. Under new regulations implemented after Sept. 11, 2001, it has become extremely difficult and in some cases impossible for Canadians to travel with firearms to the US. This has kept many Canadians from hunting in the states. It has also prevented some from traveling overseas to hunt, as their itineraries included travel through the US with firearms, and the new regulations prevented that completely. I know of one Canadian citizen who was in jail for months for crossing a few feet past an unmanned border to fill his truck with gas before going moose hunting. This is something that people in that town have done for years.

When I crossed back into the United States from this trip, I was harassed at the US border, where they searched my truck and trailer and detained me for well over an hour.

It's a changing world, of that there is little doubt, and common sense is not playing a big role in our new direction. But too, we are distracted or frightened enough that we are letting the changes lead us to the wrong results. Hunters are not now, and never were, the enemy.

I was talking with a handgun manufacturer recently and he made an interesting comment. He told me he was working on tort reform legislation when one of the lawmakers made a profound comment. It seems that this guy was not part of the gun debate until recently, and he asked the question, "What happened?" He added, "It used to be that owning a gun was a point of pride in America, a good thing, a symbol of our freedom. Now it's somehow become evil and gun owners are looked at with spite and hatred. How did that happen?"

I don't know, but it affects us all and it's not just in America. If you have plans to hunt in Canada, you should be prepared for it. My hope is that it is only temporary and with the long publishing life of most books, that you will be reading this and chuckling at how dated it all has become.

I learned later that, as has become the custom as soon as I leave camp, bucks started falling like autumn leaves. In the next 10 days, the Benoits, all their friends, and even all the cameramen shot big trophy bucks. There were bucks literally running up to guys and begging to be shot. It seems that the only person who hunted with them on this trip for any length of time and didn't fill his tag was me.

By now this has become a joke. It happens every time I hunt with them, and if the Benoits are having a rough go of it and the bucks are coming hard, all they need to do to reverse their fortunes is send me home. As soon as I leave one of their camps, big bucks come out of the woodwork and surrender.

Glad I can be of service, guys.